Jefferson in His Own Time

WRITERS IN THEIR OWN TIME

Joel Myerson, *series editor*

JEFFERSON

in His Own Time

A Biographical Chronicle of His Life, Drawn from Recollections, Interviews, and Memoirs by Family, Friends, and Associates

EDITED BY

Kevin J. Hayes

University of Iowa Press,
Iowa City

University of Iowa Press, Iowa City 52242

www.uiowapress.org
Printed in the United States of America

The University of Iowa Press is a member of Green Press Initiative and is committed to preserving natural resources.

Printed on acid-free paper

Library of Congress Cataloging-in-Publication Data
Jefferson in his own time: a biographical chronicle of his life, drawn from recollections, interviews, and memoirs by family, friends, and associates / edited by Kevin J. Hayes.
p. cm.—(Writers in their own time)
Includes bibliographical references and index.
ISBN: 978-1-60938-120-2, 1-60938-120-3 (pbk)
ISBN: 978-1-60938-138-7, 1-60938-138-6 (ebook)
1. Jefferson, Thomas, 1743–1826—Friends and associates.
2. Jefferson, Thomas, 1743–1826—In literature.
3. United States—History—1783–1865—Sources. I. Hayes, Kevin J.
E332.15.J44 2012
973.4'6092—dc23
2012004392

FOR MYUNG-SOOK

Contents

Introduction

THOMAS JEFFERSON was a funny guy. Whenever I tell people this, they respond with quizzical looks. "What do you mean by funny?" they ask. "How was Jefferson funny?" They react this way because history, which has largely ignored Jefferson's delightful sense of humor, has conditioned them to react this way. Perhaps no one has been more reluctant to acknowledge Jefferson's capacity for humor than his most prominent biographer, Dumas Malone. Writing the article about Jefferson for the tenth volume of the *Dictionary of American Biography* (1933), Malone asserted, "Though sanguine in temperament, he was as serious-minded and almost as devoid of humor as any Puritan."[1] Not only is Malone's statement unfair to Jefferson, it also slights the New England Puritans, many of whom, starting with William Bradford, did have fine senses of humor.

Malone made this statement before he began his six-volume biography of Jefferson, but, having formed a negative opinion toward Jefferson's sense of humor, he never altered it. As he composed his biography, Malone did encounter some examples of humor, especially Jefferson's fondness for tall talk, but he downplayed them. In his first volume, Malone wrote, "In Jefferson himself, however, little humor had appeared as yet except in the form of elaborate exaggeration." Discussing Jefferson's daughter Martha in his second volume, Malone asserted that she "retained the natural gaiety of youth and manifested a more active sense of humor than her father did." Even when he could not deny an instance of Jefferson's humor, Malone interpreted it as a temporary aberration. Discussing a humorous episode in *The Anas,* Jefferson's record of conversations during his time as George Washington's secretary of state, Malone asserted that Jefferson, in this instance, demonstrated "more humor than he normally displayed." And in volume four, Malone blatantly stated that Jefferson "was not conspicuously a man of humor."[2]

Other biographers have followed suit. Typically, popular biographies accept the conclusions of scholarly ones. The popularizers take others' research and abbreviate it, simplifying without essentially changing its impetus. Consequently, many biographers after Malone have accepted without question his conclusions about Jefferson's humor. Malone himself reinforced his negative attitude toward Jefferson's humor near the end of his life. When Merrill Peterson asked him to write a biographical sketch for a new reference work in the mid eighties, Malone agreed. This new article, written fifty-three years after his *Dictionary of American Biography* article, repeats word-for-word the sentence about both Jefferson and the Puritans being devoid of humor.[3]

Gathered together, the letters, accounts, and reminiscences of those who knew Thomas Jefferson personally tell a much different story. Here's a sample of what they have to say. Dr. Samuel L. Mitchill,[†] who frequently dined at the White House, told his wife that President Jefferson could "both hear and relate humorous stories as well as any other man of social feeling." Elsewhere, Mitchill commented that Jefferson's "temper was prone at times to mirth and recreative pleasantry."[4] Realizing Jefferson's fondness for tall talk, John Quincy Adams[†] observed, "Mr. Jefferson tells large stories." Stage comedian John Bernard,[†] also a frequent dinner guest at Jefferson's table, recalled, "With specimens of his humor I could fill pages." (Would that he had.) Ellen Randolph Coolidge[†] boasted about her grandfather: "Mr. Jefferson had decidedly one of the evenest and most cheerful tempers I ever knew. He enjoyed a jest, provided it were to give pain to no one, and we were always glad to have any pleasant little anecdote for him—when he would laugh as cheerily as we could do ourselves, and enter into the spirit of the thing with as much gaiety." T. P. H. Lyman concurred: "His conversation was instructive and delightful; stately where it should be so, but in general, easy, familiar, sprightly and entertaining; always, however, good humoured, and calculated to amuse without wounding." And Alexander H. H. Stuart said, "I have never met any one who presided at his own table, with the same playful grace and urbanity."[5]

Jefferson's sense of humor is just one of many different aspects of his personality that surviving letters and reminiscences reveal. The earliest documents that record personal impressions of him are letters written in 1775 by fellow delegates to the Continental Congress. Though Jefferson grew up in Virginia, attended the College of William and Mary, read law under George Wythe, practiced law for several years, and served in the House of

Thomas Jefferson, detail of a mural by Constantino Brumidi in the U.S. Capitol. Library of Congress, Prints and Photographs Division, reproduction number LC-DIG-det-4a26387.

Burgesses, few remembered him in any of these capacities. Since he was never a great public speaker, Jefferson left no lasting impressions on those who saw him at the bar or in the colonial legislature.

A few brief comments about Jefferson's student days survive. One anecdote circulated in the family of Jefferson's teacher, the Reverend James Maury. In 1760, most likely, Jefferson's grammar school classmate and future brother-in-law Dabney Carr challenged him to a horse race. Such a race would hardly be fair. Carr's horse was extremely fast, and Jefferson's pony was notoriously slow. Jefferson accepted the challenge—provided he could choose the date. Once Carr agreed, Jefferson told him when he would race: February 30! It's not a great joke, but the Maurys found it funny enough to keep retelling it for decades.[6] John Page, a fellow student at William and Mary, remembered a different side of Jefferson, recalling his scholarly bent during their time at college together: "I was too sociable, and fond of the conversation of my friends, to study as Mr. Jefferson did, who could tear himself away from his dearest friends, to fly to his studies."[7]

It was really Jefferson's writing ability that prompted others to start recording their impressions of him. Coming to Philadelphia as a delegate to the Continental Congress in 1775, he aroused much curiosity on the part of other delegates. Save for Elbridge Gerry and Charles Thomson, no one outside the Virginia contingent knew him personally.[8] But all knew him as the author of *A Summary View of the Rights of British America,* which had been published in Williamsburg the previous August and reprinted elsewhere. The writing skills Jefferson demonstrated in this work had earned him the respect of other congressional delegates even before he reached Philadelphia. Describing his arrival to a correspondent, Samuel Ward, a delegate from Rhode Island, wrote: "Yesterday the famous Mr. Jefferson a Delegate from Virginia in the Room of Mr. [Peyton] Randolph arrived. I have not been in Company with him yet, he looks like a very sensible spirited fine Fellow and by the Pamphlet which he wrote last Summer he certainly is one."[9]

In the coming days, Jefferson got to know many of the delegates personally. As they interacted, he impressed them not only with his capacity for hard work but also with the range and depth of his linguistic knowledge. Speaking with John Adams, James Duane of New York characterized Jefferson by his erudition, calling him "the greatest Rubber off of Dust" he had ever met. "He has learned French, Italian, Spanish and wants to learn

Benjamin Rush, engraved print by Charles Balthazar Julien Fevret de Saint-Mémin, 1802. Library of Congress, Prints and Photographs Division, reproduction number LC-USZ62-54697.

German."[10] Though Jefferson actively served in the Continental Congress and wrote the Declaration of Independence, his diligence as a delegate prompted few additional comments from his fellow delegates—with the exception of Benjamin Rush.

Rush did not leave a sustained reminiscence of Jefferson, but his writings are peppered with poignant remarks that offer insights into his personality and conversation. The two men first met soon after Jefferson came to Philadelphia to serve in the Continental Congress. A quarter century later, Rush wrote to Jefferson: "I shall always recollect with pleasure the many delightful hours we have spent together, from the day we first met on the banks of the Skuikill in the year 1775 to the day in which we parted. If the innocent and interesting subjects of our occasional conversations should be a delusive one, the delusion is enchanting."[11] Rush, who joined the Continental Congress just in time to sign the Declaration of Independence in the summer of 1776, remembered serving with Jefferson in Congress, as well. One particular comment Jefferson made stuck with him. Rush recalled: "While Congress were deliberating upon the measure of sending Commissioners to France I asked him what he thought of being one of them. He said 'he would go to hell to serve his country.'"[12] Like few others, Rush captures Jefferson's profound dedication to the American cause.

Jefferson himself used to tell a tall tale about the signing of the Declaration of Independence. General John Spear Smith explained to nineteenth-century biographer Henry S. Randall:

> Whilst the question of Independence was before Congress, it had its meetings near a livery stable. The members wore short breeches and silk stockings, and with handkerchief in hand, they were diligently employed in lashing the flies from their legs. So very vexatious was this annoyance, and to so great an impatience did it arouse the sufferers, that it hastened, if it did not aid, in inducing them to promptly affix their signatures to the great document, which gave birth to an entire republic.
>
> This anecdote I had from Mr. Jefferson, at Monticello, who seemed to enjoy it very much, as well as to give great credit to the influence of the flies. He told it with much glee, and seemed to retain a vivid recollection of the severity of an attack, from which the only relief was signing the paper, and flying from the scene.[13]

As wartime governor of Virginia, Jefferson had many different responsibilities. For one, he had to house and feed the four thousand Hessian troops that had been taken prisoners of war at Saratoga and sent to Virginia. He welcomed the German officers to his home and even lent them books from his library. One of them, possibly Baron von Geismar or maybe Johann Ludwig von Unger, wrote a letter home. An excerpt of the letter appeared in a Hamburg newspaper, which Jacob Rubsamen, a German-speaking Virginian, translated and sent to Jefferson. As the letter reveals, Jefferson saw no reason why these enemy combatants should not be treated with civility, even hospitality.

The Hessian officer's comments show Jefferson's scientific curiosity as well as his personal generosity. Jefferson gave him free access to his library. In the process of creating a compass on the ceiling of his parlor that would help discern the strength and direction of the wind, Jefferson also sought the help of this artistically talented German. During his visits to Monticello, the officer enjoyed hearing Mr. Jefferson play the violin with Mrs. Jefferson on the pianoforte. The account provides a rare view of Martha Jefferson, whom this officer calls "in all Respects a very agreable Sensible and Accomplished Lady."[14]

The fullest account of Jefferson to emerge from the war years is that of the Marquis de Chastellux.[†] An officer in the French army, Chastellux obtained leave to journey through the continent, an odyssey he documented in *Travels in North-America.* This travelogue includes a detailed account of Jefferson at Monticello after he had finished his last term as governor and decided to devote himself to home and family. Chastellux portrayed Thomas and Martha, then pregnant with their daughter Lucy Elizabeth, as a picture of happiness and harmony. All that would soon change. Shortly after Chastellux left Monticello, Martha gave birth. It was a difficult birth from which she never recovered. Martha Jefferson passed away on 6 September 1782. Nearly ten, their daughter Martha,[†] or Patsy, as she was called in her youth, was old enough to remember her father's profound grief upon the death of his wife. Her intimate reminiscence captures her father's emotional turmoil.

The death of his wife put Jefferson back onto the national stage. Reelected delegate to the Continental Congress in 1783, he and Patsy traveled to Philadelphia, where he found a place for her to live and enrolled her in school. Congress convened in Philadelphia this year only to adjourn and reconvene in Annapolis. Jefferson thus moved to Annapolis, where he became an inspiration to younger delegates. Serving with the author of the *Declaration of Independence,* the junior members of Congress received a thorough grounding in the study of natural law and natural rights.[15] Explaining to a correspondent how he spent his time, David Howell, a representative from Rhode Island, wrote, "I sometimes read. Gov. Jefferson, who is here a Delegate from Virginia, and one of the best members I have ever seen in Congress, has a good Library of French books, and has been so good as to lend me [some]."[16]

The surviving comments of G. K. Van Hogendorp, a young Dutchman who had come to Annapolis while Congress was in session, provide further insight into Jefferson's personal demeanor: "He has the shyness that accompanies true worth, which is at first disturbing and which puts off those who seek to know him. Those who persist in knowing him soon discern the man of letters, the lover of natural history, Law, Statecraft, Philosophy, and the friend of mankind."[17] This description is remarkably similar to the one Chastellux penned in his journal. Both men noticed an initial diffidence that warmed into affectionate friendship.

In 1784, Congress appointed Jefferson minister to France to join John Adams and Benjamin Franklin to negotiate treaties of amity and commerce in Europe. Leaving Annapolis, he went to Philadelphia to collect his daughter and then proceeded to Boston, where they sailed for France. In Paris, he enrolled her at L'Abbaye Royale de Penthémont, a prestigious convent school. During their time in France, her sister Lucy contracted whooping cough and perished in Virginia. Jefferson ultimately arranged to have Mary, his only other surviving child, join him in Paris.

Jefferson's time in France let him make new friendships and renew some old ones. He became reacquainted with both Benjamin Franklin and John Adams. He especially enjoyed the company of John Adams and his family, all of whom left accounts of him. John Quincy Adams† and his sister Abigail,† or "Nabby," sometimes visited Jefferson at his Paris home. Both John Adams and Thomas Jefferson shared a disgust of the pomp that went with the Court of France. Jefferson could not mask his contempt for all forms of ceremony. Mrs. Adams observed: "Mr. Jefferson who is really a man who abhors this shew and parade full as much as Mr. Adams, yet he has not been long enough enured to it, to Submit with patience, or bear it without fretting."[18] Instead of fussing, Jefferson would gradually channel his dislike of ceremony into humor.

His time in Paris was rich and rewarding. He entertained frequently at his Parisian home and developed his capacity for witty table talk. The French he befriended left a lasting impact on him. Throughout the rest of his life, he would often speak fondly about the people he knew in Paris. He and his daughters stayed in France until the last week of September 1789, when they sailed for Virginia. At Le Havre, Jefferson met a seafaring man from Massachusetts named Nathaniel Cutting. Known to posterity as a diarist, Captain Cutting tirelessly recorded the incidents of everyday life to create a lasting record of his seafaring adventures. His diary says much about the Jefferson family, as well. Since it took several days to find passage

Thomas Jefferson, President of the United States, stipple engraving by Cornelius Tiebout, after a painting by Rembrandt Peale, 1801. Library of Congress, Prints and Photographs Division, reproduction number LC-DIG-ppmsca-15715.

from Le Havre to the Isle of Wight, Cutting spent much time in their company, even postponing his own journey to stay with them.[19]

After saying his final good-byes, Cutting reflected upon the friendship he had formed with the Jeffersons. His emotional words and affectionate tone affirm the devotion Jefferson could inspire in articulate, sensitive men: "I never remember to have experienced so much regret at parting from a Family with whom I had so short an acquaintance. I have found Mr. Jefferson a man of infinite information and sound Judgement, becoming gravity, and engaging affability mark his deportment. His general abilities are such as would do honor to any age or Country."[20]

Upon their return to Virginia, Jefferson learned from the newspapers that George Washington had appointed him secretary of state. He left Monticello for New York to accept his new responsibilities in February 1790. On his way there he stopped in Philadelphia to see old friends, including Benjamin Franklin, who had left France in 1785. Jefferson now found him on his deathbed and related the visit in his autobiography, an account which constitutes an important contribution to the story of Franklin in his own time.[21] Jefferson also renewed his friendship with another signer, Benjamin Rush, who described Jefferson's physical appearance: "He was plain in his dress and unchanged in his manners." Rush also recorded snippets of their conversation, especially what Jefferson had to say about James Madison: "He said Mr. Madison 'was the greatest man in the world'; that Dr. [John] Witherspoon, his master, had said of him 'that he never knew him do or say an improper thing' when at School."[22]

While serving as secretary of state, Jefferson realized that what Washington and others were saying deserved to be recorded. Consequently, he created *The Anas,* which amounts to notes on conversations that occurred during his time as secretary of state. That work constitutes an invaluable contribution to the story of Washington in his own time.[23] No one was there to record Jefferson's contributions to the conversation, however. Still, some anecdotes from the period survive.

One American in Paris heard nineteenth-century French historian Edouard de Laboulaye repeat a story about a conversation that supposedly occurred between Washington and Jefferson. Influenced by the French, Jefferson attacked the bicameral system of legislation: "Washington replied that Jefferson was much better informed than himself on such topics, but that he would adhere to the experience of England and America. 'You yourself,' said the General, 'have proved the excellence of two houses this very moment.' 'I,' said Jefferson; 'how is that, General?' 'You have,' replied the heroic sage, 'turned your hot tea from the cup into the saucer, to get it cool. It is the same thing we desire of the two houses.'"[24]

Such third-hand anecdotes must always be taken with a grain of salt, but they still possess cultural value regardless of their authenticity. They show Jefferson and Washington as familiar characters in traditional narrative. In American legend, men like Thomas Jefferson and George Washington become symbolic figures representing the ideas and ideals of a nation.

Senator William Maclay, whose most lasting contribution to posterity is the diary he kept while serving in the First Federal Congress, had the opportunity to meet Jefferson on the evening of Monday, 24 May 1790. Maclay vividly recorded his impressions of the secretary of state:

> Jefferson is a slender man; has rather the air of stiffness in his manner; his clothes seem too small for him; he sits in a lounging manner, on one hip commonly, and with one of his shoulders elevated much above the other; his face has a sunny aspect; his whole figure has a loose, shackling air. He had a rambling, vacant look, and nothing of that firm, collected deportment which I expected would dignify the presence of a secretary or minister. I looked for gravity, but a laxity of manner seemed shed about him. He spoke almost without ceasing. But even his discourse partook of his personal demeanor. It was loose and rambling, and yet he scattered information wherever he went, and some even brilliant sentiments sparkled from him. The information which he gave us respecting foreign ministers, etc., was all high-spiced. He had been long enough abroad to catch the tone of European folly. He gave us a sentiment which seemed rather to savor of quaintness: "It is better to take the highest of the lowest than the lowest of the highest."[25]

The following May, Jefferson and Madison took a vacation together, traveling through upstate New York, sailing over Lake Champlain, and continuing through Vermont to the Canadian border. Madison's correspondence recalls one particular comment Jefferson made during the trip. Many Americans they met were curious about how the newly ratified Constitution would work. At a dinner party, people discussed different ways of selecting a president of the United States. Even with Jefferson and Madison present, one dinner guest had the audacity to assert that the office of president should be filled through hereditary means rather than by any sort of elective process. The person spoke at some length, arguing against a popu-

Thomas Jefferson, ink drawing, by John Marshal, ca. 1800–1830. Library of Congress, Prints and Photographs Division, reproduction number LC-DIG-ppmsca-22813.

lar choice and on behalf of birth in order to provide a more suitable head of government. After listening to the man for some time, Jefferson, with a smile, commented that "he had heard of a university somewhere in which the Professorship of Mathematics was hereditary." Finishing the anecdote, Madison concluded by recording the reaction of the other dinner guests: "The reply, received with acclamation, was a coup de grace to the Anti-Republican Heretic."[26]

After the nation relocated its seat of government from New York to Philadelphia, Jefferson once again had the opportunity to renew his friendship with Benjamin Rush. One morning the two had breakfast with Henry Drinker, a Quaker importer and shipowner. Rush recorded in his commonplace book: "Breakfasted this morning with Mr. Jefferson, and read to him and Mr. Drinker an account of the maple tree and sugar etc., and received some useful hints from each of them on the subject. Was charmed with Mr. Jefferson's conversation. It was full of instruction upon all subjects. He read several extracts from his Journal of his travels in France. . . . He added that a good climate was the richest natural gift of heaven to man."[27]

Rush also enjoyed Jefferson's wit. He recorded one anecdote Jefferson told in 1793. Rush's manuscript notebook is damaged at this point, but Jefferson retold the same anecdote at a White House dinner in 1809, when a dinner guest recorded it in detail.[28]

One of the present kings of Europe, Jefferson explained, was quite fond of hunting. Just as he was outfitted for the hunt and ready to leave his palace, a courtier announced that several strangers had arrived. Before the ceremony of introducing them was over, the king's patience had reached its limits. He turned to a courtier and said, "Oh, how I hate ceremony." With a bow, the courtier replied, "Sire, you forget that you are yourself ceremony."

The fact that Jefferson related this same anecdote at least twice within a sixteen-year period reveals much. For one thing, it suggests that he most likely told it several other times. It has the quality of a stock anecdote, one he would retell whenever the occasion arose, that is, whenever he felt the need to illustrate his disgust of ceremony. When he told it during his presidency, it was in response to a comment from the Danish minister, who had expressed his belief that the president of the United States should be surrounded by an atmosphere of ceremony.

At the end of 1793, Jefferson resigned as secretary of state and returned to Monticello, assuming he had left public life behind him for good. He was ready to devote himself to his home and farm. A detailed picture of life at Monticello comes from one of his former slaves, Isaac Jefferson. Virginia historian Charles W. Campbell interviewed Isaac Jefferson in 1847 and recorded many of his observations. Rather than record it in the first person, Campbell wrote it in the third person. The text itself suggests that he embellished the account considerably, almost giving it the aura of an antebellum plantation novel. Still, Isaac Jefferson provides a unique perspective. Talking about the lightning rod atop Monticello, for example, Isaac remembered something Thomas Jefferson had said about Benjamin Franklin after an electrical storm: "If it hadn't been for that Franklin the whole house would have gone."[29] To be sure, anyone who builds a house on top of a mountain must be grateful to the inventor of the lightning rod.

Isaac Jefferson's reminiscence is one of a handful of accounts from Jefferson's former slaves. Together these provide a much different perspective of life at Monticello than those of family, friends, and neighbors.[30] One of the best is that of Peter F. Fossett, who was born into slavery at Monticello in 1815 and served as a house slave during his adolescence. Fossett had a keen mind, as the interview he granted a reporter for the New York *Sunday World* indicates.[†] Besides recounting his personal experiences—he vividly remembered Lafayette's visit to Monticello and the frequent visits of James Madison and James Monroe—Fossett also reports details of events that occurred before he was born. His remarks clearly show that stories about Jefferson and Monticello circulated among the slave population. Recalling the invasion of Monticello during the Revolutionary War, Isaac Jefferson had observed that the British troops "marched up to the palace with drums beating; it was an awful sight—seemed like the Day of Judgment was come."[31] Fossett's account suggests that dramatic stories about the British invasion continued to circulate orally among the Monticello slaves long after the event.

In 1796, Jefferson was elected vice president of the United States. He had not campaigned for the office. Back then, the president and vice president did not run on the same ticket. Instead, whoever came in second in the electoral balloting became vice president. In this election year, John Adams received the most electoral votes, Jefferson the second most. With the seat of government temporarily located in Philadelphia, the position of vice president gave Jefferson numerous intellectual opportunities. The day before he was inaugurated vice president, in fact, he was installed as president of the

Thomas Jefferson, a Philosopher, a Patriot, and a Friend, aquatint etched by Michal Sokolnicki, after a painting by Tadeusz Kosciuszko, ca. 1800–1816. Library of Congress, Prints and Photographs Division, reproduction number LC-USZ62-23011.

American Philosophical Society, the leading scientific organization in the nation. He carried out his responsibilities in both roles with diligence but also found time to see old friends and entertain visitors.

The travelogue of Richard Parkinson, a British agriculturalist touring America, suggests that Monticello was still on Jefferson's mind, even as he served as vice president. When the two met in Philadelphia, Jefferson spoke about agriculture at length. Parkinson wrote:

> This gentleman, being very fond of the subject of agriculture, was kind enough to ask me to step into his room any time when I should find him at leisure. On such occasions a most pleasant man I found him. His travels having been chiefly into France, I was much edified by hearing what was the practice there;—and likewise what sort of agriculture he carried on in that part of Virginia where he lived. He made me a present of the mold-board of a plough he had invented himself; and told me of some red peas, which he offered to give me. He invited me to go to visit him, and showed me every possible civility. He told me the average crops of wheat in Virginia and Maryland were nearly three bushels and a half per acre.[32]

Samuel Harrison Smith,† a publisher and newspaper editor, became one of Jefferson's best friends in Philadelphia. In 1800, Jefferson convinced Smith to move his publishing business to the nation's newly established capital. The move was a huge financial gamble on Smith's part because it depended on Jefferson being elected to the presidency, which was by no means a sure thing. With the electoral votes tied between Jefferson and Aaron Burr, it was up to the House of Representatives to decide who became president. Finally, on the thirty-sixth ballot, Jefferson was elected. Margaret Bayard Smith†—Samuel Harrison Smith's wife—had not met Jefferson in Philadelphia but came to know him in Washington and became one of his best friends and most ardent supporters. In addition, she left a delightful firsthand account of him.

Filled with numerous anecdotes and table talk, her reminiscence also relates what Jefferson did after being inaugurated. He had not lost his disgust for ceremony. There was no inaugural ball: that tradition would not begin until the next president's inauguration at the behest of his wife, Dolley Madison. Since the Adamses had yet to vacate the White House, Jefferson simply walked back to the boardinghouse where he had been staying, took the same seat at the dinner table he always took, and partook of the same meal as all the other boarders.

Early biographer B. L. Rayner related a different version of this anecdote, quoting a Baltimore man who happened to be at the boardinghouse for dinner that evening.[33] Accidentally seated next to President Jefferson, the man expressed his desire to congratulate him.

"I would advise you," Jefferson answered with a smile, "to follow my example on nuptial occasions, when I always tell the bridegroom I will wait till the end of the year before offering my congratulations."

Jefferson's casual manner sometimes unsettled visitors to the White House, but he was usually able to disarm others and put them at ease. Writing in the second year of his presidency, Robert Troup observed, "Jefferson is the supreme director of measures—he has no levee days—observes no ceremony—often sees company in an undress, sometimes with his slippers on—always accessible to, and very familiar with, the sovereign people."[34] Troup, a stalwart Federalist and thus politically opposed to Jefferson, was not writing from personal knowledge. Rather, he was synthesizing stories about Jefferson that had been circulating orally since he became president. Regardless, Troup's remarks are on target. Many critics found Jefferson's lack of decorum inappropriate for the leader of a nation.

When Jefferson returned to Monticello during his presidency, and even more so after he retired from public life, numerous curiosity seekers came to visit. Thoughtful ones secured letters of introduction, but many people just showed up at his door to meet him and view his renowned home. As Benjamin Rush's son Richard told a correspondent upon his visit to Monticello, "I need not tell you with what open doors he lives, as you well know his mountain is made a sort of Mecca."[35] Samuel Whitcomb, an itinerant bookseller soliciting subscriptions for a new book, was one of many visitors who left accounts of their experience. When he knocked, Whitcomb was astonished to find Jefferson himself opening the door.[36] Among the visitors' accounts, few were more influential than the one by John Edwards Caldwell,[†] who actually spent less than an hour at Monticello. Caldwell related the visit as part of his self-published, but anonymous travel narrative, *A Tour through Part of Virginia in the Summer of 1808.*

In itself this book made little impact, but when the *Cape Fear Recorder,* a Wilmington, North Carolina, newspaper, reprinted Caldwell's account under the title, "The Sage of Monticello," in 1816, it caught fire. Under that title, it was reprinted throughout the United States.[37] Coined by his detractors during the run-up to the 1800 presidential election, the phrase, "The Sage of Monticello," was originally used in an ironic way as a pejorative, implying that perhaps Thomas Jefferson was not as sagacious as his supporters made him out to be.[38] Caldwell's account dispelled any negative connotations the phrase may have retained after Jef-

Monticello, Charlottesville, Virginia, designed by Thomas Jefferson, 1770–1826, and photographed, ca. 1906. Library of Congress, Prints and Photographs Division, reproduction number LC-USZ62-126974.

ferson's presidency and genuinely portrayed him as a philosopher of the mountaintop.

Every time Jefferson had returned to Monticello from Washington, his daughter Martha—his only surviving daughter, Mary having passed away in 1804—moved from Edgehill, her husband's nearby estate, to Monticello, bringing her numerous children along. They made the sound of laughter a daily occurrence at Monticello, and their famous grandpa loved to be with them, leading them in games and teaching them what he knew. Granddaughters Ellen[†] and Virginia[†] both left vivid accounts of their childhood memories of Thomas Jefferson. Martha's devotion to her father created some tension between her and her husband, Thomas Mann Randolph, but the two ultimately reconciled, and she gave birth to even more children at Monticello. When George Wythe Randolph, her twelfth child, was born in 1818, her father quipped, "My dear! We shall have to send you back to the convent!"[39]

Jefferson often brought his grandchildren to Poplar Forest. Located in Bedford County about seventy-five miles from Monticello, the Poplar Forest property had belonged to Jefferson ever since the death of his father-in-law John Wayles. Throughout that time, it had remained a working farm. It never really became a vacation retreat until Jefferson began building here during his second term as president.

Few visitors outside the family came to Poplar Forest, but there are exceptions, most notably an Englishman turned Illinois pioneer George Flower. In 1816, Flower came to the United States to explore the possibility of emigrating. Returning from his journey to Illinois, Flower stopped by Poplar Forest, where he found Jefferson and two of his granddaughters. Though he did not know Flower personally, Jefferson had heard of him, having read the work of his European traveling companion, Morris Birkbeck, whose *Notes on a Journey through France* appealed to Jefferson for its emphasis on agriculture. Jefferson had a copy of Birkbeck's *Notes* in his retirement library at Monticello. Birkbeck had dedicated the book to Flower, whom he calls "my agreeable and intelligent fellow-traveller."[40]

In his account, Flower provides a good description of both Poplar Forest and Jefferson:

> His house was built after the fashion of a French chateau. Octagon rooms, floors of polished oak, lofty ceilings, large mirrors, betokened his French taste, acquired by his long residence in France. Mr. Jefferson's figure was rather majestic: tall (over six feet), thin, and rather high-shouldered; manners, simple, kind, and courteous. His dress, in color and form, was quaint and old-fashioned, plain and neat—a dark pepper-and-salt coat, cut in the old quaker fashion, with a single row of large metal buttons, kneebreeches, gray-worsted stockings, shoes fastened by large metal buckles—such was the appearance of Jefferson when I first made his acquaintance, in 1816. His two granddaughters—Misses Randolph—well-educated and accomplished young ladies, were staying with him at the time.[41]

Flower also visited Monticello. Despite the grandeur of Jefferson's home and its beautiful setting, what Flower enjoyed most was Jefferson's conversation: "The chief charm of the visit was in the evening conversations with Mr. Jefferson, who gave me the inner history of events, before only known to me, as to the world generally, in the published records or outside history, which is all that the public is generally allowed to see."[42]

The Rotunda at the University of Virginia, designed by Thomas Jefferson, 1826, and photographed by the Detroit Publishing Company, ca. 1900. Library of Congress, Prints and Photographs Division, reproduction number LC-DIG-det-4a17618.

At dinner one day, Jefferson provided "many amusing anecdotes of the early days of American freedom." Flower recorded one of Jefferson's anecdotes that concerned George Washington: "Two members from one of the northern states waited on Gen. Washington in their official capacity. As they entered the house they espied Mrs. Washington crossing the Hall. With respectful Hommage they enquired if his majesty was at home. Martha Washington replied, the General's upstairs, if you mean him." Jefferson had been telling this story for at least seventeen years. Joshua Brookes, who visited Monticello in 1799, recorded the same anecdote.[43]

The creation of the University of Virginia was the great project of Jefferson's retirement. He chose its location, secured its funding, designed its buildings and its curriculum, planned and catalogued its library holdings, arranged to hire its professors, and served as its rector. As if that were not enough, sometimes he could be found with masonry tools in hand, demonstrating techniques to the workmen who were building it. Many visitors during the 1820s had the opportunity to see the university as it emerged from the wooded hills of Albemarle County. In addition, the arrival of the faculty and students in 1825 added a new set of commentators who left personal impressions of Jefferson.

Dr. Robley Dunglison,† the university's first professor of medicine, also became Jefferson's personal physician and attended him in his final illness. Henry Tutwiler,† who was among the very first class that matriculated in 1825, left an account of dinner at Monticello. Jefferson, according to Tutwiler, made it a point to invite each of the university students to dinner at least once. George Long,† the youngest professor, lived into the 1870s and, therefore, left one of the latest reminiscences of Thomas Jefferson.

The year 1843 marked the centennial of Thomas Jefferson's birth. At the time, Albert Gallatin, his former secretary of treasury, was the last surviving member of his cabinet. The organizers of a centennial celebration gra-

Robley Dunglison, M.D., engraved print by A. H. Ritchie after a daguerreotype by M. P. Simons, 1846. Library of Congress, Prints and Photographs Division, reproduction number LC-USZ62-98482.

ciously requested Gallatin to attend, but the state of his health prevented him. In his letter refusing their request, Gallatin mentioned his personal friendship with Jefferson, "which during a period of thirty years was never interrupted, or even obscured by a single cloud."[44] Gallatin's letter is respectful, yet frustrating: it offers no specific details about Jefferson, no stories, no anecdotes, just an encomium of friendship.

Privately, Albert Gallatin spoke about Jefferson in much greater detail. John Russell Bartlett, who ran a bookshop in lower Manhattan, befriended Gallatin—a frequent customer—and remembered his attachment to Jefferson, which showed in his home and his conversation. Bartlett remembered an engraved miniature portrait of Jefferson on Gallatin's desk and a set of Jefferson's collected writings on his shelf, which Gallatin asked to have rebound in luxurious full calf. In conversation, Gallatin mentioned Jefferson frequently. Bartlett wrote, "He often spoke of Mr. Jefferson, and related many anecdotes of him." Gallatin never wrote down those anecdotes, nor did Bartlett, who admitted, "Their particulars have escaped my recollection."[45] Written documents are the stuff of history. For those who knew Jefferson personally but did not write down their encounters of him, their memories, and his anecdotes, died with them.

Except where otherwise noted, the following articles come from their earliest published versions. They have been silently emended to provide readers with clear, straightforward texts. Throughout this volume, essay titles enclosed in brackets have been supplied by the editor, though they are usually derived from key passages in the corresponding essays. Bibliographic details for all sources referenced in the headnotes appear in the list of works cited at the volume's end. Bibliographic information for each essay appears in an unnumbered note following its text. The superscript daggers (†) you see before you in this introduction are not daggers of the mind. Rather, they indicate authors whose accounts have been included in this volume.

This book can trace its beginnings to the American Literature Association Symposium on Biography held in Puerto Vallarta, Mexico, where I presented a talk on Thomas Jefferson's sense of humor. Between the moonlight and the margaritas, I learned much about the art of biography from my colleagues, who encouraged me to delve more deeply into the subject of Jefferson's humor. I especially thank Joel Myerson, the editor of Writers in Their Own Time, who invited me to edit this volume as part of the series. I completed much of my research on this project at the Robert H. Smith International Center for Jefferson Studies (ICJS) at Monticello. I am grateful to the ICJS not only for providing a research fellowship, but also for giving Myung-Sook and me pleasant accommodations in the form of a country cottage where the deer came to our doorstep. I would also like to thank Andrew O'Shaughnessy, the director of the ICJS, and his kind and helpful staff.

Having dinner in Charlottesville one evening with Andrew and other notable Jefferson scholars, including Frank Cogliano and Peter Onuf, I had an opportunity to test out some of my ideas. When I told them I intended to depict Jefferson as a funny guy, Frank exclaimed, "Why, you're a revisionist!" Previously, I had never thought of myself as such. "Revisionist" had seemed like a pejorative term ever since I first heard the word in graduate school. Remember what Dale Gribble says on *King of the Hill:* "Damn revisionists, why can't they ever make history better?" If I am a revisionist, then perhaps I am one Dale Gribble might like. I hesitate to use his qualitative term (and I'm unsure whether I would want his endorsement), but I am trying to make literary history more appealing, more human.

The ICJS is also the home of *The Papers of Thomas Jefferson: Retirement Series.* J. Jefferson Looney and his crack team of editors, especially Ellen Hickman and Lisa Francavilla, helped me considerably. At the University of Iowa Press I would like to thank Holly Carver, Catherine Cocks, and Charlotte Wright for all their help in bringing this volume to fruition. Finally, I thank my wife Myung-Sook, who has provided encouragement and moral support for this and all my other concurrent projects. Her capacity to inspire continues to amaze me.

Notes

1. Dumas Malone, "Jefferson, Thomas," *Dictionary of American Biography,* ed. Allen Johnson and Dumas Malone, 20 vols. (New York: Scribner, 1928–1937), 10: 31.

2. Dumas Malone, *Jefferson and His Time,* 6 vols. (Boston: Little, Brown, 1948–1981), 1: 105, 2: 131, 3: 115, 4: 136.

3. Dumas Malone, "The Life of Thomas Jefferson," *Thomas Jefferson: A Reference Biography,* ed. Merrill D. Peterson (New York: Scribner, 1986), p. 21.

4. Samuel L. Mitchill, *A Discourse on the Character and Services of Thomas Jefferson, More Especially as Promoter of Natural and Physical Sciences* (New York: G. and C. Carvill, 1826), p. 41.

5. T. P. H. Lyman, *The Life of Thomas Jefferson, Esq. L.L.D. Late Ex. President of the*

United States (Philadelphia: D. and S. Neall, 1826), p. 107; Alexander H. H. Stuart to W. J. Campbell, 3 August 1886, quoted in Betty L. Goss, "Jefferson and Humor," unpublished research report, Monticello.

6. Diary of Ann Maury, 28 October 1831, quoted in Goss, "Jefferson and Humor."

7. John Page, "Governor Page," *Virginia Register and Literary Notebook* 3 (July 1850): 151.

8. Kevin J. Hayes, *The Road to Monticello: The Life and Mind of Thomas Jefferson* (New York: Oxford University Press, 2008), p. 167.

9. Samuel Ward to Henry Ward, 22 June 1775, *Letters of Delegates to Congress, 1774–1789,* ed. Paul Hubert Smith and Ronald M. Gephart, 26 vols. (Washington: Library of Congress, 1976–2000), 1: 535.

10. John Adams, *Diary and Autobiography of John Adams,* ed. L. H. Butterfield et al., 4 vols. (Cambridge, MA: Belknap Press of Harvard University Press, 1961), 2: 218.

11. Benjamin Rush to Thomas Jefferson, 6 October 1800, *Letters of Benjamin Rush,* ed. L. H. Butterfield, 2 vols. (Philadelphia: for the American Philosophical Society by Princeton University Press, 1951), 2: 826.

12. Benjamin Rush, *The Autobiography of Benjamin Rush, His "Travels through Life" Together with his Commonplace Book for 1789–1813,* ed. George W. Corner (Princeton: for the American Philosophical Society by Princeton University Press, 1948), p. 151.

13. John Spear Smith to Henry S. Randall, undated, quoted in Henry S. Randall, *The Life of Thomas Jefferson,* 3 vols. (New York: Derby and Jackson, 1858), 3: 680–681.

14. Jacob Rubsamen to Thomas Jefferson, 1 December 1780, *The Papers of Thomas Jefferson,* ed. Julian P. Boyd, et al., 38 vols. to date (Princeton: Princeton University Press, 1950–), 4: 174.

15. Hayes, *Road to Monticello,* p. 268.

16. David Howell to Jonathan Arnold, 21 February 1784, *Letters of Delegates to Congress,* 21: 380.

17. Quoted in *Papers,* 7: 82.

18. Abigail Adams to Cotton Tufts, 8 September 1784, *Adams Family Correspondence,* ed. L. H. Butterfield, et al., 10 vols. to date (Cambridge, MA: Belknap Press of Harvard University Press, 1963–), 5: 458.

19. Hayes, *The Road to Monticello,* pp. 383–387.

20. "Extract from the Diary of Nathaniel Cutting," *Papers,* 15: 498.

21. Thomas Jefferson, "Anecdotes of Doctor Franklin, 1818 and 1821," *Franklin in His Own Time: A Biographical Chronicle of His Life, Drawn from Recollections, Interviews, and Memoirs by Family, Friends, and Associates,* ed. Kevin J. Hayes and Isabelle Bour (Iowa City: University of Iowa Press, 2011), pp. 132–140.

22. Rush, *Autobiography,* p. 181.

23. Hayes, *Road to Monticello,* pp. 404–417.

24. Francis Lieber to General Garfield, 11 December 1871, *The Life and Letters of Francis Lieber,* ed. Thomas Sergeant Perry (Boston: James R. Osgood, 1882), p. 417.

25. William Maclay, *Journal of William Maclay, United States Senator from Pennsylvania, 1789–1791,* ed. Edgar S. Maclay (New York: D. Appleton, 1890), p. 272.

26. James Madison to Margaret B. Smith, September 1830, *The Writings of James Madison,* ed. Gaillard Hunt, 9 vols. (New York: G. P. Putnam's Sons, 1900–1910), 9: 406.

27. Rush, *Autobiography,* p. 194.

28. Noble Cunningham, Jr., "The Diary of Frances Few, 1808–1809," *Journal of Southern History* 29 (1963): 351.

29. Charles W. Campbell, "Memoirs of a Monticello Slave," *Jefferson at Monticello,* ed. James A. Bear, Jr. (Charlottesville: University Press of Virginia, 1967), p. 3.

30. For a good survey, see Lucia Stanton, "The Other End of the Telescope: Jefferson through the Eyes of His Slaves," *William and Mary Quarterly* 57 (2000): 139–152.

31. Campbell, "Memoirs," p. 8.

32. Richard Parkinson, *A Tour in America, in 1798, 1799, and 1800: Exhibiting Sketches of Society and Manners, and a Particular Account of the American System of Agriculture, with Its Recent Improvements,* 2 vols. (London: for J. Harding and J. Murray, 1805), 1: 82–83.

33. B. L. Rayner, *Life of Thomas Jefferson* (Boston: Lilly, Wait, Colman, and Holden, 1834), p. 304.

34. Robert Troup to Rufus King, 9 April 1802, *The Life and Correspondence of Rufus King: Comprising his Letters, Private and Official, His Public Documents, and His Speeches,* ed. Charles R. King, 6 vols. (New York: G. P. Putnam's Sons, 1894–1900), 4: 103.

35. Richard Rush, "Call It Olympus," *Visitors to Monticello,* ed. Merrill D. Peterson (Charlottesville: University Press of Virginia, 1989), pp. 72–73.

36. William Peden, "A Book Peddler Invades Monticello," *William and Mary Quarterly,* 3d ser. 6 (1949): 632.

37. The impact of this article has largely gone unnoticed. In 1816 alone, it appeared in the *Providence Patriot* (21 September), *Daily National Intelligencer* [Washington, D.C.] (10 October), *National Register* [Washington, D.C.] (12 October), *National Advocate* [New York] (15 October), *Boston Daily Advertiser* (18 October), *The Repertory* [Boston] (19 October), *Farmer's Repository* [Charlestown, West Virginia] (23 October), *Rhode Island Republican* (23 October), *Burlington Gazette* (24 October), *Boston Weekly Messenger* (24 October), *Pittsfield Sun* (31 October), *Farmer's Cabinet* [Amherst, New Hampshire] (2 November), *Otsego Herald* (7 November), *American Advocate* [Hallowell, Maine] (16 November), *The Eagle* [Maysville, Kentucky] (22 November), *New-Hampshire Patriot* (31 December), and undoubtedly numerous others.

38. The earliest recorded usage of the phrase that I have located is Asbury Dickins, *The Claims of Thomas Jefferson to the Presidency, Examined at the Bar of Christianity* (Philadelphia: Asbury Dickins, 1800), p. 50.

39. Ellen Wayles Harrison (one of Jefferson's great-granddaughters), quoted in Goss, "Jefferson and Humor."

40. Nathaniel P. Poor, *President Jefferson's Library* (Washington: Gales and Seaton, 1829), lot 324; Thomas Jefferson to George Flower, 12 September 1817, *The Writings of Thomas Jefferson,* ed. Andrew A. Lipscomb and Albert Ellery Bergh, 20 vols. (Washington: Thomas Jefferson Memorial Association, 1903), 15: 142; Morris Birkbeck, *Notes on a Journey through France, from Dieppe through Paris and Lyons, to the Pyrennees, and*

back through Toulouse, in July, August, and September, 1814, Describing the Habits of the People, and the Agriculture of the Country (Philadelphia: M. Carey, 1815), p. 4.

41. George Flower, *History of the English Settlement in Edwards County, Illinois, Founded in 1817 and 1818, by Morris Birkbeck and George Flower,* ed. E. B. Washburne (Chicago: Fergus, 1882), p. 43.

42. Flower, *History of the English Settlement,* pp. 44–45.

43. Quoted in Otto L. Schmidt, "The Mississippi Valley in 1816 through an Englishman's Diary," *Mississippi Valley Historical Review* 14 (1927): 155; quoted in R. W. G. Vail, "A Dinner at Mount Vernon from the Unpublished Journal of Joshua Brookes (1773–1859)," *New York Historical Society Quarterly* 31 (1947): 82.

44. Albert Gallatin to George Plitt and Others, 8 April 1843, *The Writings of Albert Gallatin,* ed. Henry Adams, 3 vols. (1879; reprinted, New York: Antiquarian Press, 1960), 2: 603.

45. John Russell Bartlett, "Reminiscences of Albert Gallatin," *Proceedings of the New York Historical Society* 7 (1849): 291–292.

Chronology

1743	13 APRIL. Thomas Jefferson born at Shadwell plantation in Goochland (later Albemarle) County, Virginia, to Peter Jefferson, a planter and surveyor, and Jane Randolph Jefferson
1752	Begins attending a local school run by the Reverend William Douglas
1757	17 AUGUST. Peter Jefferson dies
1758–1760	Attends the boarding school of the Reverend James Maury in Fredericksville Parish, twelve miles from Shadwell
1760–1762	Attends College of William and Mary in Williamsburg, studying mathematics and philosophy with William Small and becoming part of the circle of Virginia Governor Francis Fauquier
1762	Begins reading law under George Wythe in Williamsburg
1764	Comes of age and inherits 2,750 acres from his father's estate
1765	Passes his bar exam and returns to Shadwell
1766	Travels through Annapolis, Philadelphia, and New York
1767	Begins practicing law in Albemarle and Augusta counties
1768	Levels Monticello, a mountain near Shadwell on land he inherited from his father
1769	Admitted to practice law before the General Court of Virginia MAY. Takes his seat in the Virginia House of Burgesses as representative from Albemarle County, in which capacity he continues to serve until 1776
1770	Construction begins at Monticello 1 FEBRUARY. Shadwell burns. Most of Jefferson's papers and books are destroyed

NOVEMBER. Moves to Monticello

1772 1 JANUARY. Marries Martha Wayles Skelton, a widow, aged twenty-three, whose dowry nearly doubles his land, which includes Poplar Forest, the estate in Bedford County he would later make his vacation retreat
27 SEPTEMBER. Daughter Martha (Patsy) born

1774 AUGUST. *Summary View of the Rights of British America* published

1775 27 MARCH. Elected delegate to the Second Continental Congress to replace Peyton Randolph
20 JUNE. Arrives in Philadelphia to serve in the Continental Congress
JUNE–JULY. Drafts "A Declaration of the Causes and Necessity for Taking Up Arms"
JULY. Drafts "Resolutions of Congress on Lord North's Conciliatory Proposal"
AUGUST. Attends Virginia Convention at Richmond
1 OCTOBER. Returns to Philadelphia to continue serving in the Continental Congress until December

1776 31 MARCH. His mother, Jane Randolph Jefferson, dies
14 MAY. Arrives in Philadelphia to attend the Continental Congress, remaining until September
7 JUNE. Richard Henry Lee, acting on instructions from the Virginia government, moves a resolution in Congress calling for a declaration of independence; Congress appoints the "Committee of Five" to draft the declaration. The committee includes Jefferson, John Adams, Benjamin Franklin, Robert Livingston, and Roger Sherman. The committee asks Jefferson to draft the document
JUNE. Submits his draft of the Declaration of Independence to the committee, which makes several changes
28 JUNE. The committee submits to Congress the emended draft, "A Declaration by the Representatives in General Congress Assembled"
1–4 JULY. Congress debates the draft, making several additional changes before approving the Declaration of Independence

	4 JULY. Philadelphia printer John Dunlap prints copies of the Declaration of Independence 11 OCTOBER. Starts attending Virginia Assembly as a member of the House of Delegates
1777	16 MAY. Begins correspondence with John Adams
1778	1 AUGUST. Daughter Mary (Maria) is born
1779	1 JUNE. Elected governor of Virginia 18 JUNE. Submits report of the Committee of Revisors to the Virginia House, which includes Statute for Religious Freedom and various other bills revising the penal code and the educational system. The Virginia General Assembly eventually passes the Statute for Religious Freedom on 16 January 1786
1780	21 JANUARY. Elected member of the American Philosophical Society 2 JUNE. Reelected governor of Virginia OCTOBER. Begins writing what would become *Notes on the State of Virginia*
1781	6–10 JANUARY. Benedict Arnold leads an invasion of Virginia, burning Richmond and forcing Governor Jefferson and others to flee the capital 2 JUNE. Second term as governor expires, but before a new governor can be elected, a detachment from British General Lord Cornwallis's army attacks Charlottesville and Monticello; Jefferson and his family flee
1782	6 SEPTEMBER. Martha Jefferson dies after an illness of several months following the birth of her sixth child, Lucy Elizabeth, on 8 May
1783	6 JUNE. Elected delegate to Congress from Virginia DECEMBER. Begins attending Congress at Annapolis
1784	1 MARCH. Submits to Congress "Plan for Government of the Western Territory" MARCH–MAY. Drafts "Notes on Coinage," which proposes replacing the English system of pounds sterling, shillings, and pence with a decimal system 7 MAY. Appointed minister plenipotentiary to join John Adams

and Benjamin Franklin in negotiating treaties of amity and commerce with European nations
JUNE–JULY. Travels throughout the eastern states
5 JULY. Sails for Europe from Boston, accompanied by his daughter Martha, now twelve
3 AUGUST. Arrives in Le Havre and continues to Paris

1785 Publishes first edition of *Notes on the State of Virginia* in Paris

1786 MARCH–APRIL. Visits England and tours the English countryside with John Adams
LATE SUMMER. John Trumbull introduces Jefferson to Maria Cosway

1787 MARCH–JUNE. Travels through the south of France and in northern Italy
JULY. Jefferson's daughter Mary, now nine, arrives in Paris

1788 MARCH–APRIL. Jefferson travels through Holland and central Europe

1789 5 MAY. Jefferson attends the opening of the French Estates-General and its debates at Versailles
JULY. Lafayette and other French liberals meet secretly at Jefferson's home, the Hôtel de Langeac, to discuss a new French constitution
26 SEPTEMBER. The United States Senate confirms George Washington's appointment of Jefferson to the position of secretary of state
28 SEPTEMBER. Leaves France for Virginia

1790 23 FEBRUARY. Daughter Martha marries her second cousin Thomas Mann Randolph at Monticello
21 MARCH. Assumes the duties of secretary of state in New York City, where the federal government is located
4 JULY. Submits to Congress "Report on Weights and Measures"

1791 MAY–JUNE. Tours the northern states with James Madison

1793 DECEMBER. Resigns his position as secretary of state, effective 31 December

1794 WINTER–SUMMER. Returns to Monticello

1796	7 DECEMBER. Elected vice president, having received the second-largest number of electoral votes. John Adams is elected president
1797	3 MARCH. Installed as president of the American Philosophical Society in Philadelphia 4 MARCH. Inaugurated vice president of the United States. Presiding over the Senate, he begins compiling rules of parliamentary practice 13 OCTOBER. Daughter Mary weds her cousin John Wayles Eppes
1800	3 DECEMBER. Electors meet in their states and cast votes for the next president of the United States. A tie vote between Jefferson and Aaron Burr throws the election into the House of Representatives
1801	Publishes *A Manual of Parliamentary Practice,* which becomes the procedural handbook for the Senate and, indeed, for legislatures around the globe 11 FEBRUARY. The House of Representatives meets separately and continues balloting for six days 17 FEBRUARY. On the thirty-sixth ballot, Jefferson is elected president and Aaron Burr becomes vice president 4 MARCH. Jefferson is the first president inaugurated in Washington, D.C. MAY. The pasha of Tripoli declares war on the United States MAY 20. Sends a naval squadron to Tripoli
1802	1 JANUARY. Replies to a letter from Connecticut's Danbury Baptist Association, in which he articulates his views on the separation of church and state
1803	18 JANUARY. Asks Congress for funds for an expedition to explore the Mississippi River and beyond in search of a route to the Pacific 30 APRIL. Robert Livingston, ambassador to France, and James Monroe, special envoy, conclude a treaty of cession in Paris in which the United States purchases from France the whole of the Louisiana territory for fifteen million dollars, nearly doubling the size of the United States 4 JULY. News of the purchase of the Louisiana territory is announced in the United States

1804	17 APRIL. Daughter Mary Jefferson Eppes dies from complications in childbirth MAY. The expedition led by Meriwether Lewis and William Clark departs NOVEMBER. Reelected president in a landslide
1805	4 MARCH. Inaugurated as president for a second term
1806	19 APRIL. Nominates James Monroe and William Pinckney as joint commissioners to Great Britain
1807	JUNE–JULY. After the British warship *Leopard* attacks the American ship *Chesapeake* off the Virginia coast, Jefferson releases a proclamation closing American ports to all British ships except those with emergencies or on diplomatic missions 14 DECEMBER. The Nonimportation Act becomes effective, and on 18 December, the Senate passes the Embargo Act, closing all American ports to foreign trade and incensing Jefferson's political opponents at home
1809	1 MARCH. Signs the Non-Intercourse Act, which effectively repeals the Embargo Act of 1807 but continues restrictions on trade with Great Britain 4 MARCH. Retires from public office, and James Madison is inaugurated president MARCH. Leaves Washington and returns to his home, Monticello
1813	JULY. After years of estrangement, Jefferson and John Adams resume their personal correspondence, which would continue through the remainder of their lives
1814	21 SEPTEMBER. Jefferson offers to sell his library of nearly 6,700 volumes to the federal government to replace the original congressional library, destroyed when the British burned the Capitol in Washington, D.C.
1815	JANUARY. Congress purchases Jefferson's library for $23,950, and he ships it to Washington by wagon in May. His library becomes the basis of the Library of Congress
1817	4 MARCH. James Monroe is inaugurated as president 6 OCTOBER. The cornerstone is laid for Central College, which will become the University of Virginia

1818	4 FEBRUARY. Jefferson writes an introduction for a collection of letters, confidential notes, and reports written while he was secretary of state, which grandson, Thomas Jefferson Randolph, would name *The Anas* 1–4 AUGUST. Chairs a commission meeting at Rockfish Gap, Virginia, to plan the University of Virginia
1821	JANUARY–JULY. Begins writing his autobiography, which would remain unfinished at the time of his death
1824	APRIL. Prepares instructions for recruiting faculty in Europe for the University of Virginia 3–15 NOVEMBER. Lafayette visits Monticello and enjoys a dinner in his honor at the rotunda on the campus of the University of Virginia
1825	7 MARCH. The University of Virginia opens
1826	4 JULY. Dies shortly after noon on the fiftieth anniversary of the Declaration of Independence. Later that same day John Adams dies in Massachusetts

Jefferson in His Own Time

[A Conversation Always Varied and Interesting] (1782)

François Jean, Marquis de Chastellux

A professional soldier, polished author, and brilliant conversationalist, the Marquis de Chastellux was equally at home on the battlefield, at his desk, or in the Paris salons. He was an accomplished author, having already written a number of works including, most importantly, *De la félicité publique* (1772), a groundbreaking study of social history and the history of social institutions. Chastellux first came to America as a major general in the French Expeditionary Forces, third in command under General Rochambeau. During the American Revolution, Chastellux occasionally obtained leave from the service to travel through the United States and witness democracy in its genesis. In one trip, he traveled from Newport, Rhode Island, to Philadelphia. Since the French navy sailed with a printing press, Chastellux had a small edition of his travel journal printed to distribute to friends. *Voyage de Newport à Philadelphie,* as he titled this volume of travels, shows his powers of observation and his keen understanding of the American way of life. During another trip, he took a tour of Virginia. He combined the text of the Newport edition with his Virginia journal and published them together as *Voyages . . . dans l'Amérique Septentrionale* or, as the English translation was titled, *Travels in North-America.* A delightfully picaresque account of his American experiences, Chastellux's *Voyages* is the finest travel narrative to emerge from the era of the Revolutionary War.

On his tour through Virginia, Chastellux and his sizeable entourage approached Monticello on Saturday, 13 April 1782. Unsure of the precise route, they encountered an Irish emigrant and horsetrader, who led them to the foot of the Southwest Mountains. What Chastellux wrote about Jefferson's home constitutes the most detailed account of Monticello as it stood in the early 1780s. His description indicates what Jefferson had finished up to this point as well as what he had yet to complete when he remodeled it during the 1790s. Furthermore, Chastellux's account verifies that Jefferson not only designed the building, but he was also helping to build it. His description indicates how Monticello looked before Jefferson remodeled it during the 1790s.

Chastellux's characterization of Jefferson's manner jibes with what many others would say. He seemed cold at first but, among kindred spirits, he quickly warmed up. During the four days Chastellux spent at Monticello the conversation embraced many subjects and took many different directions. Chastellux's digressions are included in the following extract because, as he admits, they closely resemble his conversation with Jefferson. Not all the time the two spent together at Monticello was filled with conversation, however. They also played chess, as their subsequent correspondence confirms. Whether talking about literature, playing games of skill, or walking through the woods, Chastellux came to know Jefferson well enough during his time at Monticello to write a flattering character sketch of him, which Jefferson, as he told its author, "read with a continued blush from beginning to end, as it presented me a lively picture of what I wish to be, but am not. No, my dear Sir," he continued, "the thousand millionth part of what you there say, is more than I deserve" (Jefferson, *Papers* 8: 467).

ON THE SUMMIT [. . .] we discovered the house of Mr. Jefferson, which stands pre-eminent in these retirements; it was himself who built it and preferred this situation; for although he possessed considerable property in the neighbourhood, there was nothing to prevent him from fixing his residence wherever he thought proper. But it was a debt nature owed to a philosopher and a man of taste, that in his own possessions he should find a spot where he might best study and enjoy her. He calls his house Monticello, (in Italian, Little Mountain,) a very modest title, for it is situated upon a very lofty one, but which announces the owner's attachment to the language of Italy; and above all to the fine arts, of which that country was the cradle, and is still the asylum. As I had no farther occasion for a guide, I separated from the Irishman; and after ascending by a tolerably commodious road, for more than half an hour, we arrived at Monticello. This house, of which Mr. Jefferson was the architect, and often one of the workmen, is rather elegant, and in the Italian taste, though not without fault; it consists of one large square pavilion, the entrance of which is by two porticos ornamented with pillars. The ground floor consists chiefly of a very large lofty saloon, which is to be decorated entirely in the antique style: above it is a library of the same form, two small wings, with only a ground floor, and attic story, are joined to this pavillion, and communicate with the kitchen, offices, etc. which will form a kind of basement story over which runs a terrace. My object in this short description is only to show the difference between this, and the other houses of the country; for we may safely aver, that Mr. Jefferson is the first American who has consulted the fine arts to know how he should shelter himself from the weather. But it is on himself alone I ought to bestow my time. Let me describe to you a man, not yet forty, tall, and with a mild and pleasing countenance, but whose mind and understanding are ample substitutes for every exterior grace. An American, who without ever having quitted his own country, is at once a musician, skilled in drawing, a geometrician, an astronomer, a natural philosopher, legislator, and statesman. A senator of America, who sat for two years in that famous Congress which brought about the revolution; and which is never mentioned without respect, though unhappily not without regret: a governor of Virginia, who filled this difficult station during the invasions of [Benedict] Arnold, of [William] Phillips, and of [Lord] Cornwallis; a philosopher, in voluntary retirement from the world, and public business, because he loves the world, inasmuch only as he can flatter himself with being useful to mankind; and the minds of his countrymen are not yet in a condition either to bear the light, or to suffer contradiction. A mild and amiable wife, charming children, of whose education he himself takes charge, a house to embellish, great provisions to improve, and the arts and sciences to cultivate; these are what remain to Mr. Jefferson, after having played a principal character on the theatre of the new world, and which he preferred to the honourable commission of Minister Plenipotentiary in Europe. The visit which I made him was not unexpected, for he had long since invited me to come and pass a few days with him, in the centre of the mountains; notwithstanding which I found his first appearance serious, nay even cold; but before I had been two hours with him we were as intimate as if we had passed our whole lives together; walking, books, but above all, a conversation always varied and interesting, always supported by that sweet satisfaction experienced by two persons, who in communicating their sentiments and opinions, are invariably in unison, and who understand each other at the first hint, made four days pass away like so many minutes.

This conformity of sentiments and opinions on which I insist, because it constitutes my own eulogium, (and self-love must somewhere show itself,) this conformity, I say, was so perfect, that not only our taste was similar, but our predilections also, those partialities which cold methodical minds ridicule as enthusiastic, whilst sensible and animated ones cherish and adopt the glorious appellation. I recollect with pleasure that as we were conversing one evening over a bowl of punch, after Mrs. Jefferson had retired, our conversation turned on the poems of Ossian. It was a spark of electricity which passed rapidly from one to the other; we recollected the passages in those sublime poems, which particularly struck us, and entertained my fellow travellers, who fortunately knew English well, and were qualified to judge of their merit, though they had never read the poems. In our enthusiasm the book was sent for, and placed near the bowl, where, by their mutual aid, the night far advanced imperceptibly upon us. Sometimes natural philosophy, at others politics or the arts, were the topics of our conversation, for no object had escaped Mr. Jefferson; and it seemed as if from his youth he had placed his mind, as he has done his house, on an elevated situation, from which he might contemplate the universe.

The only stranger who visited us during our stay at Monticello, was Colonel Armand [Charles-Armand Tuffin, marquis de La Rouërie], whom I have mentioned in the first part of my Journal; he had been in France the preceding year with Colonel [John] Laurens, but returned soon enough to be present at the siege of York, where he marched as a volunteer at the attack of the redoubts. His object in going to France, was to purchase clothing and accoutrements complete for a regiment he had already commanded, but which had been so roughly handled in the campaigns to the southward, that it was necessary to form it anew: he made the advance of the necessaries to Congress, who engaged to provide men and horses. Charlotteville, a rising little town, situated in a valley two leagues from Monticello, being the quarter assigned for assembling this legion, Colonel Armand invited me to dine with him the next day, where Mr. Jefferson and I went, and found the legion under arms. It is to be composed of 200 horse and 150 foot. The horse was almost complete and very well mounted; the infantry was still feeble, but the whole were well clothed, well armed, and made a very good appearance. We dined with Colonel Armand, all the officers of his regiment, and a *wolf* he amuses himself in bringing up, which is now ten months old, and is as familiar, mild, and gay as a young dog; he never quits his master, and has constantly the privilege of sharing his bed. It is to be wished that he may always answer so good an education, and not resume his natural character as he advances to maturity. He is not quite of the same kind with ours, his skin is almost black, and very glossy; he has nothing fierce about the head, so that were it not for his upright ears and pendent tail, one might readily take him for a dog. Perhaps he owes the singular advantage of not exhaling a bad smell, to the care which is taken of his toilet; for I remarked that the dogs were not in the least afraid of him, and that when they crossed his trace, they paid no attention to it. But it appears improbable, that all the neatness in the world can deceive the instinct of those animals, which have such a dread of wolves, that they have been observed, in the King's garden at Paris, to raise their coats and howl at the smell only of two mongrels, engendered by a dog and a she-wolf. I am inclined therefore to believe, that this peculiarity belongs to the species of black wolf, for they have our species also in America; and in Europe we may possibly have the black kind, for so it may be conjectured at least from the old proverb: "He is as much afraid of me as of a *grey* wolf," which implies that there are also black ones.

Since I am on the subject of animals, I shall mention here some observations which Mr. Jefferson enabled me to make upon the wild beasts which are common in this country. I have been a long time in doubt whether to call them roebucks, stags, or deer, for in Canada they are known by the first name, in the eastern provinces by the second, and in the southern by the third. Besides, in America, their nomenclatures are so inaccurate, and their observations so slight, that no information can be acquired by examining the people of the country. Mr. Jefferson amused himself by raising a score of these animals in his park; they are become very familiar, which happens to all the animals of America; for they are in general much easier to tame than those of Europe. He amuses himself by feeding them with Indian corn, of which they are very fond, and which they eat out of his hand. I followed him one evening into a deep valley, where they are accustomed to assemble towards the close of the day, and saw them walk, run, and bound: but the more I examined their paces, the less I was inclined to annex them to any particular species in Europe; they are absolutely of the same colour as the roebuck, and never change even when they are tamed, which often happens to deer. Their horns, which are never more than a foot and a half long, and have more than four branches on each side, are more open and broader than those of the roebuck; they take an oblique direction in front; their tails are from eight to ten inches long, and when they leap they carry them almost vertical like the deer; resembling those animals not only in their proportions, but in the form of their heads which are longer and less frizzled than those of the roebuck. They differ also from that species, as they are never found in pairs. From my own observations, in short, and from all I have been able to collect on the subject, I am convinced that this kind is peculiar to America, and that it may be considered something betwixt the deer and roebuck.[1] Mr. Jefferson being no sportsman, and not having crossed the seas, could have no decided opinion on this part of natural history; but he has not neglected the other branches. I saw with pleasure that he had applied himself particularly to meteorological observation, which, in fact, of all the branches of philosophy, is the most proper for the Americans to cultivate, from the extent of their country, and the variety of their situations, which give them in this point a great advantage over us, who in other respects have so many over them. Mr. Jefferson has made, with Mr. [James] Madison, a well informed professor of mathematics, some correspondent observations on the reigning winds at Williamsburgh, and Monticello; and although these two places are at the distance only of fifty leagues, and not separated by any chain of mountains, the difference of their results was, that for 127 observations on the northeast wind at Williamsburgh, there were only 32 at Monticello, where the northwest wind in general supplies the place of the northeast. This latter appears to be a sea-wind, easily counteracted by the slightest obstacle, insomuch that twenty years since it was scarcely ever felt beyond West-Point; that is to say beyond the conflux of the Pawmunkey and the Matapony, which unite and form York river, near thirty-five miles from its mouth. Since the progress of population and agriculture has considerably cleared the woods, it penetrates so far as Richmond, which is thirty miles farther. It may hence be observed, first, that the winds vary infinitely in their obliquity, and in the height of their region. Secondly, that nothing is more essential than the manner in which we proceed in the clearing of a country, for the salubrity of the air, nay even the order of the seasons, may depend on the access which we allow the winds, and the direction we may give them. It is a generally received opinion at Rome, that the air is less healthy since the felling of a large forest situated between that city and Ostia, which defended it from the winds known in Italy by the names of the *Scirocco* and the *Libico.* It is believed in Spain also, that the excessive droughts, of which the Castilians complain more and more, are occasioned by the cutting down of the woods, which used to attract and break the clouds in their passage. There is yet a very important consideration upon which I thought it my duty to fix the attention of the learned in this country, whatever diffidence I may have of my own knowledge in philosophy, as well as on every other subject. The greatest part of Virginia is very low and flat, and so divided by creeks and great rivers, that it appears absolutely redeemed from the sea, and an entire new creation; it is consequently very swampy, and can be dried only by the cutting down a great quantity of wood; but as on the other hand it can never be so drained as not still to abound with mephitical exhalations; and of whatever nature these exhalations may be, whether partaking of fixed or inflammable air, it is certain that vegetation absorbs them equally, and that trees are the most proper to accomplish this object.[2] It appears equally dangerous either to cut down or to preserve a great quantity of wood; so that the best manner of proceeding to clear the country, would be to disperse the settlements as much as possible, and to leave some groves of trees standing between them. In this manner the ground inhabited would be always healthy; and as there yet remain considerable marshes which they cannot drain, there is no risk of admitting the winds too easily, as they would serve to carry off the exhalations.

But I perceive my journal is something like the conversation I had with Mr. Jefferson; I pass from one object to another, and forget myself as I write, as it happened not unfrequently in his society. I must now quit the friend of nature, but not nature herself, who expects me in all her splendour at the end of my journey; I mean the famous *Bridge of Rocks* [The Natural Bridge], which unites two mountains, the most curious object I ever yet beheld, as its construction is the most difficult of solution. Mr. Jefferson would most willingly have conducted me thither, although this wonder is upwards of eighty miles from him, and he had often seen it; but his wife being expected every moment to lie-in, and himself as good a husband, as he is an excellent philosopher and a virtuous citizen, he only acted as my guide for about sixteen miles, to the passage of the little river Medium, where we parted, and I presume, to flatter myself, with mutual regret.

Notes

1. I have been lately assured, that when these animals grow old, their horns are as large as those of the stag, but their flesh has certainly the same taste with that of the deer in England [Chastellux's note].

2. This discovery the world owes to Doctor Franklin [Chastellux's note].

From François Jean, Marquis de Chastellux, *Travels in North-America, in the Years 1780–81–82,* trans. George Grieve (New York: White, Gallaher, and White, 1827), pp. 227–234.

[A Man of Great Sensibility and Parental Affection] (1784–1785)

Abigail Adams Smith

Abigail Adams Smith (1765–1813), the oldest child of John and Abigail Adams, traveled abroad in her late teens with her mother. Her father and brother—John Adams and John Quincy Adams—were already in Europe. Together, the Adams family settled in Auteuil on the outskirts of Paris. Like her father and brother, Nabby, as she was known among friends and family, kept a diary during their time in Paris. Her description brings alive their experience. She and her brother would frequently go into the city, where they were always welcome at the home of Thomas Jefferson, who also visited them at Auteuil. Jefferson did what he could to expose them to the culture of Paris. When two novitiates were scheduled to take the veil at the convent where his daughter Martha studied, he invited Nabby to attend. She described the ceremony in considerable detail. Seldom have Jefferson's biographers treated this episode. He disappears from her description, but it is important to realize that he was present throughout the ceremony; he saw what she saw. Though the two viewed the ceremony from different perspectives—she was a devout New England Protestant, he disliked and distrusted any and all forms of ceremony, religious and otherwise—they both witnessed the event with shared skepticism.

Nabby Adams was never one who rushed to personal judgment. In the first reference to Jefferson that occurs in her diary, she expresses no opinion of him. Later she decides that he was "an agreeable man." Upon seeing him react to the news of the death of his daughter Lucy from whooping cough, Nabby Adams concluded that Jefferson was a sensitive man and a good parent. When John Adams was appointed ambassador to Great Britain, Nabby moved with her parents to London, where she became acquainted with Colonel William Stephens Smith, whom she wed on 12 June 1786. She and her husband returned to New York in 1788. She died of breast cancer in August 1813 at her parents' home in Quincy, Massachusetts. Her death occurred after her father and Jefferson had reconciled their political differences and resumed their correspondence. Informing Jefferson of her death, John Adams called her "a monument to Suffering and to Patience" (Cappon, *Adams-Jefferson Letters*, 366). Jefferson, having experienced the death of more than one daughter and remembering the time he spent with Nabby Adams in Paris, understood their loss and wrote Adams a touching letter of condolence.

[15 AUGUST 1784] THIS DAY, BY INVITATION, we dined with Mr. [Thomas] Barclay, in a friendly way, without form or ceremony. Mr. Jefferson and daughter dined with us, and two gentlemen who were not to be known. The dinner was in the French style; there is no such thing here as preserving our taste in any thing; we must all sacrifice to custom and fashion. I will not believe it possible to do otherwise; for my papa, with his firmness and resolution, is a perfect convert to the mode in every thing, at least of dress and appearance. Mrs. B. is a fine woman; the more I see of her, the greater is my approbation of her. She has a firm hold of my heart, from her kindness and attention to my father, when he was sick of the fever last fall; I shall ever feel a grateful remembrance of her goodness. [. . .]

[22 August 1784] Mr. Jefferson, Col. [David] Humphreys, and a Polish gentleman, lately from America, dined with us. Col. H. is appointed by Congress, Secretary of the Commercial Commission—he was an aid to General Washington. He seems about 30, his appearance is soldier-like. I have not seen enough of these people to form a judgment, or to make any remarks with justice. [. . .]

[30 September 1784] Went to Paris, and dined by invitation with Mr. Jefferson; met Mr. and Mrs. B., Mrs. Barclay. Mr. J. is an agreeable man. Col. H. is I dont know what—a sensible man I believe—but his address is not very agreeable; he is I believe a very worthy character. Mrs. B. has a most pleasing address, and a very happy turn of expression, with a good deal of politeness—she will not fail to please. Mr. B. is an agreeable man—he is delicately attentive, and his behaviour to Madame is very pleasing. [. . .]

[13 October 1784] Came home and found Mr. Jefferson again. He is an agreeable man; we should be obliged to him for taking the trouble to come out; if he had not had business, I fancy he would not have come to-day.

Thursday, 14th Oct. 1784.—Mr. Jefferson sent us cards yesterday to admit us to see the ceremony of taking the veil, in the convent where his daughter is to receive her education. We rose at seven, dressed, and went into Paris, and breakfasted with Madame Barclay. At nine we went to the Church, where we found a number of persons of our acquaintance. Upon this occasion we were admitted to the altar where the priest performs, which at other times is not allowed. It was separated from the place of the nuns and those of the convent, by iron grates. The place in which they were, was a large apartment, with seats around. The floor was covered with an elegant carpet—here were the nuns only. When we first went they were repeating their prayers; presently the curtains were drawn aside, the lady abbess and other nuns, with all the pensioners, came. The candles were lighted—each nun held a lighted candle in her hand; the two nuns who were to take the veil, came forward, attended by two English ladies who were pensioners; each held a large lighted torch in her hand—they were elegantly dressed, and in all the vanities of the world.

The two nuns were in fine, white woollen dresses, made like a parson's robes, loose and flowing; their veils were white; they appeared first with a different made robe on; it was rather a cloak very long; their hair all shaved off; a white cap and veil. They came and kneeled before the altar; there was much singing and chanting of prayers. It is impossible to describe the many different manners and forms, alternately kneeling and rising. The priest came to the altar and made many signs that I did not understand. There were three who assisted; one of them delivered a sermon in French. He began by expatiating upon the goodness of the king; then on the excellence of every particular class of people, from the throne to the footstool. He told them this was a very good world to live in, and that it was very wrong to quit it. After dwelling a long time upon its excellence, he told them a false philosophy had got into the world, and everything was becoming bad; every one was guided by self interest, and they had the happiest prospect in quitting it. At the same time, he represented to them the disagreeableness of their situation; that they would be confined, and that very possibly their actions would be wrongly construed. If they should be gay, the nuns would say of them, that they had not yet quitted the world. If they were grave, they might say, that they were unhappy and repented of their vows. After this the nuns went round and took leave of all the others, and kissed them. Then they laid down upon their faces, and there was brought in, by eight pensioners, a pall of black, crossed with white, which was held over them; the priest then read some part of the ceremony. The nuns chanted their prayers. This was an affecting sight; I could not refrain from tears; every one seemed affected around, particularly the French. One of the priests seemed affected; the others appeared as insensible as statues of lead or wood. This ceremony lasted half an hour, while these poor girls were lying on their faces; and when they rise, it is called rising to the resurrection, after having been dead to the world. Then they went to the old abbess; she put upon them the nun's habit. While this was performing, the countenance of first of the nuns, who was French, and of one of the first families in the kingdom, which had been without a smile and entirely inattentive to every thing but her devotion, was lighted up with a smile, and she appeared very pleasing. The other was an Irish girl; her countenance was not very expressive; it seemed calm, and without any appearance of the least degree of perturbation of spirits. The first, I observed, blushed often, and seemed affected. After the robe was put on, there were more reading and prayers; then the priest sprinkled the veil destined for them with holy water, and perfumed it with frank incense. The abbess then put it on them while they kneeled before her; then followed more prayers and reading; then the abbess pinned upon each of their heads a wreath of flowers; this was a part of the ceremony, as none of the nuns but them had them. A candle was then put into their hands and mass was said, which, with the prayers and the whole ceremony, was performed in Latin, of which I suppose they understood as much as I did.

When the priest in his sermon, invited all the others who were present, to follow the example of these nuns, I observed the English girl, who held the candle for one of them, look very sharp upon the other English girl, whose countenance expressed that she knew better than all this — that she had no such intention — quite right she.

The relations of the two victims appeared less affected than any one present. It is very probable they are the victims of pride or wickedness. Thus these two girls are destined to pass their lives within the walls of this convent. They are not so strict as formerly. Miss Jefferson told me they were very cheerful and agreeable. They seemed to take pleasure in contributing to the happiness of the pensioners. There were three princesses who are here for their education, and were distinguished from the others by a blue ribbon over the shoulder.

This is considered the best and most genteel convent in Paris. Most of the English, who send their children here for their education, put them into this convent. There are a number now here. [. . .]

[27 January 1785] A small company to dine to-day; the Abbé Arneau, Mr. Dash a Swedish gentleman, Col. H., and Mr. Jefferson; Miss J. we expected; but the news of the death of one of Mr. J.'s children in America, brought by the Marquis de la Fayette, prevented. Mr. J. is a man of great sensibility, and parental affection. His wife died when this child was born, and he was almost in a confirmed state of melancholy; confined himself from the world, and even from his friends, for a long time; and this news has greatly affected him and his daughter. She is a sweet girl, delicacy and sensibility are read in every feature, and her manners are in unison with all that is amiable and lovely; she is very young. Col. H. has taken the most effectual means of gaining my good opinion; no more reflections upon the stiffness of his manners must proceed from me; he presented me today with a copy of a poem written by himself, and addressed to the army, while he was Aid de Camp to General Washington, which he has had printed since he came to Paris [*Poem Addressed to the Armies of the United States of America*]. I confess I had not formed an idea of his being a poet. This was no doubt owing to my want of penetration. It is well written, and the verse is easy. [. . .]

February 7th. To-day we dined with Mr. Jefferson. He invited us to come and see all Paris, which was to be seen in the streets to-day, and many masks, it being the last day but one, of the Carnival, and to go to the mask ball in the evening; which we did not attend. I had but little curiosity to go; the description of those who have seen it, has not given me spirit enough to spend all the night to be perhaps not gratified. The ball begins at one o'clock in the morning, and lasts until six. There are no characters supported at them here, as in England, nor are there any variety in the dresses. Mrs. B. says it is the only amusement that is not superior here, to what they have in London. She is so delighted with Paris, that she says she shall never go to America with her own consent; she expects to be carried, in the spring. I confess I cannot form an idea of this disposition. She has, I believe, by this time, laid the foundation of a future life of unhappiness. Miss Jefferson dined with us — no other company. [. . .]

[30 March 1785] Yesterday Madame de la Fayette wrote a very polite card to mamma, informing her that the King would come to-day to the Church of

Notre Dame to assist in the Te Deum, which would be sung in that Church, to return thanks for the birth of a prince; and to offer us places in her father's tribune at the Church, and to-day we went. The hour she appointed us to meet at her house was two o'clock; we dined early and went. From Auteuil to the Barrier we met a number of people; but from the Barrier to the Marquis', and from thence to Notre Dame—which was at least three miles—I cannot attempt to describe the appearance; every street was so crowded, that had it not been for the police, which upon every public occasion are as numerous as the people—they are obliged to be very strict—it would not have been possible for a carriage to have passed. I believe I may say with truth there were millions of people. Mr. Jefferson, who rode from the Marquis' with us, supposed there were as many people in the streets as there were in the State of Massachusetts, or any other of the States. Every house was full—every window and door, from the bottom to the top. Before the Church there is a large square, which was lined with troops, drawn up in rows, and appeared very well. The Church of Notre Dame is of very ancient architecture; it is the most beautiful building I have seen. The churches have no pews, but are filled with chairs and benches. There are a variety of chapels in them, in which there always is a representation of the Virgin Mary and the child Jesus. On one side of the chapel there were seats, where all the judges were seated, dressed in crimson velvet robes, and large wigs. On the other side were lawyers in black habits; their dress is much the same as in our country, except that they wear their hair long behind, and without being tied, but waving, which is very graceful.

On one side of the altar were a number of ladies of rank; on the other side, were the ambassadors and public ministers; before the altar were placed seats, and under a canopy was a crimson velvet cushion, and seats all round with each a crimson velvet cushion; this was for his majesty to kneel upon. There were the bishops with the archbishop at their head, dressed in purple robes, with skirts which came as low as their knees, of the richest lace. There were a number of others of a different order, dressed with cloaks, wrought with gold. Among these was the Abbé de Bourbon, an illegitimate son of Louis 15th. He appeared to be about 27 years old, a very handsome man. I observed all the gentlemen of the court paid particular attention to him. Madame de la Fayette observed, she thought it was too magnificent, and there was too much noise and bustle for the Church; she said it was not peaceful enough. I was charmed with her behaviour to her company; the

Marquis was with the King; she had to arrange the company when we went to Church, which she did, paying particular attention to every one. In the eve the whole city of Paris was illuminated. Papa was here at the first ceremony of this kind, when the first princess was born. The decorations at that time were superior to this. It was impossible not to make many reflections upon this august and superb ceremony, and upon the sentiments the people discovered for their King. But in this government I should judge it was right and necessary. If the man who has the whole kingdom at his disposal, is not respected, and thought of next to their God, he will not long sustain his power. And however wrong it may be, it is unavoidable.

From *Journal and Correspondence of Miss Adams, Daughter of John Adams, Second President of the United States, Written in France and England, in 1785,* ed. Caroline Amelia Smith De Windt, 2 vols. (New York: Wiley and Putnam, 1841–1842), 1: 14–16, 20, 23–27, 44–45, 46–47, 65–68.

[A Stock of Information Not Inferior to That of Any Man] (1799)

François Alexandre Frédéric,

Duc de La Rochefoucauld-Liancourt

A French social reformer, the duc de La Rochefoucauld-Liancourt (1747–1827) established a model farm at Liancourt, erected spinning machines on his estate, and founded a school of arts and crafts for the sons of soldiers, which eventually became L'École des Enfants de la Patrie. After he and Jefferson met in Paris, Jefferson invited him to visit Monticello. During the French Revolution, Rochefoucauld fled France for England, where Arthur Young, the most prominent British agricultural reformer of the day, welcomed him. From England, Rochefoucauld came to America. In 1796, he visited Monticello. Given his interests in agriculture and arts and crafts, he found much to admire. He described his visit in detail in *Travels through the United States of North America.* More than half of his account of Monticello, in fact, is devoted to Jefferson's agricultural improvements. He caught Jefferson at a propitious time. Having retired from his position as George Washington's secretary of state, Jefferson could now devote his time and energy to the improvement of his farm. Rochefoucauld describes Jefferson's innovative schemes for preventing erosion, planting seed, rotating crops, harvesting corn, and protecting grain from disease, pestilence, and erosion. Only after describing the farm in detail does Rochefoucauld describe Jefferson's other accomplishments. He creates an intriguing picture. As Rochefoucauld portrays him, Jefferson is a farmer first and a statesman second.

Monticello is situated four miles from Milford, in that chain of mountains which stretches from James's-River to the Rappahannock, twenty-eight miles in front of the Blue-Ridge, and in a direction parallel to those mountains. This chain, which runs uninterrupted in its small extent, assumes successively the names of the West, South, and Green Mountains.

It is in the part known by the name of the South-Mountains [Southwest Mountains] that Monticello is situated. The house stands on the summit of the mountain, and the taste and arts of Europe have been consulted in the formation of its plan. Mr. Jefferson had commenced its construction before the American revolution; since that epocha his life has been constantly engaged in public affairs, and he has not been able to complete the execution to the whole extent of the project which it seems he had at first conceived. That part of the building which was finished has suffered from the suspension of the work, and Mr. Jefferson, who two years since resumed the habits and leisure of private life, is now employed in repairing the damage occasioned by this interruption, and still more by his absence; he continues his original plan, and even improves on it, by giving to his buildings more elevation and extent. He intends that they should consist only of one story, crowned with balustrades; and a dome is to be constructed in the centre of the structure. The apartments will be large and convenient; the decoration, both outside and inside, simple, yet regular and elegant. Monticello, according to its first plan, was infinitely superior to all other houses in America, in point of taste and convenience; but at that time Mr. Jefferson had studied taste and the fine arts in books only. His travels in Europe have supplied him with models; he has appropriated them to his design; and his new plan, the execution of which is already much advanced, will be accomplished before the end of next year, and then his house will certainly deserve to be ranked with the most pleasant mansions in France and England.

Mr. Jefferson's house commands one of the most extensive prospects you can meet with. On the east side, the front of the building, the eye is not checked by any object, since the mountain on which the house is seated commands all the neighbouring heights as far as the Chesapeak. The Atlantic might be seen were it not for the greatness of the distance, which renders that prospect impossible. On the right and left the eye commands the extensive valley that separates the Green, South and West Mountains from the Blue-Ridge, and has no other bounds but these high mountains, of which, on a clear day, you discern the chain on the right upwards of a hundred miles, far beyond James's-River; and on the left as far as Maryland, on the other side of the Potowmack. Through some intervals, formed by the irregular summits of the Blue-Mountains, you discover the Peaked-Ridge, a chain of mountains placed between the Blue and North Mountains, another more distant ridge. But in the back part the prospect is soon interrupted by a mountain more elevated than that on which the house is seated. The bounds of the view on this point, at so small a distance, form a pleasant resting-place; as the immensity of prospect it enjoys is, perhaps, already too vast. A considerable number of cultivated fields, houses, and barns, enliven and variegate the extensive landscape, still more embellished by the beautiful and diversified forms of mountains, in the whole chain of which not one resembles another. The aid of fancy is, however, required to complete the enjoyment of this magnificent view; and she must picture to us those plains and mountains such as population and culture will render them in a greater or smaller number of years. The disproportion existing between the cultivated lands and those which are still covered with forests as ancient as the globe, is at present much too great: and even when that shall have been done away, the eye may perhaps further wish to discover a broad river, a great mass of water—destitute of which, the grandest and most extensive prospect is ever destitute of an embellishment requisite to render it completely beautiful.

On this mountain, and in the surrounding valleys, on both banks of the Rivanna, are situated the five thousand acres of land which Mr. Jefferson possesses in this part of Virginia. Eleven hundred and twenty only are cultivated. The land left to the care of stewards has suffered as well as the buildings from the long absence of the master; according to the custom of the country it has been exhausted by successive culture. Its situation on declivities of hills and mountains renders a careful cultivation more necessary than is requisite in lands situated in a flat and even country; the common routine is more pernicious, and more judgement and mature thought are required, than in a different soil. This forms at present the chief employment of Mr. Jefferson. But little accustomed to agricultural pursuits, he has drawn the principles of culture either from works which treat on this subject, or from conversation. Knowledge thus acquired often misleads, and is at all times insufficient in a country where agriculture is well understood; yet it is preferable to mere practical knowledge, in a country where a bad practice prevails, and where it is dangerous to follow the routine, from which it is so difficult to depart. Above all, much good may be expected, if a contemplative mind, like that of Mr. Jefferson, which takes the theory for its guide, watches its application with discernment, and rectifies it according to the peculiar circumstances and nature of the country, climate and soil, and conformably to the experience which he daily acquires.

Pursuant to the ancient rotation, tobacco was cultivated four or five successive years; the land was then suffered to lie fallow, and then again succeeded crops of tobacco. The culture of tobacco being now almost entirely relinquished in this part of Virginia, the common rotation begins with wheat, followed by Indian corn, and then again wheat, until the exhausted soil loses every productive power; the field is then abandoned, and the cultivator proceeds to another, which he treats and abandons in the same manner, until he returns to the first, which has in the mean time recovered some of its productive faculties. The disproportion between the quantity of land which belongs to the planters and the hands they can employ in its culture, diminishes the inconveniences of this detestable method. The land, which never receives the least manure, supports a longer or shorter time this alternate cultivation of wheat and Indian corn, according to its nature and situation, and regains, according to the same circumstances, more or less speedily the power of producing new crops. If in the interval it be covered with heath and weeds, it frequently is again fit for cultivation at the end of eight or ten years; if not, a space of twenty years is not sufficient to render it capable of production. Planters who are not possessed of a sufficient quantity of land to let so much of it remain unproductive for such a length of time, fallow it in a year or two after it has borne wheat and Indian corn, during which time the fields serve as pasture, and are hereupon again cultivated in the same manner. In either case the land produces from five to six bushels of wheat, or from ten to fifteen bushels of Indian corn, the acre. To the produce of Indian corn must also be added one hundred pounds of leaves to every five bushels, or each barrel, of grain. These leaves are given as fodder to the cattle. It was in this manner that Mr. Jefferson's land had always been cultivated, and it is this system which he has very wisely relinquished. He has divided all his land under culture into four farms, and every farm into six fields of forty acres. Each farm consists, therefore, of two hundred and eighty acres. His system of rotation embraces seven years, and this is the reason why each farm has been divided into seven fields. In the first of these seven years wheat is cultivated; in the second, Indian corn; in the third, pease or potatoes; in the fourth, vetches; in the fifth, wheat; and in the sixth and seventh, clover. Thus each of his fields yields some produce every year, and his rotation of successive culture, while it prepares the soil for the following crop, increases its produce. The abundance of clover, potatoes, pease, etc. will enable him to keep sufficient cattle for manuring his land, which at present receives hardly any dung at all, independently of the great profit which he will in future derive from the sale of his cattle.

Each farm, under the direction of a particular steward or bailiff, is cultivated by four negroes, four negresses, four oxen, and four horses. The bailiffs, who in general manage their farms separately, assist each other during the harvest, as well as at any other time, when there is any pressing labour. The great declivity of the fields, which would render it extremely troublesome and tedious to carry the produce, even of each farm, to one common central point, has induced Mr. Jefferson to construct on each field a barn, sufficiently capacious to hold its produce in grain; the produce in forage is also housed there, but this is generally so great, that it becomes necessary to make stacks near the barns. The latter are constructed of trunks of trees, and the floors are boarded. The forests and slaves reduce the expence of these buildings to a mere trifle.

Mr. Jefferson possesses one of those excellent threshing-machines, which a few years since were invented in Scotland, and are already very common in England. This machine, the whole of which does not weigh two thousand pounds, is conveyed from one barn to another in a waggon, and threshes from one hundred and twenty to one hundred and fifty bushels a day. A worm, whose eggs are almost constantly deposited in the ear of the grain, renders it necessary to thresh the corn a short time after the harvest; in this case the heat, occasioned by the mixture of grain with its envelope, from which it is disengaged, but with which it continues mixed, destroys the vital principle of the egg, and protects the corn from the inconveniences of its being hatched. If the grain continued in the ears, without being speedily beaten, it would be destroyed by the worm, which would be excluded from the eggs. This scourge, however, spreads no farther northwards than the Potowmack, and is bounded to the west by the Blue Mountains. A few weeks after the corn has been beaten, it is free from all danger, winnowed and sent to market. The Virginia planters have generally their corn trodden out by horses; but this way is slow, and there is no country in the world where this operation requires more dispatch than in this part of Virginia. Besides the straw is bruised by the treading of horses. Mr. Jefferson hopes that his machine, which has already found some imitators among his neighbours, will be generally adopted in Virginia. In a country where all the inhabitants possess plenty of wood, this machine may be made at a very trifling expence.

Mr. Jefferson rates the average produce of an acre of land, in the present state of his farm, at eight bushels of wheat, eighteen bushels of Indian corn, and twenty hundred weight of clover. After the land has been duly manured, he may expect a produce twice, nay three times more considerable. But his land will never be dunged as much as in Europe. Black cattle and pigs, which in our country are either constantly kept on the farm, or at least return thither every evening, and whose dung is carefully gathered and preserved either separate or mixed, according to circumstances, are here left grazing in the woods the whole year round. Mr. Jefferson keeps no more sheep than are necessary for the consumption of his own table. He cuts his clover but twice each season, and does not suffer his cattle to graze in his fields. The quantity of his dung is therefore in proportion to the number of cattle which he can keep with his own fodder, and which he intends to buy at the beginning of winter to sell them again in spring; and the cattle kept in the vicinity of the barns where the forage is housed, will furnish manure only for the adjacent fields.

From an opinion entertained by Mr. Jefferson, that the heat of the sun destroys, or at least dries up in a great measure, the nutritious juices of the earth, he judges it necessary that it should be always covered. In order therefore to preserve his fields, as well as to multiply their produce, they never lie fallow. On the same principle he cuts his clover but twice a season, does not let the cattle feed on the grass, nor encloses his fields, which are merely divided by a single row of peach trees.

A long experience would be required to form a correct judgement, whether the loss of dung which this system occasions in his farms, and the known advantage of fields enclosed with ditches, especially in a declivous situation, where the earth from the higher grounds is constantly washed down by the rain, are fully compensated by the vegetative powers which he means thus to preserve in his fields. His system is entirely confined to himself; it is censured by some of his neighbours, who are also employed in improving their culture with ability and skill, but he adheres to it, and thinks it is founded on just observations.

Wheat, as has already been observed, is the chief object of cultivation in this country. The rise, which within these two years has taken place in the price of this article, has engaged the speculations of the planters, as well as the merchants. The population of Virginia, which is so inconsiderable in proportion to its extent, and so little collected in towns, would offer but a very precarious market for large numbers of cattle. Every planter has as many of them in the woods, as are required for the consumption of his family. The negroes, who form a considerable part of the population, eat but little meat, and this little is pork. Some farmers cultivate rye and oats, but they are few in number. Corn is sold here to the merchants of Milford or Charlotte-Ville, who ship it for Richmond, where it fetches a shilling more per bushel than in other places. Speculation or a pressing want of money may at times occasion variations in this manner of sale, but it is certainly the most common way. Money is very scarce in this district, and, bank-notes being unknown, trade is chiefly carried on by barter; the merchant, who receives the grain, returns its value in such commodities as the vender stands in need of.

Mr. Jefferson sold his wheat last year for two dollars and a half per bushel. He contends, that it is in this district whiter than in the environs of Richmond, and all other low countries, and that the bushel, which weighs there only from fifty-five to fifty-eight pounds, weighs on his farm from sixty to sixty-five.

In addition to the eleven hundred and twenty acres of land, divided into four farms, Mr. Jefferson sows a few acres with turnips, succory, and other seeds.

Before I leave his farm, I shall not forget to mention, that I have seen here a *drilling-machine,* the name of which cannot be translated into French but by *machine à semer en paquets.* By Mr. Jefferson's account, it has been invented in his neighbourhood. If this machine fully answers the good opinion which he entertains of it, the invention is the more fortunate, as by Arthur Young's assertion not one good drilling-machine is to be found in England. This machine, placed on a sort of plough-carriage, carries an iron, which gently opens the furrow as deeply as is required. Behind this iron, and in the upper part of the machine, is a small trough, containing the grain which is intended to be sown. This grain is taken out of the trough by a row of small receivers, sewed on a leather band, or ribbon, and turning round two pivots placed above each other at the distance of from seven to eight inches. The small receivers take the grain from the trough, and turn it over into a small conduit, which conveys it into the furrow made by the iron. The distance of one of those receivers from another determines that of the places in which the grain is deposited in the ground; and a harrow, fixed on the machine behind the conduits through which the seed falls into the furrow, covers it again. The *endless* chain of the receivers, which forms the merit of the machine, may be compared with that which is used for drawing water from a great depth, or still more properly with a heaver of flour in Evans's mills. It is put in motion by a light wheel, which moves along the ground as the machine advances, and is fixed in such a manner that it is not obstructed in its movements by the inequalities of the ground, nor even by the stones which it may find in its way. If this machine really answers the intended purpose, it is difficult to conceive why it should not have been invented before, as it is extremely simple, composed of movements well known, and of powers frequently employed. In my opinion it admits, however, of great improvements.

My readers will undoubtedly find that I bestow peculiar attention on agriculture, by speaking of Mr. Jefferson as a farmer, before I mention him in any other point of view.

They must be very ignorant of the history of America, who know not that Mr. Jefferson shared with George Washington, Franklin, John Adams, Mr. [John] Jay, and a few others, the toils and dangers of the revolution, in all its different stages; that in the famous congress which guided and consolidated it, he displayed a boldness and firmness of character, a fund of talents and knowledge, and a steadiness of principles, which will hand down his name to posterity with glory, and ensure to him for ever the respect and gratitude of all friends of liberty. It was he, who in that famous congress, so respectable, and so much respected—in that congress, ever inaccessible to the seduction, fear, and apparent weakness of the people—who jointly with Mr. [Richard Henry] Lee, another deputy of Virginia, proposed the declaration of independence. It was he, who, supported principally by John Adams, pressed the deliberation on the subject, and carried it, bearing down the wary prudence of some of his colleagues, possessed of an equal share of patriotism, but less courage. It was he, who was charged with drawing up this master-piece of dignified wisdom, and patriotic pride. It was he, who being afterwards appointed governor of Virginia at the period of the invasion of Arnold and Cornwallis, acquired a peculiar claim on the gratitude of his fellow-citizens. It was he, who, as the first ambassador of the United States in France, filled at that momentous epocha that distinguished post to the satisfaction of both nations. In fine, it was he, who as Secretary of State in 1792, when the ridiculous and disorganizing pretentions of Mr. [Edmond Charles] Genêt, and the lofty arrogance of the . . . minister, endeavoured alternately to abuse the political weakness of the United States, induced his government to speak a noble and independent language, which would have done credit to the most formidable power. The long correspondence carried on with these two designing agents would, from its just, profound, and able reasoning, be alone sufficient to confer on its author the reputation of an accomplished statesman.

Since the beginning of 1794, Mr. Jefferson has withdrawn from public affairs. This was the time when the malevolent sentiments of . . . were displayed against the United States in the strongest manner, and when her unjust proceedings were resented with the utmost indignation from one end of America to the other. This was the most important epocha of the policy of the United States, because they proposed to act with energy and vigour. The preference which under those circumstances the President was accustomed to give to the advice of Mr. [Alexander] Hamilton, which continually carried along with it the opinion not only of General [Henry] Knox, but also of Mr. [Edmund] Randolph, then attorney-general of the Union, over that of Mr. Jefferson, caused him to embrace this resolution. Immediately after this step, Mr. Jefferson was considered by the ruling party as the leader of Opposition; he was suspected of revolutionary views; he was accused of an intention to overturn the constitution of the United States, of being the enemy of his country, and of a wish to become a tribune of the people. It is sufficient to know that Mr. Jefferson is a man of sense, to feel the absurdity of these scandalous imputations; and whoever is acquainted with his virtue, must be astonished at their having ever been preferred against him. His speeches are those of a man firmly attached to the maintenance of the Union, of the present constitution, and of the independence of the United States. He is the declared enemy of every new system the introduction of which might be attempted, but he is a greater enemy of a kingly form of government than of any other. He is clearly of opinion, that the present constitution should be carefully preserved, and defended against all infringements arising from an extension of the prerogatives of the executive power. It was framed and accepted on republican principles, and it is his wish that it should remain a republican constitution. On several occasions I have heard him speak with great respect of the virtues of the President, and in terms of esteem of his sound and unerring judgement.

But the spirit of party is carried to excess in America; men who embrace the opinion of Mr. Jefferson, attack their opponents with imputations, no doubt, equally unfounded. In all party-proceedings neither reason nor justice can be expected from either side, and very seldom strict morality with respect to the means employed to serve the favourite cause; one cause alone appears good; every thing besides is deemed bad, nay criminal, and probity itself serves to mislead probity. Personal resentments assume the colour of public spirit, and frequently, when the most odious acts of injustice have been committed, and the most atrocious calumnies spread, but few members of the party are in the secret, and know that they are the effusions of injustice and false representation. The truth of these observations being evident to all men who have lived amidst parties, should lead to mutual toleration and forbearance.

In private life Mr. Jefferson displays a mild, easy and obliging temper, though he is somewhat cold and reserved. His conversation is of the most agreeable kind, and he possesses a stock of information not inferior to that of any other man. In Europe he would hold a distinguished rank among men of letters, and as such he has already appeared there; at present he is employed with activity and perseverance in the management of his farms and buildings; and he orders, directs, and pursues in the minutest detail every branch of business relative to them. I found him in the midst of the harvest, from which the scorching heat of the sun does not prevent his attendance. His negroes are nourished, clothed, and treated as well as white servants could be. As he cannot expect any assistance from the two small neighbouring towns, every article is made on his farm; his negroes are cabinet-makers, carpenters, masons, bricklayers, smiths, etc. The children he employs in a nail-manufactory, which yields already a considerable profit. The young and old negresses spin for the clothing of the rest. He animates them by rewards and distinctions; in line, his superior mind directs the management of his domestic concerns with the same abilities, activity, and regularity, which he evinced in the conduct of public affairs, and which he is calculated to display in every situation of life. In the superintendence of his household he is assisted by his two daughters, Mrs. *Randolph* and Miss *Mary,* who are handsome, modest, and amiable women. They have been educated in France. Their father went often with them to the house of Madame *d'Enville,* my dear and respectable aunt, where they became acquainted with my family, and as the names of many of my friends are not unknown to them, we were able to converse of them together. It will be easily conceived, that this could not but excite in my mind strong sensations, and recollections, sometimes painful, yet generally sweet. Fifteen hundred leagues from our native country, in another world, and frequently given up to melancholy, we fancy ourselves restored to exigence, and not utter strangers to happiness, when we hear our family and our friends mentioned by persons who have known them, who repeat their names, describe their persons, and express themselves on so interesting a subject in terms of kindness and benevolence.

Mr. [Thomas Mann] Randolph is proprietor of a considerable plantation, contiguous to that of Mr. Jefferson's; he constantly spends the summer with him, and, from the affection he bears him, he seems to be his son rather than his son-in-law. Miss Maria constantly resides with her father; but as she is seventeen years old, and is remarkably handsome, she will, doubtless, soon find, that there are duties which it is still sweeter to perform than those of a daughter. Mr. Jefferson's philosophic turn of mind, his love of study, his excellent library, which supplies him with the means of satisfying it, and his friends, will undoubtedly help him to endure this loss, which moreover is not likely to become an absolute privation, as the second son-in-law of Mr. Jefferson may, like Mr. Randolph, reside in the vicinity of Monticello, and, if he be worthy of Miss Maria, will not be able to find any company more desirable than that of Mr. Jefferson.

The situation of Monticello exempts this place from the pestilential effluvia which produce so many diseases in the lower countries. From its great elevation it enjoys the purest air; and the sea-breeze, which is felt on shore about eight or nine o'clock in the morning, reaches Monticello at one or two in the afternoon, and somewhat refreshes the atmosphere, but the sun is intolerable from its scorching heat; as indeed it is in all the southern States. The places that enjoy some advantage over others are those which, like Monticello, are exposed to its direct rays, without experiencing their reflection from more elevated mountains, or neighbouring buildings.

Mr. Jefferson, in common with all landholders in America, imagines that his habitation is more healthy than any other; that it is as healthful as any in the finest parts of France; and that neither the ague, nor any other bilious distempers are ever observed at Monticello. This is undoubtedly true, because he asserts it, in regard to himself, to his family, and his negroes, none of whom is attacked by these maladies; but I am, nevertheless, of opinion, that an European, who during this season should expose himself too much to the air from nine in the morning until six at night, would not long enjoy a good state of health. During the seven days I continued there, not one passed without some moments of rain, and yet the intensity of the heat was not in the least abated by it.

In Virginia mongrel negroes are found in greater number than in Carolina and Georgia; and I have even seen, especially at Mr. Jefferson's, slaves, who, neither in point of colour nor features, shewed the least trace of their original descent; but their mothers being slaves, they retain, of consequence, the same condition. This superior number of people of colour is owing to the superior antiquity of the settlement of Virginia, and to the class of stewards or bailiffs, who are accused of producing this mongrel breed. They are liable to temptation, because they are young, and constantly amidst their slaves; and they enjoy the power of gratifying their passions, because they are despots. But the public opinion is so much against this intercourse between the white people and the black, that it is always by stealth, and transiently, the former satisfy their desires, as no white man is known to live regularly with a black woman.

Before I close this article I must say, that during my residence at Monticello I witnessed the indignation excited in all the planters of the neighbourhood by the cruel conduct of a master to his slave, whom he had flogged to such a degree as to leave him almost dead on the spot. Justice pursues this barbarous master, and all the other planters declared loudly their wish, that he may be severely punished, which seems not to admit of any doubt.

But it is time to take leave of Mr. Jefferson, whose kind reception has perfectly answered what I had a right to expect from his civility, from our former acquaintance in France, and from his particular connection with my relations and friends. Mr. Jefferson is invited by the republican party, named anti-federalists, to succeed George Washington in the President's chair of the United States, the latter having publicly declared, that he will not continue in this place, although he should be re-elected by the majority of the people of the United States.

From *Travels through the United States of North America, the Country of the Iroquois, and Upper Canada in the Years 1795, 1796, and 1797*, 2 vols. (London: for R. Phillips by T. Davison, 1799), 2: 69–82.

[Fourth of July at the President's Mansion] (1801 and 1803)

SAMUEL HARRISON SMITH

Samuel Harrison Smith (1772–1845) received an excellent education, taking his BA at the University of Pennsylvania in 1787 and his MA in 1790. After completing his studies, he went into the publishing business but did not stop thinking about education. When the American Philosophical Society sponsored an essay contest, Smith wrote an essay proposing a system of education based on free public schools. It tied for first place, caught the attention of the president of the American Philosophical Society, Thomas Jefferson, and initiated a lasting friendship between the two men. Smith became a stalwart supporter of Jefferson's policies. In 1800, he married his second cousin Margaret Bayard. On Jefferson's invitation later that year, the Smiths moved from Philadelphia to Washington, D.C., where Mr. Smith reestablished his publishing business. The move involved considerable risk: Smith's financial success depended on Jefferson winning the presidency, which was, needless to say, by no means certain. In Washington, Smith started the triweekly *National Intelligencer,* which is widely considered the finest American political newspaper of the nineteenth century. Living in Washington, Mr. and Mrs. Smith frequently dined at the White House. The following extracts describe Fourth of July parties he attended at the White House in 1801 and 1803. The first comes from a letter to Mary Ann Smith, the second from a letter to his wife, who had left Washington to escape the summer heat. Jefferson announced the cession of Louisiana at the 1803 Fourth of July party, which consequently turned out to be a grand celebration.

Samuel Harrison Smith to Mary Ann Smith, 5 July 1801

Mr. Craven, a neighbour and acquaintance of ours, departing for Phila. to-morrow, I cannot deny myself the pleasure of passing a few minutes with you, chiefly to draw a picture, which I know will give your patriotic heart delight, a picture of Mr. Jefferson in which he was exhibited to the best advantage. About 12 o'clock yesterday, the citizens of Washington and Geo. Town waited upon the President to make their devoirs. I accompanied Mr. Sumpter. We found about 20 persons present in a room where sat Mr. J. surrounded by the five Cherokee chiefs. After a conversation of a few minutes, he invited his company into the usual dining room, whose four large sideboards were covered with refreshments, such as cakes of various kinds, wine, punch, etc. Every citizen was invited to partake, as his taste dictated, of them, and the invitation was most cheerfully accepted, and the consequent duties discharged with alacrity. The company soon increased to near a hundred, including all the public officers and most of the respectable citizens, and strangers of distinction. Martial music soon announced the approach of the marine corps of Capt. Burrows, who in due military form saluted the President, accompanied by the President's March played by an excellent band attached to the corps. After undergoing various military evolutions, the company returned to the dining room, and the band from an adjacent room played a succession of fine patriotic airs. All appeared to be cheerful, all happy. Mr. Jefferson mingled promiscuously with the citizens, and far from designating any particular friends for consultation, conversed for a short time with every one that came in his way. It was certainly a proud day for him, the honours of which he discharged with more than his usual care. At two o'clock, after passing two hours in this very agreeable way, the company separated.

Samuel Harrison Smith to Margaret Bayard Smith, 5 July 1803

Yesterday was a day of joy to our citizens and of pride to our President. It is a day which you know he always enjoys. How much more must he have enjoyed it on this occasion from the great event that occasioned it. The news of the cession of Louisiana only arrived about eight o'clock of the night preceding, just in time to be officially announced on this auspicious day. Next to the liberty of his country, peace is certainly the dearest to his heart. How glad then must that heart be which with loving participancy in obtaining and securing the one, has placed the other on an impregnable basis. This mighty event forms an era in our history, and of itself must render the administration of Jefferson immortal. At an early hour the city was alive, — a discharge of eighteen guns saluted the dawn, the military assembled exhibiting a martial appearance, at 11 o'clock an oration was delivered by Capt. Sprig (well written but poorly pronounced), at twelve company began to assemble at the President's; it was more numerous than I have before marked it, enlivened too by the presence of between forty and fifty ladies clothed in their best attire, cakes, punch, wine etc in profusion. After partaking of these mingled pleasures the company separated about two, and at three, the greater part assembled at Stille's to the number of near 100. Before dinner I had the honor of reading the Declaration of Independence; pleased as I was with the distinction I confess I was not sorry when it was over, not having been perfectly well for a few days I was not without some apprehension of being unable to perform the duty with decency, and tho' I did not have the ambition to be eloquent, yet I felt anxious to escape the implication of inability. As it happened, however, the reading went off very well, and I was complimented for the precision and spirit with which it was delivered and I was pleased with learning that not a word was missed in the utmost parts of the room. Margaret, there is no person on earth but yourself to whom I could speak so frankly. Receive this very openness as a coincidence of my unbounded confidence, confidence which nothing but love and esteem strong as my heart entertains for its best heaven, could inspire. At dinner our toasts were politics, our songs convivial. At nine I left the company, part of which remained, I believe, till daylight.

From Margaret Bayard Smith, *The First Forty Years of Washington Society, Portrayed by the Family Letters of Mrs. Samuel Harrison Smith (Margaret Bayard) from the Collection of Her Grandson, J. Henley Smith,* ed. Gaillard Hunt (New York: Scribner, 1906), pp. 30–31, 38–39.

[Visiting the President's Mansion] (1802–1803)

Samuel L. Mitchill

Dr. Samuel L. Mitchill (1764–1831) exemplified Jefferson's notion of a natural aristocracy. A bright, well-educated man, he excelled as both a physician and a scientist, yet he also recognized a responsibility to his nation and served in both the U.S. House of Representatives and the Senate. Born on Long Island, New York, Mitchill studied medicine at the University of Edinburgh, where he took his MD in 1786. Returning home, he practiced medicine, studied law, and became active in local politics. Appointed professor of natural history, chemistry, and agriculture at Columbia College in 1792, he began a career in academia that would last a lifetime. A member of the American Philosophical Society, Mitchill served as its vice president when Jefferson was president of the society. Mitchill brought his learning to his role as legislator. Jefferson called him the "Congressional Dictionary."

Mitchill greatly respected Jefferson and delivered a eulogy upon the request of the New York Lyceum of Natural History, published as *A Discourse on the Character and Services of Thomas Jefferson, More Especially as Promoter of the Natural and Physical Sciences* (1826). The letters to his wife Catherine reprinted below date from Mitchill's first two terms in the House, during which time he had several opportunities to visit the White House. When these letters were first published in *Harper's Magazine* in 1879, the last one was misdated 4 January 1802. The date is corrected here and the letter restored to its proper chronological order.

The following letters reveal much about Jefferson—perhaps more than Mitchill himself realized. Mitchill described Jefferson's physical appearance and personality, bringing to life the social gatherings at the White House. Though Jefferson's library has been studied in considerable detail, the precise makeup of the library he kept at the White House remains a mystery. Mitchill identified three books Jefferson had on a mantlepiece at the White House: one volume of *L'Encyclopédie méthodique;* a Spanish/Latin volume of Tacitus's works, which Jefferson had created by conflating a Latin text with a separately published Spanish translation; and the handsome Greek and Latin Deuxponts edition of Plato with annotations by the fifteenth-century Italian philosopher Marsilio Ficino (Sowerby, nos. 4889, 81, 1311). Mitchill also recorded Jefferson's capacity for humor, but Jefferson's humor, even his use of tall talk, could be quite subtle, and, in one instance, Mitchill did not realize when Jefferson was joking. When Mitchill asked about the beautiful prospect Jefferson had described in *Notes on the State of Virginia,* Jefferson said that John Adams had troops blow up the precipice from which he had viewed the scene, thus rendering the description in *Notes* false. Mitchill reacted to what Jefferson said with indignance. He did not realize the president was pulling his leg.

Samuel L. Mitchill to Catherine Mitchill, 19 January 1802

I promised you in a former letter some account of Thomas Jefferson, now President of the United States.

I have had several opportunities of seeing and conversing with him since my arrival at Washington. He is tall in stature and rather spare in flesh. His dress and manners are very plain; he is grave, or rather sedate, but without any tincture of pomp, ostentation, or pride, and occasionally can smile, and both hear and relate humorous stories as well as any other man of social feelings. At this moment he has a rather more than ordinary press of care and solicitude, because Congress is in session, and he is anxious to know in what manner the Representatives will act upon his Message, and how the communications he expects soon to make to the Senate will be received by that branch of the national legislature.

He has been many years a widower, and has never, that I know of, showed any disposition to form a second matrimonial connection. His children are two daughters, one of whom is the wife of an old fellow student with me at the University of Edinburgh, Thomas Mann Randolph.

Waiting one morning in the parlor for the President, who at the moment of my arrival was engaged with the Secretary of the Navy, Mr. Robert Smith, I amused myself a few minutes in looking at the books which occupied one end of the mantel-piece. There were three volumes—one was a volume of the French Encyclopedia, in the original; the second was a tome of the Roman historian Tacitus, with the Latin text on one page and a translation into Spanish on the other; and the third was one of the elegant copies of that celebrated edition of the works of Plato which was printed a few years ago at Deuxponts. Mr. Jefferson had been at Deuxponts, and there had purchased the works of Plato and Aristophanes. He is more deeply versed in human nature and human learning than almost the whole tribe of his opponents and revilors.

He has generally a company of eight or ten persons to dine with him every day. The dinners are neat and plentiful, and no healths are drunk at table, nor are any toasts or sentiments given after dinner. You drink as you please, and converse at your ease. In this way every guest feels inclined to drink to the digestive or the social point, and no further. Our company on one occasion were Dr. [William] Eustis and General [Joseph] Varnum, of Massachusetts; Mr. John Randolph, of Virginia; General John Smith and myself, from New York, Representatives; and Mr. [Abraham] Baldwin, of Georgia, and Mr. [John] Breckinridge, of Kentucky, Senators, the former being the pro-temporary president of the Senate. The President and his secretary, Captain [Meriwether] Lewis, completed the party.

Mr. Jefferson has interested himself very much in propagating the cow-pox. He has even inoculated many persons with his own hand, and talks on the subject with the intelligence of a physician, so ardent is his philanthropy and such his zeal to extirpate the small-pox.

I have seen the great "mammoth cheese" which has been presented to him. It weighs upward of twelve hundred pounds, and is as large as a burr millstone!

On New-Year's morning the ladies generally went to visit him, and made a grand show. At the same time a body of Miami and Potawatamie Indian chiefs were there.

Samuel L. Mitchill to Catherine Mitchill, 10 February 1802

I write you a few lines for the sake of writing. I have news enough to commit to paper, but have not time at present to do so. I am sitting in Congress, where public debates are sounding in my ears. I am in very tolerable health—am to dine this afternoon with President Jefferson, and the day after to-morrow with Citizen Pichon, the charge d'affaires of the French government, who lives at Georgetown, about three miles from my residence.

I recommend to you Jefferson's *Notes on Virginia*. The work is not large. You may borrow it at the library, and read all the parts you will find necessary in a few evenings. I asked Mr. Jefferson some questions about the sublime prospect he has described in that work of the passage of the Potomac through the mountains. My chief object was to be directed to the proper place for observation—the place where he himself stood when there. He told me the place no longer existed, for during the reign of Federalism under Adams's administration, the spot, which was a projecting point of rock on the brow of the mountain, had been industriously blown up and destroyed by gunpowder! A company of Federal troops quartered there were several days employed in boring and blasting the rock to pieces, doubtless with the intention of falsifying his account, and rendering it incredible by putting it out of the power of any subsequent traveller to behold the like from the same point of view. What shameful, what vandalic revenge is this!

Samuel L. Mitchill to Catherine Mitchill, 4 January 1803

New-Year's Day was a time of great parade in the city of Washington. The weather being fine, gave every body an opportunity of exhibiting. The great place of resort was the President's mansion. There was no visiting, as at New York, from house to house through a whole circle of acquaintance, or of public men who keep open houses; but everybody crowded to Mr. Jefferson's, and after having made their appearance there, returned home.

It was Saturday, and that is commonly a busy day with Congressmen. They then must meet on their committees of business, and consider the subjects intrusted to them, that after examination they may make judicious reports to the body that appoints them. Being engaged myself that morning on the Committee for Naval Affairs, I could not go to the President's till after one o'clock. The reading of voluminous papers and the discussion of their merits occupied all the earlier part of the day. However, late as it was, I went to pay my respects and make one of the crowd on this occasion, which occurs but once a year.

I rode from the Capitol, and proceeding along Pennsylvania Avenue, met many gentlemen on their return. In some of the carriages ladies were to be seen, for the Secretaries of the Treasury, Navy, State, etc., with their families, had sallied forth to pay their homage to the Executive, and so had the foreign ministers.

Arriving late, I met a whole troop of ladies and their attendant gallants coming down the outside stairs and going to their carriages. On passing the great hall and entering the withdrawing-room, I found still a large party there. The President was standing near the middle of the room, to salute and converse with visitors. The male part of them walked about or made groups for conversation, while the ladies received the bows and adorations of the gentlemen. Among the ladies were the President's two daughters, Mrs. Randolph and Mrs. Eppes, to whom I paid my obeisance; then to Mrs. [Dolley] Madison and her sister, Miss Paine [Anna Payne]; then to Mrs. [Hannah] Gallatin and Miss Nicholson, besides a number of others. Beaux growing scarce or inattentive, toward the last I had to officiate myself, and to escort several of the fair creatures in succession to their carriages. Several belles from Virginia and elsewhere were brought out on this gala day, and it was allowed on all hands that the company made a brilliant appearance. After the room was cleared, I went into another apartment with the President, and had a conference with him about the best method of preserving our public ships from decay, etc., and then withdrew.

From "Dr. Mitchill's Letters from Washington, 1801–1813," *Harper's New Monthly Magazine* 58 (April 1879): 743–744.

[Large Stories] (1804–1809)

John Quincy Adams

John Quincy Adams (1767–1848), the sixth president of the United States, was the son of the second president, a member of the diplomatic corps of the first and fourth presidents, good friends with the third, and secretary of state to the fifth. As a boy he accompanied his father John Adams on his diplomatic missions to Europe. Living at Auteuil with his family in 1784, he frequently went into Paris and visited Jefferson. In 1785, he returned to Boston to further his education, graduating from Harvard College in 1787. (Jefferson had recommended he attend William and Mary instead.) John Quincy Adams subsequently read law with Theophilus Parsons. He embarked on a diplomatic career of his own when President Washington appointed him minister to the Netherlands. In London on 26 July 1797, he married Louisa Catherine Johnson, daughter of the U.S. Consul. That same year his father appointed him minister plenipotentiary to Berlin but recalled him after being defeated in the presidential election of 1800. Back home, John Quincy Adams became active in local politics and, in April 1803, was appointed to fill a vacant seat in the U.S. Senate. His support of Jefferson's policies antagonized the Federalist Party that had supported his appointment to the Senate.

One of the greatest diarists in the history of American literature, John Quincy Adams began keeping a diary in 1779, when he was twelve, and continued it for the next sixty-eight years, until just a few months before he died. What follows is a selection from his diary dating from his time in the Senate, when he often dined at the White House. Adams recognized Jefferson as a teller of tall tales and even attributed a motive to his hyperbolic humor: to excite wonder. In one conversation, he asked Jefferson about a geographical point he had made in *Notes on the State of Virginia*. Adams knew the work well, having read it at least twice before. Adams's diary also adds another volume to Jefferson's White House library: François Le Vaillant's *Histoire naturelle des perroquets* (1804–1805; not in Sowerby). In his diary, Adams provides a brief account of James Madison's inauguration and the first-ever inaugural ball that followed. He expanded his account of these events in a letter to his wife, which records that he and Jefferson found time to discuss classical verse at the event, the first and perhaps the last time an ex-president and a future one discussed Greek and Latin poetry at an inaugural ball.

The Diary of John Quincy Adams

[23 November 1804] Dined with the President. Mrs. Adams did not go. The company were Mr. R[obert] Smith, Secretary of the Navy, and his lady, Mr. and Mrs. Harrison, Miss Jenifer and Miss Mouchette, Mr. [Daniel] Brent, and the President's two sons-in-law [Thomas Mann Randolph and John W. Eppes], with Mr. [William] Burwell, his private secretary. I had a good deal of conversation with the President. The French Minister just arrived had been this day first presented to him, and appears to have displeased him by the profusion of gold lace on his clothes. He says they must get him down to a plain frock coat, or the boys in the streets will run after him as a sight. I asked if he had brought his *Imperial* credentials, and was answered he had. Mr. Jefferson then turned the conversation towards the French Revolution, and remarked how *contrary to all expectation* this great *bouleversement* had turned out. It seemed as if every thing in that country for the last twelve or fifteen years had been A DREAM; and who could have imagined that such an *ébranlement* would have come to this? He thought it very much to be wished that they could now return to the Constitution of 1789, and call back *the Old Family*. For although by that Constitution the Government was much too weak, and although it was defective in having a Legislature in only one branch, yet even thus it was better than the present form, where it was impossible to perceive *any limits*. I have used as near as possible his very words; for this is one of the most unexpected phases in the waxing and waning opinions of this gentleman concerning the French Revolution. He also mentioned to me the extreme difficulty he had in finding fit characters for appointments in Louisiana, and said he would now give *the creation* for a young lawyer of good abilities, and who could speak the French language, to go to New Orleans as one of the Judges of the Superior Court in the Territory. The salary was about two thousand dollars. We had been very lucky in obtaining one such Judge, in Mr. [J. B.] Prevost, of New York, who had accepted the appointment, and was perfectly well qualified, and he was in extreme want of another. I could easily have named a character fully corresponding to the one he appeared so much to want. But if his observations were meant as a *consultation* or an intent to ask whether I knew any such person I could recommend, he was not sufficiently explicit. Though if they were not, I know not why he made them to me. He further observed that both French and Spanish ought to be made primary objects of acquisition in all the educations of our young men. As to Spanish, it was so easy that he had learned it, with the help of a *Don Quixote* lent him by Mr. Cabot, and a grammar, in the course of a passage to Europe, on which he was but nineteen days at sea. But Mr. Jefferson tells large stories. At table he told us that when he was at Marseilles he saw there a Mr. Bergasse, a famous manufacturer of wines, who told him that he would make him any sort of wine he would name, and in any quantities, at six or eight sols the bottle. And though there should not be a drop of the genuine wine required in his composition, yet it should so perfectly imitate the taste, that the most refined connoisseur should not be able to tell which was which. You never can be an hour in this man's company without something of the marvellous, like these stories. His genius is of the old French school. It conceives better than it combines. He showed us, among other things, a Natural History of Parrots, in French, with colored plates very beautifully executed. [. . .]

[11 January 1805] Dined at the President's, with my wife. General [Samuel] Smith and his brother, of the navy [Robert Smith], Mr. William Smith, formerly a member of Congress, from Baltimore, Mr. Williams and his two daughters, Mrs. Hall and Mrs. Hewes, were there. So was the Vice-President [James Madison]. The President appeared to have his mind absorbed by some other object, for he was less attentive to his company than usual. His itch for telling prodigies, however, is unabated. Speaking of the cold, he said he had seen Fahrenheit's thermometer, *in Paris,* at twenty degrees below zero; and that, not for a single day, but that for six weeks together it stood *thereabouts.* "Never once in the whole time," said he, "so high as zero, which is *fifty* degrees below the freezing point." These were his own words. He knows better than all this; but he loves to excite wonder. Fahrenheit's thermometer never since Mr. Jefferson existed was at twenty degrees below zero in Paris. It was never for six weeks together so low as twenty degrees above zero. Nor is Fahrenheit's zero fifty degrees below the freezing point. I asked him upon what foundation he had, in his *Notes on Virginia,* spoken of the river Potomac as common to Virginia and Maryland. He said that it was on *the compact* between the two States—that the charter of Maryland had included the bed of the river, but the compact had made it common. It is singular, however, if this be the case, that among the vouchers expressly given in the book this compact is not at all mentioned, though a compact with Pennsylvania is. He added, however, that as to all the arguments inferred from these facts in the debate of the House of Representatives (alluding to Mr. J. Randolph's arguments) he considered them as mere metaphysical subtleties, and that they ought to have no weight. This conversation was interrupted by the entrance of General Turreau [Louis-Marie, Baron Turreau de Garambouville] and Captain Marin; immediately after which we took leave. [. . .]

[30 November 1805] Paid visits this morning to the President, whom I found at home, and the Secretaries of State and of the Navy, whom I did not see. Called also on Mr. [Samuel Allyne] Otis at his office, where I met Mr. [William] Plumer. At the President's door I met Mr. Israel Smith and Mr. [John] Gaillard, who were on the same visit as myself. The President mentioned a late act of hostility committed by a French privateer near Charleston, South Carolina, and said that we ought to assume as a principle that the neutrality of our territory should extend to the Gulf Stream, which was a natural boundary, and within which we ought not to suffer any hostility to be committed. Mr. Gaillard observed that on a former occasion in Mr. Jefferson's correspondence with Genet, and by an Act of Congress at that period, we had seemed only to claim the usual distance of three miles from the coast; but the President replied that he had then assumed that principle because Genet by his intemperance forced us to fix on some point, and we were not then prepared to assert the claim of jurisdiction to the extent we are in reason entitled to; but he had then taken care expressly to reserve the subject for future consideration, with a view to this same doctrine for which he now contends. I observed that it might be well, before we ventured to assume a claim so broad, to wait for a time when we should have a force competent to maintain it. But in the mean time, he said, it was advisable *to squint at it,* and to accustom the nations of Europe to the idea that we should claim it in future. The subject was not pushed any farther. [. . .]

[4 March 1809] I went to the Capitol, and witnessed the inauguration of Mr. Madison as President of the United States. The House was very much crowded, and its appearance very magnificent. He made a very short speech, in a tone of voice so low that he could not be heard, after which the official oath was administered to him by the Chief-Justice of the United States, the four other Judges of the Supreme Court being present and in their robes. After the ceremony was over I went to pay the visit of custom. The company was received at Mr. Madison's house; he not having yet removed to the President's house. Mr. Jefferson was among the visitors. The Court had adjourned until two o'clock. I therefore returned to them at that hour. Mr. [Luther] Martin closed the argument in the cause of Fletcher and Peck; after which the Court adjourned. I came home to dinner, and in the evening went with the ladies to a ball at Long's, in honor of the new President. The crowd was excessive—the heat oppressive, and the entertainment bad. Mr. Jefferson was there. About midnight the ball broke up.

John Quincy Adams to Louisa Catherine Adams, 5 March 1809

The oath of office was yesterday administered to the new President in the chamber of the Representatives. He delivered a short speech, which you will without doubt see in the newspapers before you can receive this letter. It is in very general terms, and was spoken in a tone of voice so low that scarcely any part of it was heard by three-fourths of the audience.

The body of the House was excessively crowded and the galleries were equally thronged, which gave it altogether a very magnificent appearance. The city was very much crowded with strangers, and I believe I may say without exaggeration that in the course of the day yesterday I saw more people than in the whole time I have ever been here.

Immediately after the ceremony was performed the President and his lady received company at their own house. I paid my visit with your mamma and Mr. and Mrs. Hellen. It was not at the President's house, which Mr. Jefferson has not yet left. He was with the company who visited his successor.

In the evening there was a ball at Long's on the Capitol Hill, the house which last winter was kept by Stelle. The crowd there was excessive; the rooms suffocating and the entertainment bad. Your sister Hellen literally took me with her, for I should not have gone but at special invitation that I would attend her. The President and his family were also there, and also Mr. Jefferson. I had some conversation with him in the course of the evening, in the course of which he asked me whether I continued as fond of Poetry as I was in my youth. I told him, yes; that I did not perceive I had lost any of my relish for good poetry, though my taste for the minor poets, and particular for amatory verses, was not so keen as it had been when I was young. He said he was still fond of reading Homer, but did not take much delight in Virgil.

From *Memoirs of John Quincy Adams, Comprising Portions of His Diary from 1795 to 1848,* ed. Charles Francis Adams, 12 vols. (Philadelphia: J. B. Lippincott, 1874–1877), 1: 316–317, 330–331, 375–376, 544.

From *Writings of John Quincy Adams,* ed. Worthington Chauncey Ford, 7 vols. (New York: Macmillan, 1913–1917), 3: 288–289.

[The Marks of Intense Thought and Perseverance] (1807)

JOSEPH STORY

U.S. Supreme Court justice and Harvard law professor Joseph Story (1779–1845) was born in Marblehead, Massachusetts, the son of Dr. Elisha Story and Mehitable Pedrick Story. Graduating from Harvard in 1798, Joseph Story returned to Marblehead to read law. Admitted to the bar in 1801, he began practicing law in Salem, Massachusetts. Though initially a proponent of Jefferson's politics, Story opposed the embargo President Jefferson had imposed on American exports as an economic sanction against the European powers. In 1811, President Madison nominated Story to the U.S. Supreme Court, despite Jefferson's misgivings. Story took his seat on the Supreme Court on 3 February 1812 and served on it until his death. As Jefferson anticipated, Story sided with John Marshall, opposing states' rights and perpetrating a judicial nationalism that sought to expand federal powers broadly. While serving on the bench of the nation's highest court, Story also cultivated a career as a law professor at Harvard. The law school there had been wallowing for years, but once Story took over the program in 1829, it flourished. Almost single-handedly, he built Harvard Law School into one of the most dynamic programs of legal education in the United States. In addition, his podium became a forum for perpetuating his judicial nationalism. The extract below comes from a letter Story wrote to his friend Judge Samuel Fay. It records his first meeting with Jefferson, a happier time before their political views began to diverge.

Joseph Story to Samuel P. P. Fay, 30 May 1807

Jefferson is tall and thin, of a sallow complexion, with a fine, intelligent eye. Dr. M. [Samuel Mitchill] yesterday introduced me, and we spent a half hour with him, in which time he conversed in a very easy, correct, and pleasant style. His language is peculiarly appropriate, and his manner very unaffected. The negligence of his dress a little surprised me. He received us in his slippers, and wore old-fashioned clothes, which were not in the nicest order, or of the most elegant kind; a blue coat, white worked cassimere waistcoat and corduroy breeches, (I beg your pardon, I mean *small clothes,*) constituted his dress. You know Virginians have some pride in appearing in simple habiliments, and are willing to rest their claim to attention upon their force of mind and suavity of manners. The President is a little awkward in his first address, but you are immediately at ease in his presence. His manners are inviting and not uncourtly; and his voice flexible and distinct. He bears the marks of intense thought and perseverance in his countenance. The miniature lately published by Field in Boston is a very excellent likeness. I visited him again this morning in company with Mr. Madison, at whose house I breakfasted, and conversed with him upon politics in a perfectly familiar manner. His smile is very engaging and impresses you with cheerful frankness. His familiarity, however, is tempered with great calmness of manner and with becoming propriety. Open to all, he seems willing to stand the test of inquiry, and to be weighed in the balance only by his merit and attainments. You may measure if you please, and cannot easily misjudge. On the whole, I confess he appears to me a clear and intelligent man, ready and discriminating, but more formed by philosophical reflection, than by rapid, enterprising, overbearing genius. If he chooses, he cannot fail to please. If he cannot awe, he will not sink into neglect. The current of his thoughts is gentle and uniform, unbroken by the torrent of eloquence, and unruffled by the fervor of vivid internal flame. Take this passing sketch and color it to your own fancy.

From William W. Story, *Life and Letters of Joseph Story, Associate Justice of the Supreme Court of the United States, and Dane Professor of Law at Harvard University,* 2 vols. (Boston: Charles C. Little, 1851), 1: 151–152.

[The Habitation of Philosophy and Virtue] (1809 and 1837)

Margaret Bayard Smith

The defining year in the life of Margaret Bayard Smith (1778–1844) was 1800, not necessarily because it was the year she married Samuel Harrison Smith but because it was the year he decided to relocate his thriving business as newspaper editor and publisher from Philadelphia to Washington, D.C. Once she reached their new home, Margaret Bayard Smith became a fixture on Washington's social and literary scene. An avid novel reader since girlhood, she ultimately turned to writing novels herself, starting with *A Winter in Washington; or, Memoirs of the Seymour Family* (1824), a work drawing on her own experiences in the political and social world of the nation's capital. Toward the end of her life, she started writing her reminiscences as a legacy for her family, not necessarily intending to publish them. In 1906, Gaillard Hunt combined her reminiscences, her detailed notebooks, and a selection from her correspondence to create *The First Forty Years of Washington Society*, the source of the following text.

Mr. Smith had become good friends with Jefferson when they lived in Philadelphia during Jefferson's vice presidency, but Mrs. Smith did not meet him until December 1800, two months after they moved to Washington. She composed the first selection below as part of her reminiscences in 1837. Written decades after the experience and after Smith had turned novelist, it must be taken with a grain of salt. Nonetheless, it captures Jefferson's personality and outlook. The Smiths were frequent guests at the White House throughout Jefferson's presidency. When he left Washington for Monticello after James Madison's inauguration in 1809, he invited the Smiths to Monticello, an offer they readily accepted. They visited that summer and spent four days there, an experience Mrs. Smith chronicled in considerable detail in her notebook. In his essay on Margaret Bayard Smith for the *American National Biography*, Donald B. Cole calls her description of Jefferson a classic.

Reminiscences

"And is this," said I, after my first interview with Mr. Jefferson, "the violent democrat, the vulgar demagogue, the bold atheist and profligate man I have so often heard denounced by the federalists? Can this man so meek and mild, yet dignified in his manners, with a voice so soft and low, with a countenance so benignant and intelligent, can he be that daring leader of a faction, that disturber of the peace, that enemy of all rank and order?" Mr. Smith, indeed, (himself a democrat) had given me a very different description of this celebrated individual; but his favourable opinion I attributed in a great measure to his political feelings, which led him zealously to support and exalt the party to which he belonged, especially its popular and almost idolized leader. Thus the virulence of party-spirit was somewhat neutralized, nay, I even entertained towards him the most kindly dispositions, knowing him to be not only politically but personally friendly to my husband; yet I did believe that he was an ambitious and violent demagogue, coarse and vulgar in his manners, awkward and rude in his appearance, for such had the public journals and private conversations of the federal party represented him to be.[1]

In December, 1800, a few days after Congress had for the first time met in our new Metropolis, I was one morning sitting alone in the parlour, when the servant opened the door and showed in a gentleman who wished to see my husband. The usual frankness and care with which I met strangers, were somewhat checked by the dignified and reserved air of the present visitor; but the chilled feeling was only momentary, for after taking the chair I offered him in a free and easy manner, and carelessly throwing his arm on the table near which he sat, he turned towards me a countenance beaming with an expression of benevolence and with a manner and voice almost femininely soft and gentle, entered into conversation on the commonplace topics of the day, from which, before I was conscious of it, he had drawn me into observations of a more personal and interesting nature. I know not how it was, but there was something in his manner, his countenance and voice that at once unlocked my heart, and in answer to his casual enquiries concerning our situation in our *new home,* as he called it, I found myself frankly telling him what I liked or disliked in our present circumstances and abode. I knew not who he was, but the interest with which he listened to my artless details, induced the idea he was some intimate acquaintance or friend of Mr. Smith's and put me perfectly at my ease; in truth so kind and conciliating were his looks and manners that I forgot he was not a friend of my own, until on the opening of the door, Mr. Smith entered and introduced the stranger to me as *Mr. Jefferson.*

I felt my cheeks burn and my heart throb, and not a word more could I speak while he remained. Nay, such was my embarrassment I could scarcely listen to the conversation carried on between him and my husband. For several years he had been to me an object of peculiar interest. In fact my destiny, for on his success in the pending presidential election, or rather the success of the democratic party, (their interests were identical) my condition in life, my union with the man I loved, depended. In addition to this personal interest, I had long participated in my husband's political sentiments and anxieties, and looked upon Mr. Jefferson as the corner stone on which the edifice of republican liberty was to rest, looked upon him as the champion of human rights, the reformer of abuses, the head of the republican party, which must rise or fall with him, and on the triumph of the republican party I devoutly believed the security and welfare of my country depended.

Notwithstanding those exalted views of Mr. Jefferson as a political character; and ardently eager as I was for his success, I retained my previously conceived ideas of the coarseness and vulgarity of his appearance and manners and was therefore equally awed and surprised, on discovering the stranger whose deportment was so dignified and gentlemanly, whose language was so refined, whose voice was so gentle, whose countenance was so benignant, to be no other than Thomas Jefferson. How instantaneously were all these preconceived prejudices dissipated, and in proportion to their strength, was the reaction that took place in my opinions and sentiments. I felt that I had been the victim of prejudice, that I had been unjust. The revolution of feeling was complete and from that moment my heart warmed to him with the most affectionate interest and I implicitly believed all that his friends and my husband believed and which the after experience of many years confirmed. Yes, not only was he great, but a truly good man!

The occasion of his present visit, was to make arrangements with Mr. Smith for the publication of his *Manual* for *Congress,* now called *Jefferson's manual.* The original was in his own neat, plain, but elegant hand writing. The manuscript was as legible as printing and its unadorned simplicity was emblematical of his character. It is still preserved by Mr. Smith and valued as a precious relique.

After the affair of business was settled, the conversation became general and Mr. Jefferson several times addressed himself to me; but although his manner was unchanged, my feelings were, and I could not recover sufficient ease to join in the conversation. He shook hands cordially with us both when he departed, and in a manner which said as plain as words could do, "I am your friend."

During part of the time that Mr. Jefferson was President of the Philosophical Society (in Philadelphia) Mr. Smith was its secretary. A prize offered by the society for the best system of national education, was gained by Mr. Smith. The merit of this essay, first attracted the notice of Mr. J. to its author; the personal acquaintance which then took place, led to a friendly intercourse which influenced the future destiny of my husband, as it was by Mr. Jefferson's advice, that he removed to Washington and established the *National Intelligencer.* Esteem for the talents and character of the editor first won Mr. Jefferson's regard, a regard which lasted to the end of his life and was a thousand times evinced by acts of personal kindness and confidence.

At this time Mr. Jefferson was vice-President and in nomination for the Presidency. Our infant city afforded scant accommodations for the members of Congress. There were few good boarding-houses, but Mr. Jefferson was fortunate enough to obtain one of the best. Thomas Law, one of the wealthiest citizens and largest proprietors of city property, had just finished for his own use a commodious and handsome house on Capitol hill; this, on discovering the insufficiency of accommodation, he gave up to Conrad for a boarding house, and removed to a very inconvenient dwelling on Greenleaf's point, almost two miles distant from the Capitol. And here while I think of it, though somewhat out of place, I will mention an incident that occurred which might have changed the whole aspect of the political world and have disappointed the long and deep laid plans of politicians, so much do great events depend on trivial accidents. This out-of-the-way-house to which Mr. Law removed, was separated from the most inhabited part of the city by old fields and waste grounds broken up by deep gulleys or ravines over which there was occasionally a passable road. The election of President by Congress was then pending, one vote given or withheld would decide the question between Mr. Jefferson and Mr. [Aaron] Burr.

Mr. [James] Bayard from Delaware held that vote. He with other influential and leading members went to a ball given by Mr. Law. The night was dark and rainy, and on their attempt to return home, the coachman lost his way, and until daybreak was driving about this waste and broken ground and if not overturned into the deep gullies was momentarily in danger of being so, an accident which would most probably have cost some of the gentlemen their lives, and as it so happened that the company in the coach consisted of Mr. Bayard and three other members of Congress who had a leading and decisive influence in this difficult crisis of public affairs, the loss of either, might have turned the scales, then so nicely poised. Had it been so, and Mr. Burr been elected to the Presidency, what an awful conflict, what civil commotions would have ensued.

Conrad's boarding house was on the south side of Capitol hill and commanded an extensive and beautiful view. It was on the top of the hill, the precipitous sides of which were covered with grass, shrubs and trees in their wild uncultivated state. Between the foot of the hill and the broad Potomac extended a wide plain, through which the Tiber wound its way. The romantic beauty of this little stream was not then deformed by wharves or other works of art. Its banks were shaded with tall and umbrageous forest trees of every variety, among which the superb Tulip-Poplar rose conspicuous; the magnolia, the azalia, the hawthorn, the wild-rose and many other indigenous shrubs grew beneath their shade, while violets, anemonies and a thousand other sweet wood-flowers found shelter among their roots, from the winter's frost and greeted with the earliest bloom the return of spring. The wild grape-vine climbing from tree to tree hung in unpruned luxuriance among the branches of the trees and formed a fragrant and verdant canopy over the greensward, impervious to the noon day-sun. Beautiful banks of Tiber! delightful rambles! happy hours! How like a dream do ye now appear. Those trees, those shrubs, those flowers are gone. Man and his works have displaced the charms of nature. The poet, the botanist, the sportsman and the lover who once haunted those paths must seek far hence the shades in which they delight. Not only the banks of the Tiber, but those of the Potomack and Anacosta, were at this period adorned with native trees and shrubs and were distinguished by as romantic scenery as any rivers in our country. Indeed the whole plain was diversified with groves and clumps of forest trees which gave it the appearance of a fine park. Such as grew on the public grounds ought to have been preserved, but in a government such as ours, where the people are sovereign, this could not be done. *The people,* the poorer inhabitants cut down these noble and beautiful trees for fuel. In one single night seventy tulip-Poplars were *girdled,* by which process life is destroyed and afterwards cut up at their leisure by the people. Nothing afflicted Mr. Jefferson like this wanton destruction of the fine trees scattered over the city-grounds. I remember on one occasion (it was after he was President) his exclaiming "How I wish that I possessed the power of a despot." The company at table stared at a declaration so opposed to his disposition and principles. "Yes," continued he, in reply to their inquiring looks, "I wish I was a despot that I might save the noble, the beautiful trees that are daily falling sacrifices to the cupidity of their owners, or the necessity of the poor."

"And have you not authority to save those on the public grounds?" asked one of the company. "No," answered Mr. J., "only an armed guard could save them. The unnecessary felling of a tree, perhaps the growth of centuries seems to me a crime little short of murder, it pains me to an unspeakable degree."[2]

It was partly from this love of nature, that he selected Conrad's boarding house, being there able to enjoy the beautiful and extensive prospect described above. Here he had a separate drawing-room for the reception of his visitors; in all other respects he lived on a perfect equality with his fellow boarders, and eat at a common table. Even here, so far from taking precedence of the other members of Congress, he always placed himself at the lowest end of the table. Mrs. [Margaretta] Brown, the wife of the senator from Kentucky [John Brown], suggested that a seat should be offered him at the upper end, near the fire, if not on account of his rank as vice-President, at least as the oldest man in company. But the idea was rejected by his democratic friends, and he occupied during the whole winter the lowest and coldest seat at a long table at which a company of more than thirty sat down. Even on the day of his inauguration when he entered the dining-hall no other seat was offered him by the gentlemen. Mrs. Brown from an impulse which she said she could not resist, offered him her seat, but he smilingly declined it, and took his usual place at the bottom of the table. She said she felt indignant and for a moment almost hated the levelling principle of democracy, though her husband was a zealous democrat. Certainly this was carrying equality rather too far; there is no incompatibility between politeness and republicanism; grace cannot weaken and rudeness cannot strengthen a good cause, but democracy is more jealous of power and priviledge than even despotism. [. . .]

Visit to Monticello

Monticello, August 1st, 1809.

In a visit Mr. J. made our little cottage last autumn, we were speaking of all the various charms of nature, storms of winter. "But," said he, "you can here form no idea of a snow storm. No, to see it in all its grandeur you should stand at my back door; there we see its progress—rising over the distant Allegany, come sweeping and roaring on, mountain after mountain, till it reaches us, and then when its blast is felt, to turn to our fire side, and while we hear it pelting against the window to enjoy the cheering blaze, and the comforts of a beloved family." Well, I have seen those distant mountains over which the winter storm has swept, now rearing their blue and misty heads to the clouds, and forming a sublime and beautiful horizon round one of the finest and most extended scenes the eye ever rested on.—I have seen that beloved family, whose virtues and affections are the best reward and the best treasure of their parent and their country's parent—I have seen, I have listened to, one of the greatest and best of men. He has passed through the tempestuous sea of political life, has been enveloped in clouds of calumny, the storms of faction, assailed by foreign and domestic foes, and often threatened with a wreck, of happiness and fame. But these things are now all passed away, and like the mountain on which he stands, fogs and mists and storms, gather and rage below, while he enjoys unclouded sunshine. How simple and majestic is his character, my affection for him is weighed with much veneration, that, meek, humble, gentle and kind, as he is in his manners, I cannot converse with him, with ease. My mind is busied in thinking of what he is, rather than listening to what he says. After a very delightful journey of three days, we reached Monticello on the morning of the fourth. When I crossed the Ravanna, a wild and romantic little river, which flows at the foot of the mountain, my heart beat,—I thought I had entered, as it were the threshhold of his dwelling, and I looked around everywhere expecting to meet with some trace of his superintending care. In this I was disappointed, for no vestige of the labour of man appeared; nature seemed to hold an undisturbed dominion. We began to ascend this mountain, still as we rose I cast my eyes around, but could discern nothing but untamed woodland, after a mile's winding upwards, we saw a field of corn, but the road was still wild and uncultivated. I every moment expected to reach the summit, and felt as if it was an endless road; my impatience lengthened it, for it is not two miles from the outer gate on the river to the house. At last we reached the summit, and I shall never forget the emotion the first view of this sublime scenery excited. Below me extended for above 60 miles round, a country covered with woods, plantations and houses; beyond, arose the blue mountains, in all their grandeur. Monticello rising 500 feet above the river, of a conical form and standing by itself, commands on all sides an unobstructed and I suppose one of the most extensive views any spot the globe affords. The sides of the mountain covered with wood, with scarcely a speck of cultivation, present a fine contrast to its summit, crowned with a noble pile of buildings, surounded by an immense lawn, and shaded here and there with some fine trees. Before we reached the house, we met Mr. J. on horseback, he had just returned from his morning ride, and when, on approaching, he recognized us, he received us with one of those benignant smiles, and cordial tones of voice that convey an undoubted welcome to the heart. He dismounted and assisted me from the carriage, led us to the hall thro' a noble portico, where he again bade us welcome. I was so struck with the appearance of this Hall, that I lingered to look around, but he led me forward, smiling as he said, "You shall look bye and bye, but you must now rest." Leading me to a sopha in a drawing room as singular and beautiful as the Hall, he rang and sent word to Mrs. [Martha] Randolph that we were there, and then ordered some refreshments. "We have quite a sick family," said he; "My daughter has been confined to the sick bed of her little son; my grand-daughter has lost her's and still keeps to her room and several of the younger children are indisposed. For a fortnight Mr. and Mrs. Randolph have sat up every night, until they are almost worn out." This information clouded my satisfaction and cast a gloom over our visit,—but Mrs. R. soon entered, and with a smiling face, most affectionately welcomed us. Her kind and cheerful manners soon dispersed my gloom and after a little chat, I begged her not to let me detain her from her nursery, but to allow me to follow her to it; she assented and I sat with her until dinner time. Anne,[3] (Mrs. Bankhead) who had been confined 3 weeks before and had lost her child looked delicate and interesting; Ellen, my old favorite, I found improved as well as grown. At five o'clock the bell summoned us to dinner. Mr. [Thomas Mann] Randolph, Mr. [Charles] Bankhead, and Jefferson R. were there. They are 12 in family, and as Mr. J. sat in the midst of his children and grand-children, I looked on him with emotions of tenderness and respect. The table was plainly, but genteely and plentifully spread, and his immense and costly variety of French and Italian wines, gave place to Madeira and a sweet ladies' wine. We sat till near sun down at the table, where the desert was succeeded by agreeable and instructive conversation in which every one seemed to wish and expect Mr. J. to take the chief part. As it is his custom after breakfast to withdraw to his own apartments and pursuits and not to join the family again until dinner, he prolongs that meal, or rather the time after that meal, and seems to relish his wine the better for being accompanied with conversation, and during the 4 days I spent there these were the most social hours. When we rose from table, a walk was proposed and he accompanied us. He took us first to the garden he has commenced since his retirement. It is on the south side of the mountain and commands a most noble view. Little is as yet done. A terrace of 70 or 80 feet long and about 40 wide is already made and in cultivation. A broad grass walk leads along the outer edge; the inner part is laid off in beds for vegetables. This terrace is to be extended in length and another to be made below it. The view it commands, is at present its greatest beauty. We afterwards walked round the first circuit. There are 4 roads about 15 or 20 feet wide, cut round the mountain from 100 to 200 feet apart. These circuits are connected by a great many roads and paths and when completed will afford a beautiful shady ride or walk of seven miles. The first circuit is not quite a mile round, as it is very near the top. It is in general shady, with openings through the trees for distant views. We passed the outhouses for the slaves and workmen. They are all much better than I have seen on any other plantation, but to an eye unaccustomed to such sights, they appear poor and their cabins form a most unpleasant contrast with the palace that rises so near them. Mr. J has carpenters, cabinet-makers, painters, and blacksmiths and several other trades all within himself, and finds these slaves excellent workmen. As we walked, he explained his future designs. "My long absence from this place, has left a wilderness around me." "But you have returned," said I, "and the wilderness shall blossom like the rose and you, I hope, will long sit beneath your own vine and your own fig-tree." It was near dark when we reached the house; he led us into a little tea room which opened on the terrace and as Mrs. R. was still in her nursery he sat with us and conversed till tea time. We never drank tea until near nine, afterwards there was fruit, which he seldom staid to partake of, as he always retired immediately after tea. I never sat above an hour afterwards, as I supposed Mrs. R. must wish to be in her nursery. I rose the morning after my arrival very early and went out on the terrace, to contemplate scenery, which to me was so novel. The space between Monticello and the Allegany, from sixty to eighty miles, was covered with a thick fog, which had the appearance of the ocean and was unbroken except when wood covered hills rose above the plain and looked like islands. As the sun rose, the fog was broken and exhibited the most various and fantastic forms, lakes, rivers, bays, and as it ascended, it hung in white fleecy clouds on the sides of the mountains; an hour afterwards you would scarcely believe it was the same scene you looked on. In spite of the cold air from the mountains, I staid here until the first breakfast bell rang. Our breakfast table was as large as our dinner table; instead of a cloth, a folded napkin lay under each plate; we had tea, coffee, excellent muffins, hot wheat and corn bread, cold ham and butter. It was not exactly the Virginian breakfast I expected. Here indeed was the mode of living in general that of a Virginian planter. At breakfast the family all assembled, all Mrs. R's. children eat at the family table, but are in such excellent order, that you would not know, if you did not see them, that a child was present. After breakfast, I soon learned that it was the habit of the family each separately to pursue their occupations. Mr. J. went to his apartments, the door of which is never opened but by himself and his retirement seems so sacred that I told him it was his sanctum sanctorum. Mr. Randolph rides over to his farm and seldom returns until night; Mr. Bankhead who is reading law to his study; a small building at the end of the east terrace, opposite to Mr. Randolph's which terminates the west terrace; these buildings are called pavilions. Jefferson R. went to survey a tract of woodland, afterwards make his report to his grand father. Mrs. Randolph withdrew to her nursery and excepting the hours housekeeping requires she devotes the rest to her children, whom she instructs. As for them, they seem never to leave her for an instant, but are always beside her or on her lap.

Visitors generally retire to their own rooms, or walk about the place; those who are fond of reading can never be at a loss, those who are not will some times feel wearied in the long interval between breakfast and dinner. The dinner bell rings twice, the first collects the family in time to enter the room by the time the second announces dinner to be on table, which while I was there was between 4 and 5 oclock. In summer the interval between rising from table and tea (9 oclock) may be agreeably passed in walking. But to return to my journal. After breakfast on Sunday morning, I asked Ellen to go with me on the top of the house; Mr. J. heard me and went along with us and pointed out those spots in the landscape most remarkable. The morning was show'ry, the clouds had a fine effect, throwing large masses of shade on the mountain sides, which finely contrasted with the sunshine of other spots. He afterwards took us to the drawing room, 26 or 7 feet diameter, in the dome. It is a noble and beautiful apartment, with 8 circular windows and a sky-light. It was not furnished and being in the attic story is not used, which I thought a great pity, as it might be made the most beautiful room in the house. The attic chambers are comfortable and neatly finished but no elegance. When we descended to the hall, he asked us to pass into the Library, or as I called it his sanctum sanctorum, where any other feet than his own seldom intrude. This suit of apartments opens from the Hall to the south. It consists of 3 rooms for the library, one for his cabinet, one for his chamber, and a green house divided from the other by glass compartments and doors; so that the view of the plants it contains, is unobstructed. He has not yet made his collection, having but just finished the room, which opens on one of the terraces. He showed us everything he thought would please or interest us. His most valuable and curious books—those which contained fine prints etc.—among these I thought the most curious were the original letters of Cortez to the King of Spain, a vol of fine views of ancient villas around Rome, with maps of the grounds, and minute descriptions of the buildings and grounds, an old poem written by Piers Plowman and printed 250 years ago; he read near a page, which was almost as unintelligible as if it was Hebrew; and some Greek romances. He took pains to find one that was translated into French, as most of them were translated in Latin and Italian. More than two hours passed most charmingly away. The library consists of books in all languages, and contains about twenty thousand vols, but so disposed that they do not give the idea of a great library. I own I was much disappointed in its appearance, and I do not think with its numerous divisions and arches it is as impressive as one large room would have been. His cabinet and chamber contained every convenience and comfort, but were plain. His bed is built in the wall which divides his chamber and cabinet. He opened a little closet which contains all his garden seeds. They are all in little phials, labeled and hung on little hooks. Seeds such as peas, beans, etc. were in tin cannisters, but everything labeled and in the neatest order. He bade us take whatever books we wished, which we did, and then retired to our own room. Here we amused ourselves until dinner time excepting an hour I sat with Mrs. R. by her sick baby, but as she was reading I did not sit long. After dinner Ellen and Mr. Bankhead accompanied us in a long ramble in the mountain walks. At dark when we returned, the tea room was still vacant; I called Virginia and Mary (the age of my Julia and Susan) amused myself with them until their grand papa entered, with whom I had a long and interesting conversation; in which he described with enthusiasm his retirement from public life and the pleasures he found in domestic.

Monday morning. I again rose early in order to observe the scenes around me and was again repaid for the loss of sleep, by the various appearances the landscape assumed as the fog was rising. But the blue and misty mountains, now lighted up with sunshine, now thrown into deep shadow, presented objects on which I gaze each morning with new pleasure. After breakfast Mr. J. sent E. to ask me if I would take a ride with him round the mountain; I willing assented and in a little while I was summoned; the carriage was a kind of chair, which his own workmen had made under his direction, and it was with difficulty that he, Ellen and I found room in it, and might well be called the sociable. The first circuit, the road was good, and I enjoyed the views it afforded and the familiar and easy conversation, which our sociable gave rise to; but when we descended to the second and third circuit, fear took from me the power of listening to him, or observing the scene, nor could I forbear expressing my alarm, as we went along a rough road which had only been laid out, and on driving over fallen trees, and great rocks, which threatened an overset to our sociable and a roll down the mountains to us. "My dear madam," said Mr. J., "you are not to be afraid, or if you are you are not to show it; trust yourself implicitly to me, I will answer for your safety; I came every foot of this road yesterday, on purpose to see if a carriage could come safely; I know every step I take, so banish all fear." This I tried to do, but in vain, till coming to a road over which one wheel must pass I jumped out, while the servant who attended on horseback rode forward and held up the carriage as Mr. J. passed. Poor Ellen did not dare to get out. Notwithstanding the terror I suffered I would not have lost this ride; as Mr. J. explained to me all his plans for improvement, where the roads, the walks, the seats, the little temples were to be placed. There are two springs gushing from the mountain side; he took me to one which might be made very picturesque. As we passed the graveyard, which is about half way down the mountain, in a sequestered spot, he told me he there meant to place a small gothic building,—higher up, where a beautiful little mound was covered with a grove of trees, he meant to place a monument to his friend Wythe. We returned home by a road which did not wind round the mountain but carried us to the summit by a gentle ascent. It was a good road, and my terror vanished and I enjoyed conversation. I found Mrs. R. deeply engaged in the *Wild Irish Boy* sitting by the side of her little patient; I did not stay long to interrupt her, but finding Mrs. Bankhead likewise engaged with a book, I withdrew to my own room to read my Grecian romance. At dinner Mrs. Randolph sent an apology, she hurt her eye so badly, that it produced excessive inflamation and pain, which obliged her to go to bed. After dinner I went up to sit by her, Mr. J. came up soon after and I was delighted by his tender attentions to their dear daughter. As he sat by her and held her hand, for above an hour, we had a long social conversation in which Mrs. R. joined occasionally. After he had gone, finding her disposed to sleep, I went down. It was now quite dark and too late to walk, so I took my seat in the tea room with my little girls and told them stories till the tea bell again collected the family.

Tuesday. After breakfast I went up and sat all the morning by Mrs. Randolph; she was too unwell to rise; part of the time I read, but when we were alone, conversed. Our conversation turned chiefly on her father, and on her mentioning their correspondence, I begged her to show me some of his letters. This she willingly assented to and it was a rich repast to mind and heart. Some of them were written when he was minister in France and she in a convent. These are filled with the best advice in the best language. His letters come down to the last days of his political life; in every one he expresses his longings after retirement. She was so good as to give me one of these precious letters. When I went down stairs I found Mr. J. in the hall and Mr. S., and we had a long conversation on a variety of topics. He took us a charming walk round the edge of the lawn and showed us the spots from which the house appeared to most advantage. I looked upon him as he walked, the top of this mountain, as a being elevated above the mass of mankind, as much in character as he was in local situation. I reflected on the long career of public duties and stations through which he had passed, and that after forty years spent on the tempestuous sea of political life, he had now reached the haven of domestic life. Here while the storm roared at a distance, he could hear its roaring and be at peace. He had been a faithful labourer in the harvest field of life, his labours were crowned with success, and he had reaped a rich harvest of fame and wealth and honor. All that in this, his winter of life he may enjoy the harvest he has reaped. In him I perceive no decay of mind or debility of frame and to all the wisdom and experience of age, he adds the enthusiasm and ardour of youth. I looked on him with wonder as I heard him describe the improvements he designed in his grounds, they seemed to require a whole life to carry into effect, and a young man might doubt of ever completing or enjoying them. But he seems to have transposed his hopes and anticipations into the existence of his children. It is in them he lives, and I believe he finds as much delight in the idea that they will enjoy the fruit of his present labours, as if he hoped it for himself. If full occupation of mind, heart and hands, is happiness, surely he is happy. The sun never sees him in bed, and his mind designs more than the day can fulfil, even his long day. The conversation of the morning, the letters I had read, and the idea that this was the last day I was to spend in his society, the last time I was ever to see him, filled my heart with sadness. I could scarcely look at or speak to him without tears. After dinner he went to the carpenter's shop, to give directions for a walking seat he had ordered made for us, and I did not see him again until after sun-set. I spent the interval in walking with Mr. Smith round the lawn and grave, and had just parted from him to join the children to whom I had promised another story, when as I passed the terrace, Mr. J. came out and joined us. The children ran to him and immediately proposed a race; we seated ourselves on the steps of the Portico, and he after placing the children according to their size one before the other, gave the word for starting and away they flew; the course round this back lawn was a quarter of a mile, the little girls were much tired by the time they returned to the spot from which they started and came panting and out of breath to throw themselves into their grandfather's arms, which were opened to receive them; he pressed them to his bosom and rewarded them with a kiss; he was sitting on the grass and they sat down by him, until they were rested; then they again wished to set off; he thought it too long a course for little Mary and proposed running on the terrace. Thither we went, and seating ourselves at one end, they ran from us to the pavillion and back again; "What an amusement," said I, "do these little creatures afford us." "Yes," replied he, "it is only with them that a grave man can play the fool." They now called on him to run with them, he did not long resist and seemed delighted in delighting them. Oh ye whose envenomed calumny has painted him as the slave of the vilest passions, come here and contemplate this scene! The simplicity, the gaiety, the modesty and gentleness of a child, united to all that is great and venerable in the human character. His life is the best refutation of the calumnies that have been heaped upon him and it seems to me impossible, for any one personally to know him and remain his enemy. It was dark by the time we entered the tearoom. I was glad to close the windows and shut out the keen air from the mountains. The mornings and evenings are here always cool and indeed Mrs. Randolph says it is never hot. As it was the last evening we were to pass here, Mr. J. sat longer than usual after tea. All the family except Mrs. Randolph were at tea. I gazed upon Mr. J. in the midst of this interesting circle and thought of the following lines, which I copied from one of his letters.

"When I look to the ineffable pleasures of my family society, I become more and more disgusted with the jealousies, the hatred, the rancourous and malignant passions of this scene, and lament my having ever again been drawn into public view. Tranquility is now my object; I have seen enough of political honors, to know they are but splendid torments; and however one might be disposed to render services on which many of their fellow citizens might set a value, yet when as many would deprecate them as a public calamity, one may well entertain a modest doubt of their real importance and feel the impulse of duty to be very weak," and again, in another of a later date, 1797 he says,

"Worn down here with pursuits in which I take no delight, surrounded by enemies and spies, catching and perverting every word which falls from my lips, or flows from my pen, and inventing where facts fail them, I pant for that society, where all is peace and harmony, where we love and are beloved by every object we see. And to have that intercourse of soft affections, hushed and suppressed by the eternal presence of strangers, goes very hard indeed, and the harder when we see that the candle of life is burning out and the pleasures we lose are lost forever. I long to see the time approach when I can be returning to you, tho' it be for a short time only — these are the only times existence is of any value to me, continue then to love me my ever dear daughter, and to be assured, that to yourself, your sister and those dear to you every thing in my life is directed, ambition has no hold upon me but through you, my personal affections would fix me forever with you. Kiss the dear little objects of our mutual love," etc. etc.

By these dear objects, I saw him now surrounded. I saw him in the scenes for which his heart had panted, at the time when others looked upon his elevated station with envy, and did not know that these honors which his country lavished on him and which they envied, were splendid torments, to his unambitious spirit and affectionate heart. But why then it will be asked, did he not withdraw from public life? A satisfactory answer is often found in his letters; in one he says (it was while secretary) that he had made up his mind to retire, that he had arranged his affairs for it, but contrary to all his wishes he was persuaded by his friends of the necessity of remaining, that a retreat at that time would be attributed to timidity or fear of the attacks made by the papers and might ruin the party of which he was the head. In one of his letters he says—"The real difficulty is that once being delivered into the hands of others, where feelings are friendly to the individual and warm to the public cause; how to withdraw from them, without leaving a dissatisfaction in their minds and impressions of pusilanimity with the public." From many other passages of his letters, it is evident that his own wishes were subordinated to the remonstrances of his friends and to the wish of supporting the republican cause,—on which he sincerely and honestly believed the happiness of his country to depend.

After tea, fruit as usual was brought, of which he staid to partake; the figs were very fine and I eat them with greater pleasure from their having been planted rear'd and attended by him with peculiar care, which this year was rewarded with an abundant crop, and of which we every day enjoyed the produce.

Wednesday morning. Mrs. Randolph was not able to come down to breakfast, and I felt too sad to join in the conversation. I looked on every object around me, all was examined with that attention a last look inspires; the breakfast ended, our carriage was at the door, and I rose to bid farewell to this interesting family. Mrs. R. came down to spend the last minutes with us. As I stood for a moment in the Hall, Mr. J. approached and in the most cordial manner urged me to make another visit the ensuing summer, I told him with a voice almost choked with tears, "that I had no hope of such a pleasure—this," said I, raising my eyes to him, "is the last time I fear in this world at least, that I shall ever see you—But there is another world." I felt so affected by the idea of this last sight of this good and great man, that I turned away and hastily repeating my farewell to the family, gave him my hand, he pressed it affectionately as he put me in the carriage saying, "God bless you, dear madam. God bless you." "And God bless you," said I, from the very bottom of my heart.

Mr. Smith got in, the door shut and we drove from the habitation of philosophy and virtue. How rapidly did we seem to descend that mountain which had seemed so tedious in its ascent, and the quick pulsations I then felt were now changed to a heavy oppression.

Yes, he is truly a philosopher, and truly a good man, and eminently a great one. Then there is a tranquility about him, which an inward peace could alone bestow. As a ship long tossed by the storms of the ocean, casts anchor and lies at rest in a peaceful harbour, he is retired from an active and restless scene to this tranquil spot. Voluntarily and gladly has he resigned honors which he never sought, and unwillingly accepted. His actions, not his words, preach the emptiness and dissatisfaction attendant on a great office. His tall and slender figure is not impaired by age, tho' bent by care and labour. His white locks announce an age his activity, strength, health, enthusiasm, ardour and gaiety contradict. His face owes all its charm to its expression and intelligence; his features are not good and his complexion bad, but his countenance is so full of soul and beams with such benignity, that when the eye rests on his face, it is too busy in perusing its expression, to think of its features or complexion. His low and mild voice, harmonizes with his countenance rather than his figure. But his manners,—how gentle, how humble, how kind. His meanest slave must feel as if it were a father instead of a master who addressed him, when he speaks. To a disposition ardent, affectionate and communicative, he joins manners timid, even to bashfulness and reserved even to coldness. If his life had not proved to the contrary I should have pronounced him rather a man of imagination and taste, than a man of judgement, a literary rather than a scientific man, and least of all a politician, A character for which nature never seemed to have intended him, and for which the natural turn of mind, and his disposition, taste, and feeling equally unfit him. I should have been sure that this was the case, even had he not told me so. In an interesting conversation I had one evening—speaking of his past public and present domestic life—"The whole of my life," said he, "has been a war with my natural taste, feelings and wishes. Domestic life and literary pursuits, were my first and my latest inclinations, circumstances and not my desires lead me to the path I have trod. And like a bow tho long bent, which when unstrung flies back to its natural state, I resume with delight the character and pursuits for which nature designed me.

"The circumstances of our country," continued he, "at my entrance into life, were such that every honest man felt himself compelled to take a part, and to act up to the best of his abilities."

Notes

1. Colonel John Bayard, Mrs. Smith's father, was a federalist [Gaillard Hunt's note].
2. This anecdote is given in *A Winter in Washington,* Vol. II, p. 40 [Gaillard Hunt's note].
3. Jefferson's eldest [grand]daughter [Gaillard Hunt's note].

From *The First Forty Years of Washington Society, Portrayed by the Family Letters of Mrs. Samuel Harrison Smith (Margaret Bayard) from the Collection of Her Grandson, J. Henley Smith,* ed. Gaillard Hunt (New York: Scribner, 1906), pp. 5–12, 65–81.

The Sage of Monticello (1809)

John Edwards Caldwell

John Edwards Caldwell (1769–1819) was an orphan of the American Revolution. His mother, Hannah Ogden Caldwell, was killed by a British rifleman at their New Jersey home in 1780, and his father, the Reverend John Caldwell, was killed by friendly fire the next year. The Marquis de Lafayette, an acquaintance of the Reverend Caldwell, took the reverend's orphaned son to France in December 1781 and arranged an excellent education for the boy, who did not return to America until 1791. Upon returning, he entered the mercantile trade and did a lively business in the West Indies. In 1801, Jefferson appointed him consular agent of the United States for the city of Santo Domingo and ports of the West Indies. By 1803, however, Caldwell had returned to the mercantile trade. The embargo Jefferson imposed in December 1807 as an economic sanction on Great Britain severely limited the business of American merchants. Caldwell took the loss of business in stride, deciding to use the government-imposed lull to travel through Virginia in 1808. He published an account of his journey anonymously the following year: *A Tour through Part of Virginia in the Summer of 1808.*

Caldwell's travel narrative has been the source of some confusion. A second edition, also anonymous, appeared at Belfast in 1810. In 1819, David Warden identified Caldwell as the author of the Belfast edition, but Caldwell's authorship remained largely unknown until William M. E. Rachel republished the Belfast edition in 1951. Though Caldwell's authorship was unknown, his account of Jefferson at Monticello became widely known across the United States after the *Cape Fear Recorder*, a Wilmington, North Carolina, newspaper, reprinted it in 1816 as "The Sage of Monticello." Under that title, the article was reprinted in newspapers and magazines around the country from the Carolinas to Kentucky to Maine. Furthermore, Baron de Montlezun, a French traveler who visited Monticello in 1816, translated Caldwell's account of Monticello into French and passed it off as his own in *Souvenirs des Antilles: Voyage en 1815 et 1816, aux États-Unis, et dans l'Archipel Caraïbe* (1818). Translating the baron's account back into English, J. M. Varriere and L. C. Moffett suggested the possibility that Montlezun borrowed it from another source, but made no mention of Caldwell or any of the numerous reprints. The work has been reprinted as Montlezun's own writing (Peterson, *Visitors,* 67–71). Perhaps more than any other single item, this account shaped contemporary readers' perceptions of Jefferson in retirement.

THIS VILLAGE [MILTON] IS THREE MILES from the seat of Mr. Jefferson, President of the United States; my stay there did not exceed one hour, and my opportunity of converse with this great man was much shorter than I wished; however from my own observation, and from correct and authentic information, I am enabled to give you such an account of Monticello and its philosophic owner as may afford you gratification and entertainment, and as the most minute particulars respecting so eminent a character, and whatever may concern him, must interest you, I hope I shall not be accused of prolixity. Thomas is the oldest surviving son of Peter Jefferson; he has one brother and three sisters yet living, most of them have families; he had six children, two daughters alone lived to maturity; one married to Mr. John Eppes, the other to Mr. Thomas M. Randolph; the patriotism and talents of both these gentlemen are well known to the community. Mrs. Eppes died about five years since, and left two children, one of whom is since dead. Mr. and Mrs. Randolph lived near this place; they have a large family of children, and reside with the President during his visits to Monticello. Mr. Jefferson is very regular and temperate in his mode of living; he retires to his chamber about nine o'clock, and rises before the sun, both in summer and winter, and it is not easy to conceive a more grand or sublime sight than the rising of the sun viewed from the summit of Monticello. Until breakfast (which is early) he is employed in writing, after that he generally visits his work-shops, labourers, etc. and then, until 12 o'clock, he is engaged in his study, either in drawing, writing or reading; he then rides over his plantation, returns at two, dresses for dinner and joins his company; he retires from table soon after the cloth is removed, and spends the evening in walking about, reading the papers and in conversation with such guests as may be with him. His disposition is truly amiable, easy of access, quick and ready in the dispatch of business, and so condescending and naturally pleasing in his manners and address, that no person, at all acquainted with him, can feel in his presence perplexity or embarrassment. Mr. Jefferson is seen to less advantage at the seat of government, than at this, his favourite residence.

Monticello is a conical hill; — its summit, on which stands the house, is 500 feet above the adjoining country. The view from hence is extensive, variegated and charming; to the west, the blue mountains, at a distance of about fifteen miles, bound the prospect, while to the north and east, the eye wanders in rapture over an expanse of, I think, 45 miles; and can distinguish particular objects at that distance. It is near a mile from the public road which leads between Charlottesville and Milton. In a few years, when some improvements, now begun, are complete, the approach will be worthy the taste of the proprietor.

The house is an irregular octagon, with porticoes on the east and west sides, and piazzas on the north and south ends. Its extent, including the porticoes and piazzas, is about one hundred and ten by ninety feet; the external is finished in the Doric order complete, with a ballustrade on the top of it. In the centre of the S. W. side, over the parlour, is an attic story, terminated with a dome, which has a fine effect, and forms a beautiful room inside. The internal of the house contains specimens of all the different orders, except the composite, which is not introduced; the hall is in the Ionic, the dining room, in the Doric, the parlour, in the Corinthian, and dome in the Attic; in the other rooms are introduced several different forms of these orders, all in the truest proportions, according to Palladio. On the ground floor are eleven rooms; on the second, six; and on the attic, four; there are cellars under the whole. Through the antes of the house, from N. to S. on the cellar floor, is a passage of 300 feet long, leading to two wings or ranges of building of one story, that stand equidistant from each end of the house, and extend 120 feet eastwardly from the passages, terminated by a pavillion of two stories at the end of each. The roofs of the passages, and range of buildings, form an agreeable walk, being flat and floored, and are to have a Chinese railing round them; they rise but a little height above the lawn, that they may not obstruct the view. On the south side are the kitchen, smoke house, dairy, waste house and servants' rooms; on the north are the ice house, coach houses, &c. &c. The library is extensive, and contains, as might indeed be expected, a vast collection of rare and valuable works, on all subjects, and in all languages. Mr. Jefferson has also a large collection of mathematical, philosophical, and optical instruments, and Indian curiosities. Among the latter are busts of a male and female, sitting in the Indian position; they are supposed to be of great antiquity, and to have been formed by the Indians: they were ploughed up in the state of Tennessee, are of very hard stone, but considerably defaced; there is also in the hall a representation of a battle between the Panis and Osage; also a map of the Missouri and its tributary streams, both executed by Indians on dressed Buffaloe hides; bows, arrows and quivers; poisoned lances, pipes of peace, wampum belts, mockasins, &c. &c. several dresses, and cooking utensils of the Mandan and other nations of the Missouri. The statuary in the hall consists of a collosal bust of Mr. Jefferson, by Carrachi [Giuseppe Ceracchi], it is on a truncated column, on the pedestal of which are represented the twelve tribes of Israel, and the twelve signs of the Zodiac. A full length figure of Cleopatra, in a reclining position, after she had applied the asp, and busts of Voltaire and Turgot, in plaister; there is likewise a model of one of the pyramids of Egypt. In the parlour are busts of the emperors Alexander of Russia, and Napoleon of France, sitting on columns, and a sleeping Venus. In the bow of the dining room are busts of Genl. Washington, Doctor Franklin, Marquis de La Fayette, and Paul Jones, in plaister. The collection of paintings is considered by connoisseurs to be of the first rate.—Among them is the Ascension, by Poussin, the Holy Family, by Raphael, scourging of Christ, by Reubens, Crucifixion, by Guido, and a great many other scripture and historic pieces, by the first masters; portraits, prints, medalions, medals, etc. of celebrated characters and events. The collection of natural curiosities is tolerably extensive, and consists of mammoth and other bones, horns of different kinds, a head of the mountain ram, petrifactions, chrystalizations, minerals, shells etc. In short, it is supposed there is no private gentleman in the world in possession of so perfect and complete a scientific, useful and ornamental collection. His lands adjoining Monticello are said to be about eleven thousand acres. About fifteen hundred acres of cleared land, and a proportion of his negroes are hired out; as his public duties, since he became President, have prevented his engaging in agricultural pursuits: he proposes however making a beginning next year, and no doubt the farming community will be benefited both by his observations and practice. He has a merchant mill, which he lets at a rent of 1200 dollars per annum, and a grist mill which he works himself. He has a large tract of land in Bedford county, where he raises annually about

40,000 wt. of tobacco, and grain sufficient to maintain the plantations. He keeps no stock of horses or cattle here, but uses mules for his waggons. The number of his negroes are about two hundred. His flock of sheep are valuable, although not numerous; they consist of the Cape or large tail, Shetland, and Marino breed. The only manufactories at present carried on by him, are at Bedford, of Smith's work, and at Monticello a nailery, the latter conducted by boys; but he is making arrangements for the manufacture of cotton and woolens, on his return to domestic life. The garden, though justly celebrated for variety of delicious fruit, has been much neglected, but Mr. Jefferson proposes making considerable improvements, useful and ornamental, both here, and in his pleasure grounds.

From *A Tour through Part of Virginia in the Summer of 1808: In a Series of Letters, Including an Account of Harper's Ferry, the Natural Bridge, the New Discovery Called Weir's Cave, Monticello, and the Different Medicinal Springs, Hot and Cold Baths, Visited by the Author* (New York: for the Author, 1809), pp. 26–29.

Interview with Mr. Jefferson (1812)

JOHN MELISH

John Melish (1771–1822) was born in Methven, Scotland, and studied at the University of Glasgow. In 1798, he moved to the West Indies, where he lived until 1806, when he relocated to Savannah, Georgia, to run a cotton-exporting business. He traveled throughout the South, spending some time in Washington that October. On 5 October 1806, he visited the White House and secured an interview with President Jefferson. Melish went back to Scotland in 1807 but returned to the United States two years later, eventually settling in Philadelphia, where he established a career as a publisher and mapmaker. He specialized in books pertaining to travel: atlases, geography textbooks, travel guides, travel narratives, and promotional tracts encouraging emigration to the United States. He continued to travel extensively himself. Melish shaped his adventures into a book: *Travels in the United States of America* (1812), which incorporated his 1806 interview with President Jefferson. Melish asked Jefferson if he would be willing to subscribe to *Travels*. On 14 February 1812, Jefferson replied: "I very willingly become a subscriber to your intended publication, judging from the table of contents, and your familiarity with the subjects treated of, that work cannot fail to be useful to ourselves by pointing out advantageous pursuits not yet attended to and to Great Britain by shewing what their ignorance and injustice have lost to them here, and laying open to their wiser successors the interests they yet may cherish by peace and justice, advantageously for both nations" (*Papers, Retirement Series,* 4: 494). Melish published *Travels* in December 1812 and sent Jefferson's subscription copy to him (Sowerby, no. 4034). Jefferson enjoyed it very much and sent Melish a long letter calling *Travels* "an antidote to the misrepresentations of former travellers" (*Papers, Retirement Series,* 5: 566).

IN PURSUANCE OF THE recommendation of my friends, I set out, this morning, at 8 o'clock, for the purpose of waiting on Mr. Jefferson. On my arrival at the president's house, I delivered my address to a servant, who in a few minutes returned with an answer, that Mr. Jefferson would be with me presently, and showed me into an elegant apartment. Mr. Jefferson soon entered by an inner door, and requesting me to be seated, sat down himself; and immediately, and very frankly, entered into conversation, by asking where I had landed, and how long I had been in the country. Having informed him, he remarked that I would probably be travelling to the northward; I replied that I had been to the north, and was now travelling to the southward. "And how do you like New York?" "Very much," said I; "it is one of the finest sea-ports I have seen, and, I presume, will always continue to be the first commercial city in the United States." He observed that he found that idea generally entertained by strangers; that New York was a very fine situation, and would unquestionably continue always to be a great commercial city: but it appeared to him that *Norfolk* would probably, in process of time, be the greatest sea-port in the United States, New Orleans perhaps excepted. He pointed out the circumstance of the vast confluence of waters, that constituted the outlet of the Chesapeak bay, on which Norfolk is situated, and remarked that these rivers were as yet but partially settled; but they were rapidly settling up, and, when the population was full, the quantity of surplus produce would be immense, and Norfolk would probably become the greatest depôt in the United States, except New Orleans.

The conversation next turned upon the climate and season; on which the president remarked, that the country had this summer been remarkably healthy; that no case of epidemical sickness had come to his knowledge, some few of *bilious fever* and *fever and ague* excepted, at the foot of the mountains on James' river, not far from where he lived; and which country was never known to experience any cases of the kind before. As this appeared singular, I inquired whether there was any way of accounting for it. He replied, that the way he accounted for it was this: "In ordinary seasons, there is a sufficiency of water to keep the rivers in a state of circulation, and no more; but this season there has been a long and severe drought, which, in many places, has dried them up. The water has stagnated in pools, and sends out a putrid effluvia to some distance; which, being lighter than the atmosphere, ascends even some little way up the mountains, and reaches the abodes of those who thought themselves heretofore free from attack."

I was struck with the force of this remark, and applied it to a circumstance that had come under my observation at Washington. The Capitol Hill is elevated above the river upwards of 70 feet. Between this and the river there is a low meadow, about a mile broad, abounding with swamps and shrubbery. In the autumn these swamps send out an effluvia, which often affects the health of those who live on the hill. I noticed this circumstance, and the president remarked, that it was exactly in point. He said he had frequently observed from his windows, in the morning, the vapour to rise, and it seemed to have sufficient buoyancy to carry it to the top of the hill, and no further; there it settled, and the inhabitants coming out of their warm rooms, breathed this cold contaminated vapour, which brought on agues and other complaints. He said he had frequently pointed out this to the people, and urged them to drain the swamp, but it was still neglected, although they had, besides suffering in their health, probably expended more in doctor's bills than it would have cost. "But, indeed," he continued, "mankind are exceedingly slow in adopting resolutions to prevent disease, and it is very difficult to convince them where they originate; particularly when the reasoning applied is the result of philosophical deduction."

The transition from this subject to that of the yellow fever was natural, and I introduced it by noticing [Thomas] Paine's essay on the subject [*Of the Causes of the Yellow Fever* (1807)]. The president observed, that it was one of the most sensible performances on that disease, that had come under his observation. The remarks were quite philosophical, and, not being calculated to excite any party feeling, they might have a very useful tendency.

He then made a few remarks on the nature of the yellow fever itself. He observed, that it evidently arose from breathing impure air, and impure air may be either generated in the country or imported. A case had come under his observation where it was imported. A vessel arrived at Norfolk, and the air in her hold was so pestilential, that every person who went into it was affected, and some of them died; but, on the discovery being made, the vessel was purified, and the fever did not spread. This was a local circumstance, he observed, and there may be many others, which are pernicious as far as they go, and care should be taken to prevent them. But a ship can never import a sufficient quantity of impure air to pollute a whole city, if that city be otherwise healthy, and therefore, the origin of the yellow fever, *on an extended scale,* must be sought for in an impure air, generated from filth collected in and about great cities; and it was very expedient that this view of the subject should be enforced, in order to induce mankind to attend to one of the most important concerns in life—cleanliness.

I took notice of the bad state of the road between Baltimore and Washington, and expressed my surprise that it should remain in this state, so near the capital of the United States. The president observed, that the removal of the seat of government was a recent measure, and the country was so extensive, that it would necessarily be a considerable time before good roads could be made in all directions, but as it was a most important subject, it would be attended to as fast as circumstances would permit; and the road to Baltimore, being the great thoroughfare to the northern states, would probably be one of the first that would undergo a thorough repair. He then informed me, that both this subject and that of internal navigation by canals, were under consideration at the present time, upon a very extended scale, and probably a report would soon be published relative to them; and he had little doubt, but that in less than 20 years turnpike roads would be general throughout the country; and a chain of canals would probably be cut, which would complete an inland navigation from Massachusetts to Georgia; and another to connect the eastern with the western waters.

I remarked that these would be most important improvements, and would greatly facilitate internal intercourse; and as to manufactures, I presumed it would long continue to be the policy of the country to import them. He replied, that this, like other branches, would of course find its level, and would depend upon the genius of the people; but it was astonishing, the progress that had been made in manufactures of late years. It would hardly be believed, he said, by strangers, but he had it on the best authority, that the manufactures of Philadelphia were greater in value annually, than were those of Birmingham 20 years ago; and he had no doubt but that manufactures of articles of the first necessity, would increase until they became quite general through the country.

As the non-importation act was then in dependence, I was naturally anxious to ascertain, whether matters were likely to be adjusted with Britain, and, as modestly as possible, endeavoured to turn the conversation that way. I was urged to this by two considerations. I was not sure but that part of our fall importation would come under the operation of the non-importation act, if it took place; and being fully satisfied of the friendly disposition of the whig party in Britain towards America, I would gladly have availed myself of an opportunity of expressing that opinion to the president. But on this subject Mr. Jefferson was, of course, reserved; though, from the few observations he made, I concluded that matters would ultimately be amicably adjusted. I was highly gratified by the expression of his opinion, on the character of my great favourite statesman Mr. [Charles] Fox. Accounts had that morning reached Washington, that Mr. Fox was in the last stage of his illness.—I noticed the circumstance. "Poor man," said Mr. Jefferson, "I fear by this time he is no more, and his loss will be severely felt by his country: he is a man of the most liberal and enlightened policy—a friend to his country, and to the human race."

A gentleman then called upon him, I believe General [William] Eaton, and I took my leave, highly pleased with the affability, intelligence and good sense of the President of America.

From *Travels in the United States of America, in the Years 1806 and 1807, and 1809, 1810, and 1811: Including an Account of Passages betwixt America and Britain, and Travels through Various Parts of Britain, Ireland, and Canada,* 2 vols. (Philadelphia: for the Author, 1812), 1: 201–206.

[An Italian Friend Remembers Virginia and France] (1813)

PHILIP MAZZEI

One of the most colorful characters to emerge from Revolutionary Virginia, Philip Mazzei (1730–1816), was born in Italy and studied medicine in Florence. Disgruntled with the medical profession, he traveled to England in 1756, where he established a successful mercantile business. Encouraged by Virginia merchant Thomas Adams, Mazzei (pronounced Mah-tzay-ee) left England for Tuscany in 1772, planning to outfit an agricultural venture in Virginia. He collected grape and olive cuttings and hired several local viticulturists and oenologists to accompany him. He reached Virginia in 1773 and acquired property adjacent to Monticello, which he named Colle. When news of Lexington and Concord reached Virginia, Mazzei became a thoroughgoing American patriot, writing essays for the *Virginia Gazette* advocating the American cause. In 1779, Governor Patrick Henry appointed Mazzei Virginia's agent in Europe, though his mission was largely unsuccessful. Mazzei returned to Virginia in 1783, only to discover that his vineyard and olive orchard had been destroyed during the war. Monticello was a melancholy sight, as well. Mazzei wrote, "Monticello was a sad place for me, because I often remembered the angelic deceased wife of Jefferson. She vivified that home" (Branchi, "Memoirs," 11).

Mazzei went to Paris in 1785, where he renewed his friendship with Jefferson. Well connected among the Parisian philosophes, Mazzei introduced Jefferson to many leading French intellectuals. After Jefferson returned to the United States, he and Mazzei continued to correspond. On 24 April 1796, Jefferson wrote Mazzei a letter criticizing Federalist policies and suggesting that the Federalists were manipulating George Washington. Mazzei indiscreetly shared the letter with others, and copies of it were translated into French and published in the newspapers. The letter was badly retranslated back into English and republished in America. Known as the "Mazzei Letter," the document generated much criticism of Jefferson, who never really held Mazzei accountable for his indiscretion; the two remained friends and continued to correspond.

When Mazzei was in his early eighties, he started writing his autobiography, which he completed in 1813. Dr. John Reynolds, an American physician who went to Italy to recover his health, met Mazzei toward the end of his life. Mazzei read parts of his manuscript to Reynolds and even loaned it to him to read at his leisure, as Thomas Appleton, U.S. consul at Leghorn, informed Jefferson. Mazzei left his autobiography unpublished at the time of his death on 19 March 1816. Reynolds enjoyed it so well that he proposed to publish an English translation, but he could not recruit enough subscribers to make it a viable endeavor. Reynolds advertised for subscribers in the Philadelphia *Aurora,* from which Jefferson learned about his proposal. In an 18 July 1816 letter to Thomas Appleton, Jefferson wrote an incisive character sketch of Mazzei:

> He was of solid worth; honest, able, zealous, in sound principles, moral and political constant in friendship, and punctual in all his undertakings. He was greatly esteemed in this country, and someone has inserted in our papers an account of his death, with a handsome eulogy of him, and a proposition to publish his life in one octavo volume. I have no doubt that what he has written of himself during the portion of the revolutionary period he passed with us, would furnish some good material for our history of which there is already a wonderful scarcity. (*Works,* 12: 16–18)

MR. [THOMAS] ADAMS has sold the house in which he lived, and also all his properties, and he had bought another about one hundred sixty miles above Williamsburg, in Augusta County, and about fifty miles beyond the Blue Ridge Mountains (a name given them by the first European immigrants because the atmosphere at a distance lent that color), the top of which separates Augusta County from Albemarle County, in which Mr. Jefferson is living, about twenty miles this side of the mountains.

We left together to go there. We desired to determine where it was possible to construct a house, and to have an opportunity of seeing if I might buy a tract of land next to his, if the region were suitable to me. We agreed to pass two or three days with Mr. Jefferson, who lived a very short distance off our route.

Mr. Jefferson was thirty-two years old [thirty, actually], or eleven younger than I; his wife was a widow when he married her at the age of twenty-three, and they had a baby girl a few months old. We arrived there one evening, and the following morning Jefferson and I, while the others slept, went walking in the neighborhood. He took me to the home of a poor man, who had a small house and about four hundred acres of land bordering Mr. Jefferson's, of which he had cleared and cultivated about an eighth part which he wanted to sell, for he had several sons, and by going farther inland about a hundred miles he could, with half of the money from the land which he had sold, buy a quantity sufficient to leave to each of his sons a portion equal to that which I bought.

That little house was more than sufficient for the peasants I had brought with me. It was in a small valley which sloped upward on two sides, one of which formed a *spiaggia,* and the other—longer and higher—a hill, on which we agreed to build a log cabin for myself. As the land of Mr. Jefferson bordered that which I had bought, and as he had much more than he needed, he made me a present of a tract that contained about two thousand acres.

He had other possessions in the county adjoining Albemarle, the products of which he sold for about two thousand pounds sterling, after using what he needed for himself and for his relatives.

When we returned, all the others had risen, and Mr. Adams, seeing Mr. Jefferson, said, "I see in your face that you have taken him from me, and I expected it." Jefferson, without paying any attention to him, looked at the table and said, "Let's take breakfast, and later we'll arrange everything." After breakfast, he sent a letter to his brother-in-law, Mr. Eppes, in which he told him to send us my men from the ship, together with some things described in a note, and to tell Madame Martin that soon after the arrival of my men, Mr. Adams and I would come for her and her daughter.

Mr. Adams left at once for Augusta. He did not return from his trip until after my men arrived. Jefferson knew the Italian language very well, but had never heard it spoken. Nevertheless, speaking with my men, he understood them and they understood him. I was impressed by their demonstrations of joy at the circumstance. Jefferson had among his slaves very skilful workers in every trade except tailoring. As soon as he saw the use of our spades and implements, he had them duplicated for the use of all his tenants. He liked our *carniera,* or hunting-coat, and adopted it at once. His neighbors imitated him, and the use of the coat spread with great rapidity. This was good for the tailor, because, being obliged to work for me and my men (I had to support him in everything), any other work he might find was entirely his profit. [. . .]

In every country in which I have been, I have heard the Tuscan language praised as being sweet and at the same time prolix and lacking in forcefulness. Jefferson was the first I heard to hold a different opinion. After he had translated a number of my articles for the newspaper, he told me to write in English, and that he would correct what errors I made. I believed that he was wearied of translating, but he assured me to the contrary, and he said, "You have a manner of expressing yourself in your language which I cannot translate without weakening your expression." I then wrote in English. After he had corrected the first page, it looked like a swarm of flies; but the number or errors diminished, and after I had written six or seven pages he told me that there was nothing to correct. I could not persuade myself of that, but he showed me several places where I had expressed myself with great energy; and he said that they could not be corrected without a lessening of force. "The phraseology," he continued, "is not wholly English, but you will be understood by everyone, and that is of the greatest importance." [. . .]

Arriving at Paris, I lodged in the Hotel des Colonies, Rue des Prouvaires, taking the same room as formerly. Then, I went at once to see Jefferson, who lived in a beautiful *villetta* with a charming garden, at the end of the Champs Elysees, within gunshot distance of the city wall passed on going to Versailles. I took an enjoyable and interesting walk, arriving about an hour before dinner. I had informed him of my arrival at Lorient, as soon as I landed; and I wrote to him from Nantes, also. So he expected me daily. Nevertheless, our meeting was moving to both. We had many things to say, and we had a great deal of time at our disposal, for on that day no one came to dine with him, and his secretary, Mr. [William] Short, was at dinner with the Countess de Tesse, cousin of the Marquis de la Fayette. After discoursing on public matters, we spoke about our own affairs. I found out, then, that when I sent him my letter at Boston to show to my friends in France, I had forgotten to send one for M. de Marmontel, and we agreed to visit him the next day. . . .

On the following morning, Jefferson and I went to Marmontel's home. We found him outdoors. He wanted us to go inside with him, and though

Jefferson had to pay several calls that same morning, nevertheless our conversation lasted for two hours. They had much to say, and more to ask. Jefferson, among other things, said that he did not understand why the diplomats of the European powers made a mystery of things entirely unimportant. Marmontel answered him, "It is true, they have always a lock on their mouths; but if you take off the lock, you will see that the hand-bag is empty."

When we were ready to leave, there arrived the Abbot Morellet, maternal uncle of Marmontel, and the greatest French logician, who lived in the same house. So, we remained for another half hour. From there, we went to Lavoisier's, to Condorcet's, to the Duc de la Rochefoucauld's and finally home, where, having only Mr. Short at dinner, we spoke about the affairs of our country.

From "Memoirs of the Life and Voyages of Doctor Philip Mazzei," trans. E. C. Branchi, *William and Mary College Quarterly Historical Magazine,* 2d ser. 9 (July 1929): 163–164, 168; 10 (January 1930): 14–15.

[Man of the Mountain] (1815)

GEORGE TICKNOR

Having learned that Jefferson had successfully sold his personal library to the U.S. Congress, George Ticknor (1791–1871) grew anxious to see his great collection of books before it was carted off to Washington. With his friend and traveling companion Francis Calley Gray, Ticknor planned a literary pilgrimage to Monticello. For both Ticknor and Gray, John Adams wrote letters of introduction to Jefferson. The one Adams wrote for Ticknor is a pure delight. It begins, "The most exalted of our young Genius's in Boston have an Ambition to see Monticello, its Library and its Sage." Adams predicted that Jefferson would get along famously with both young men. As you are all "gluttons for books," he continued, "I think you ought to have a Sympathy for each other" (Cappon, *Adams-Jefferson Letters,* 441). Ticknor and Gray left separate accounts of their journey to Monticello in 1815, and both imbue the ascent to Monticello in terms of a heroic quest. Gray wrote: "The forest had evidently been abandoned to nature; some of the trees were decaying from age, some were blasted, some uprooted by the wind and some appeared even to have been twisted from their trunks by the violence of a hurricane. They rendered the approach to the house even at this season of the year extremely grand and imposing" (*Thomas Jefferson in 1814,* 66–67).

Though nearly fifty years separated Thomas Jefferson and George Ticknor, the two men found one another kindred spirits. As John Adams realized, both had a great love of books. Something of a prodigy, Ticknor excelled at the study of ancient and modern languages, graduating from Dartmouth College the year he turned sixteen. After college he continued studying Latin and Greek, passed the bar, and started practicing law. The legal profession turned out to be a disappointment. The trip that took Ticknor from Boston to Monticello, with several stops in between, including one at Washington to dine with President Madison, was something of a soul-searching journey. In his old age, Jefferson inspired many young men: Ticknor was no exception. Essentially Jefferson helped him to cultivate his love of learning and make the world of books his profession. Ticknor subsequently traveled to Europe, where he expanded his horizons, broadened his education, and, while there, purchased many books for Jefferson (Hayes, *Road to Monticello,* 564–566). After a lengthy education in Europe, at the University of Gottingen and in self-directed travels, Ticknor returned to take a professorship of modern languages at Harvard.

After meeting Ticknor, Jefferson called him "the best bibliograph I have met with" (*Adams-Jefferson Letters,* 441). He was sad to see Ticknor leave so soon and encouraged him to stay longer. At the time, Ticknor attributed his friendliness to Southern hospitality, not realizing how much he meant to Jefferson. He recognized Ticknor would go far in his career. In a 14 February 1815 letter to the Marquis de Lafayette, Jefferson called Ticknor a man "of great erudition, indefatigable industry, and preparation for a life of distinction in his own country" (*Works,* 11: 463). Jefferson would correspond with Ticknor throughout the remainder of his life.

George Ticknor to Elisha Ticknor, 7 February 1815

We left Charlottesville on Saturday morning, the 4th of February, for Mr. Jefferson's. He lives, you know, on a mountain, which he has named Monticello, and which, perhaps you do not know, is a synonyme for Carter's mountain. The ascent of this steep, savage hill, was as pensive and slow as Satan's ascent to Paradise. We were obliged to wind two thirds round its sides before we reached the artificial lawn on which the house stands; and, when we had arrived there, we were about six hundred feet, I understand, above the stream which flows at its foot. It is an abrupt mountain. The fine growth of ancient forest-trees conceals its sides and shades part of its summit. The prospect is admirable. . . . The lawn on the top, as I hinted, was artificially formed by cutting down the peak of the height. In its centre, and facing the southeast, Mr. Jefferson has placed his house, which is of brick, two stories high in the wings, with a piazza in front of a receding centre. It is built, I suppose, in the French style. You enter, by a glass folding-door, into a hall which reminds you of Fielding's "Man of the Mountain," by the strange furniture of its walls. On one side hang the head and horns of an elk, a deer, and a buffalo; another is covered with curiosities which Lewis and Clarke found in their wild and perilous expedition. On the third, among many other striking matters, was the head of a mammoth, or, as Cuvier calls it, a mastodon, containing the only *os frontis,*

Mr. Jefferson tells me, that has yet been found. On the fourth side, in odd union with a fine painting of the Repentance of Saint Peter, is an Indian map on leather, of the southern waters of the Missouri, and an Indian representation of a bloody battle, handed down in their traditions.

Through this hall — or rather museum — we passed to the dining room, and sent our letters to Mr. Jefferson, who was of course in his study. Here again we found ourselves surrounded with paintings that seemed good.

We had hardly time to glance at the pictures before Mr. Jefferson entered; and if I was astonished to find Mr. Madison short and somewhat awkward, I was doubly astonished to find Mr. Jefferson, whom I had always supposed to be a small man, more than six feet high, with dignity in his appearance, and ease and graciousness in his manners. . . . He rang, and sent to Charlottesville for our baggage, and, as dinner approached, took us to the drawing-room, — a large and rather elegant room, twenty or thirty feet high, — which, with the hall I have described, composed the whole centre of the house, from top to bottom. The floor of this room is tessellated. It is formed of alternate diamonds of cherry and beech, and kept polished as highly as if it were of fine mahogany.

Here are the best pictures of the collection. Over the fireplace is the Laughing and Weeping Philosophers, dividing the world between them; on its right, the earliest navigators to America, — Columbus, Americus Vespuccius, Magellan, etc., — copied, Mr. Jefferson said, from originals in the Florence Gallery. Farther round, Mr. Madison in the plain, Quaker-like dress of his youth, Lafayette in his Revolutionary uniform, and Franklin in the dress in which we always see him. There were other pictures, and a copy of Raphael's Transfiguration.

We conversed on various subjects until dinner-time, and at dinner were introduced to the grown members of his family. These are his only remaining child, Mrs. Randolph, her husband, Colonel Randolph, and the two oldest of their unmarried children, Thomas Jefferson and Ellen; and I assure you I have seldom met a pleasanter party.

The evening passed away pleasantly in general conversation, of which Mr. Jefferson was necessarily the leader. I shall probably surprise you by saying that, in conversation, he reminded me of Dr. Freeman. He has the same discursive manner and love of paradox, with the same appearance of sobriety and cool reason. He seems equally fond of American antiquities, and especially the antiquities of his native State, and talks of them with freedom and, I suppose, accuracy. He has, too, the appearance of that fairness and simplicity which Dr. Freeman has; and, if the parallel holds no further here, they will again meet on the ground of their love of old books and young society.

On Sunday morning, after breakfast, Mr. Jefferson asked me into his library, and there I spent the forenoon of that day as I had that of yesterday. This collection of books, now so much talked about, consists of about seven thousand volumes, contained in a suite of fine rooms, and is arranged in the catalogue, and on the shelves, according to the divisions and subdivisions of human learning by Lord Bacon. In so short a time I could not, of course, estimate its value, even if I had been competent to do so.

Perhaps the most curious single specimen—or, at least, the most characteristic of the man and expressive of his hatred of royalty—was a collection which he had bound up in six volumes, and lettered "The Book of Kings," consisting of the *Memoires de la Princesse de Bareith,* two volumes; *Les Memoires de la Comtesse de la Motte,* two volumes; the *Trial of the Duke of York,* one volume; and *The Book,* one volume. These documents of regal scandal seemed to be favorites with the philosopher, who pointed them out to me with a satisfaction somewhat inconsistent with the measured gravity he claims in relation to such subjects generally.

On Monday morning I spent a couple of hours with him in his study. He gave me there an account of the manner in which he passed the portion of his time in Europe which he could rescue from public business; told me that while he was in France he had formed a plan of going to Italy, Sicily, and Greece, and that he should have executed it, if he had not left Europe in the full conviction that he should immediately return there, and find a better opportunity. He spoke of my intention to go, and, without my even hinting any purpose to ask him for letters, told me that he was now seventy-two years old, and that most of his friends and correspondents in Europe had died in the course of the twenty-seven years since he left France, but that he would gladly furnish me with the means of becoming acquainted with some of the remainder, if I would give him a month's notice, and regretted that their number was so reduced.

The afternoon and evening passed as on the two days previous; for everything is done with such regularity, that when you know how one day is filled, I suppose you know how it is with the others. At eight o'clock the first bell is rung in the great hall, and at nine the second summons you to the breakfast-room, where you find everything ready. After breakfast every one goes, as inclination leads him, to his chamber, the drawing-room, or the library. The children retire to their school-room with their mother, Mr. Jefferson rides to his mills on the Rivanna, and returns at about twelve. At half past three the great bell rings, and those who are disposed resort to the drawing room, and the rest go to the dining-room at the second call of the bell, which is at four o'clock. The dinner was always choice, and served in the French style; but no wine was set on the table till the cloth was removed. The ladies sat until about six, then retired, but returned with the tea-tray a little before seven, and spent the evening with the gentlemen; which was always pleasant, for they are obviously accustomed to join in the conversation, however high the topic may be. At about half past ten, which seemed to be their usual hour of retiring, I went to my chamber, found there a fire, candle, and a servant in waiting to receive my orders for the morning, and in the morning was waked by his return to build the fire.

To-day, Tuesday, we told Mr. Jefferson that we should leave Monticello in the afternoon. He seemed much surprised, and said as much as politeness would permit on the badness of the roads and the prospect of bad weather, to induce us to remain longer. It was evident, I thought, that they had calculated on our staying a week. At dinner, Mr. Jefferson again urged us to stay, not in an oppressive way, but with kind politeness; and when the horses were at the door, asked if he should not send them away; but, as he found us resolved on going, he bade us farewell in the heartiest style of Southern hospitality, after thrice reminding me that I must write to him for letters to his friends in Europe. I came away almost regretting that the coach returned so soon, and thinking, with General Hamilton, that he was a perfect gentleman in his own house.

Two little incidents which occurred while we were at Monticello should not be passed by. The night before we left, young Randolph came up late from Charlottesville, and brought the astounding news that the English had been defeated before New Orleans by General Jackson. Mr. Jefferson had made up his mind that the city would fall, and told me that the English would hold it permanently — or for some time — by a force of Sepoys from the East Indies. He had gone to bed, like the rest of us; but of course his grandson went to his chamber with the paper containing the news. But the old philosopher refused to open his door, saying he could wait till the morning; and when we met at breakfast I found he had not yet seen it.

One morning, when he came back from his ride, he told Mr. Randolph, very quietly, that the dam had been carried away the night before. From his manner, I supposed it an affair of small consequence, but at Charlottesville, on my way to Richmond, I found the country ringing with it. Mr. Jefferson's great dam was gone, and it would cost $30,000 to rebuild it.

There is a breathing of notional philosophy in Mr. Jefferson,—in his dress, his house, his conversation. His setness, for instance, in wearing very sharp toed shoes, corduroy small-clothes, and red plush waistcoat, which have been laughed at till he might perhaps wisely have dismissed them.

So, though he told me he thought Charron, *De la Sagesse*, the best treatise on moral philosophy ever written, and an obscure Review of Montesquieu, by Dupont de Nemours, the best political work that had been printed for fifty years,—though he talked very freely of the natural impossibility that one generation should bind another to pay a public debt, and of the expediency of vesting all the legislative authority of a State in one branch, and the executive authority in another, and leaving them to govern it by joint discretion,—I considered such opinions simply as curious *indicia* of an extraordinary character.

From *Life, Letters, and Journals of George Ticknor,* ed. Anna Ticknor, 2 vols. (1876; reprinted, Boston: Houghton Mifflin, 1909), 1: 34–38.

Monticello (1818)

Francis Hall

Francis Hall served in the British Army, 14th Light Dragoons during the Peninsular War. Wounded at the combat of Carpio in 1812, he was invalided home. He came to America in 1816, documenting his trip as *Travels in Canada, and the United States, in 1816 and 1817* (1818). Hall's travels brought him to Monticello, where he became acquainted with Thomas Jefferson, who welcomed him to spend the night. Hall included an account of the experience in *Travels,* which he padded out using an article from *Niles' Weekly Register* (11 [1817]: 337) quoting Adams's remarks about the authenticity of political speeches from the Revolutionary era.

One British reviewer appreciated Hall's *Travels,* especially his Monticello chapter, observing, "The account of the new settlements on the lakes, and of the venerable Jefferson, cannot fail to be read with singular interest" (*Monthly Magazine* 45 [1818]: 626). Others generally enjoyed the book, too. The Reverend Sydney Smith remarked, "Mr. Hall is a clever, lively man, very much above the common race of writers; with very liberal and reasonable opinions, which he expresses with great boldness,—and an inexhaustible fund of good humour. [. . .] It is certainly somewhat rare to meet with an original thinker, an indulgent judge of manners, and a man tolerant of neglect and familiarity, in a youth covered with tags, feathers, and martial foolery" (*Works of the Rev. Sydney Smith,* 1: 327–328).

Hall parlayed his knack for travel writing into two additional books: *Travels in France in 1818* (1819) and *Colombia: Its Present State* (1824). The latter book stemmed from Hall's experience as hydrographer in the service of Colombia. He subsequently ventured further south to fight in the Chilean Revolution of 1829 and met a gruesome end. Colonel Hugh Pearse explains:

> Having a Byronic aspiration to succour oppressed nationalities he and a brother officer named Devereux joined the Chilian revolutionary army as volunteers. Francis Hall received the rank of Colonel, and met his death in a tragic manner. He had made overtures to a discontented faction in a town garrisoned by Royalist troops, and had arranged a night surprise during a festival. The town guard was bribed, and Hall with a party of about

a hundred men presented himself at the gate, which was thrown open to him and his party. After entering they found to their dismay the street lined by troops, and they were taken prisoners to a man. Colonel Hall's head was cut off and placed over the gate (*The Hearseys*, 37–38).

HAVING AN INTRODUCTION to Mr. Jefferson, I ascended his little mountain on a fine morning, which gave the situation its due effect. The whole of the sides and base are covered with forest, through which roads have been cut circularly, so that the winding may be shortened or prolonged at pleasure: the summit is an open lawn, near to the south side of which, the house is built, with its garden just descending the brow: the saloon, or central hall, is ornamented with several pieces of antique sculpture, Indian arms, Mammoth bones, and other curiosities collected from various parts of the Union. I found Mr. Jefferson tall in person, but stooping and lean with old age, thus exhibiting that fortunate mode of bodily decay, which strips the frame of its most cumbersome parts, leaving it still strength of muscle and activity of limb. His deportment was exactly such as the Marquis de Chastellux describes it, above thirty years ago: "At first serious, nay even cold," but in a very short time relaxing into a most agreeable amenity; with an unabated flow of conversation on the most interesting topicks, discussed in the most gentlemanly and philosophical manner. I walked with him round his grounds, to visit his pet trees, and improvements of various kinds: during the walk, he pointed out to my observation a conical mountain, rising singly at the edge of the southern horizon of the landscape: its distance he said, was 40 miles, and its dimensions those of the greater Egyptian pyramid; so that it accurately represents the appearance of the pyramid at the same distance; there is a small cleft visible on its summit, through which, the true meridian of Monticello exactly passes: its most singular property, however, is, that on different occasions it looms, or alters its appearance, becoming sometimes cylindrical, sometimes square, and sometimes assuming the form of an inverted cone. Mr. Jefferson had not been able to connect this phenomenon with any particular season, or state of the atmosphere, except, that it most commonly occurred in the forenoon. He observed, that it was not only wholly unaccounted for by the laws of vision, but that it had not as yet engaged the attention of philosophers so far as to acquire a name; that of looming, being in fact, a term applied by sailors, to appearances of a similar kind at sea. The Blue Mountains are also observed to loom, though not in so remarkable a degree.[1]

It must be interesting to recall and preserve the political sentiments of a man who has held so distinguished a station in public life as Mr. Jefferson. He seemed to consider much of the freedom and happiness of America, to arise from local circumstances. "Our population," he observed, "has an elasticity, by which it would fly off from oppressive taxation." He instanced the beneficial effects of a free government, in the case of New Orleans, where many proprietors who were in a state of indigence under the dominion of Spain, have risen to sudden wealth, solely by the rise in the value of land, which followed a change of government. Their ingenuity in mechanical inventions, agricultural improvements, and that mass of general information to be found among Americans of all ranks and conditions, he ascribed to that ease of circumstances, which afforded them leisure to cultivate their minds, after the cultivation of their lands was completed,—In fact, I have frequently been surprised to find mathematical and other useful works in houses, which seemed to have little pretension to the luxury of learning. Another cause, Mr. Jefferson observed, might be discovered in the many court and county meetings, which brought men frequently together on public business, and thus gave them habits, both of thinking and of expressing their thoughts on subjects, which in other countries are confined to the consideration of the privileged few. Mr. Jefferson has not the reputation of being very friendly to England: we should, however, be aware, that a partiality in this respect is not absolutely the duty of an American citizen; neither is it to be expected that the policy of our government should be regarded in foreign countries, with the same complacency with which it is looked upon by ourselves: but whatever may be his sentiments in this respect, politeness naturally repressed any offensive expression of them: he talked of our affairs with candour, and apparent good-will, though leaning, perhaps, to the gloomier side of the picture. He did not perceive by what means we could be extricated from our present financial embarrassments, without some kind of revolution in our government: on my replying, that our habits were remarkably steady, and that great sacrifices would be made to prevent a violent catastrophe, he acceded to the observation, but demanded, if those who made the sacrifices, would not require some political reformation in return. His repugnance was strongly marked to the despotic principles of Bonaparte, and he seemed to consider France under Louis XVI as scarcely capable of a republican form of government; but added, that the present generation of Frenchmen had grown up with sounder notions, which would probably leap to their emancipation. [. . .]

The conversation turning on American history, Mr. Jefferson related an anecdote of the Abbé Raynal, which serves to shew how history, even when it calls itself philosophical, is written. The Abbé was in company with Dr. Franklin, and several Americans at Paris, when mention chanced to be made of his anecdote of Polly Baker, related in his sixth volume, upon which one of the company observed, that no such law as that alluded to in the story, existed in New England: the Abbé stoutly maintained the authenticity of his tale, when Dr. Franklin, who had hitherto remained silent, said, "I can account for all this; you took the anecdote from a newspaper, of which I was at that time editor, and, happening to be very short of news, I composed and inserted the whole story." "Ah! Doctor," said the Abbé, making a true French retreat, "I had rather have your stories, than other men's truths."

Mr. Jefferson preferred Botta's Italian *History of the American Revolution,* to any that had yet appeared, remarking, however, the inaccuracy of the speeches. Indeed, the true history of that period seems to be generally considered as lost: A remarkable letter on this point, lately appeared in print, from the venerable Mr. John Adams, to a Mr. Niles, who had solicited his aid to collect and publish a body of revolutionary speeches. He says, "Of all the speeches made in Congress, from 1774 to 1777, inclusive, of both years, not one sentence remains, except a few periods of Dr. Witherspoon, printed in his works." His concluding sentence is very strong. "In plain English, and in a few words, Mr. Niles, I consider the true history of the American revolution, and the establishment of our present constitutions, as lost for ever; and nothing but misrepresentations, or partial accounts of it, will ever be recovered."

I slept a night at Monticello, and left it in the morning, with such a feeling as the traveller quits the mouldering remains of a Grecian temple, or the pilgrim a fountain in the desert. It would indeed argue great torpor, both of understanding and heart, to have looked without veneration and interest, on the man who drew up the declaration of American independence; who shared in the councils by which her freedom was established;

whom the unbought voice of his fellow-citizens called to the exercise of a dignity, from which his own moderation impelled him, when such example was most salutary, to withdraw; and who, while he dedicates the evening of his glorious days to the pursuits of science and literature, shuns none of the humbler duties of private life; but, having filled a seat higher than that of kings, succeeds with graceful dignity to that of the good neighbour, and becomes the friendly adviser, lawyer, physician, and even gardener of his vicinity. This is the "still small voice" of philosophy, deeper and holier than the lightnings and earthquakes which have preceded it. What monarch would venture thus to exhibit himself in the nakedness of his humanity? On what royal brow would the laurel replace the diadem? But they who are born and educated to be kings, are not expected to be philosophers. This is a just answer, though no great compliment either to the governors or the governed.

My travels had nearly terminated at the Rivannah, which flows at the foot of Monticello: in trying to ford it, my horse and waggon were carried down the stream: I escaped with my servant, and by the aid of Mr. Jefferson's domestics, we finally succeeded in extricating my equipage from a watery grave.

Note

1. Vide for a more detailed account of this phenomenon, in *Notes on Virginia,* p. 122. [Hall's note]

From *Travels in Canada, and the United States, in 1816 and 1817* (London: Longman, Hurst, Rees, Orme, and Brown, 1818), pp. 374–385.

[A Philosophical Legislator] (1824)

Adam Hodgson

A distinguished Liverpool merchant, Adam Hodgson (1788–1862) was a partner in Rathbone, Hodgson, and Company, a firm established in 1814. This mercantile firm operated a fleet of ships sailing to America and the Baltic. The cotton trade was its primary business, but the firm also traded grain, timber, and turpentine. In 1821, Hodgson traveled to North America on behalf of the company. His commercial mission had a twofold purpose: to gather political and economic intelligence and to establish personal contacts in the transatlantic mercantile world. He described his American experience in letters to his family and business partners and subsequently collected and edited his travel correspondence as *Letters from North America, Written During a Tour in the United States and Canada* (1824). The book met with a mixed reception in the United States. Reviewing it for the *North American Review,* Jared Sparks concluded, "His book is creditable to his heart and his principles; we should be glad if as much could be said of his discretion and judgment" (234). Hodgson retired from Rathbone, Hodgson, and Company the year the book appeared, but he later became a director of the Bank of Liverpool and figured prominently in the political, social, and cultural life of Liverpool until his death.

ON THE 18TH INSTANT, I left Hayes's tavern, at the foot of the Blue ridge [. . .] and proceeded to Gooch's, an excellent inn, to breakfast, where I saw the arrival of the *Albion,* at New York, with newspapers to the 30th April, and the sentence pronounced on [Arthur] Thistlewood and his associates. We shortly afterwards passed through Charlottesville, where General [Banastre] Tarleton was near capturing Mr. Jefferson and the State Legislature, being prevented only by a private intimation, sent by a female relation of one of the officers, a few miles distant, at whose house the General and his suite had invited themselves to breakfast. Here we saw an extensive university, which the State is erecting under Mr. Jefferson's auspices, and to which it is intended to invite the ablest Professors which Europe can supply.

We arrived at Monticello, three miles farther, about eleven o'clock, ascending the South West Mountain, on which the house is situated, by a winding carriage-road through the wood. I sent in my letter to Mr. Jefferson, who soon afterwards came out and gave me a polite reception, leading me through the hall, hung with mammoth bones and Indian curiosities, to a room, ornamented with fine paintings. A young lady was playing on a piano-forte, but retired when we entered. Our conversation turned principally on the Indians, and the fine timber of the United States. With respect to the former, he considers them quite on a level, as respects intellectual character, with the Whites, and attributes the rapid civilization of the Choctaws, compared with that of the Creeks, on whom, perhaps, greater efforts have been bestowed, to the advantages possessed by the former for the growth of cotton, which had gradually induced them to spin and weave. He observed, that notwithstanding the fine specimens which have been preserved of Indian eloquence, the Indians appear to have no poetic genius; and that he had never known an Indian discover a musical taste; that, on the contrary, the Africans almost universally possess fine voices and an excellent ear, and a passionate fondness for music. With this I have often been struck, as I passed through the Southern States, especially when I have seen them assembled at public worship, or packing cotton at New Orleans. Mr. Jefferson said that he never knew a person who had resided long among the Indians, return and settle among the Whites; and I understood him to say also, that he never knew a person who left the coast for the western country, or his descendants, return to the Atlantic States. After sitting about an hour, I rose to take leave, when Mr. J. pressed me to stay to dinner, to which I assented, on condition that he would not allow me to be any restraint upon him. He said he must leave me for an hour to ride, as his health had a few months since begun to fail, for the first time. I found no difficulty, however, in amusing myself in the museum and the grounds and garden. In the former, was the only upper jaw ever yet discovered, as I was told, of a large animal now extinct, and some maps traced by the Indians on leather. The view on every side of the house, except one, where a small arc of the horizon is intercepted by a hill, is very extensive and beautiful. The Blue ridge affords an interesting variety of romantic scenery in a broken curve, extending, I believe, above 100 miles; one peak at the distance, I understood, of more than 120 miles, being sometimes visible. The horizon, on the Atlantic side, is about 40 miles distant; and bounds a flat well-wooded country, which appeared tame, when contrasted with the sublimity of the mountains. These, and especially a hill of the shape and dimensions of the largest pyramid in Egypt, which gives Mr. Jefferson a meridian line of 40 miles, frequently exhibit the phenomenon of looming.

On Mr. Jefferson's return from his ride, we had some interesting conversation respecting the university, and a favourite plan of his of dividing every county into districts, in which there should be schools, and a humble sort of college at convenient distances, a superior college, with every possible advantage, being established in the State. After dinner, when the ladies had retired, and we were quite alone, he expressed his sentiments very freely on the present situation of England, and the character of many of her public men. He then stated the views and feelings which he had entertained with respect to her while President, as well as those which had been generally entertained by the American Government; the various causes which had contributed to the unhappy misunderstanding between the two countries, and the grounds for believing that many of them were of a nature which rendered their recurrence improbable. He then described, with a good deal of spirit and minuteness, the character of the different ministers we have sent to Washington, and concluded with an earnest hope, that as the two Governments at length understood each other perfectly, the people might gradually be soothed into better humour with one another. The particulars of this very interesting conversation, which lasted two hours, and of which I have preserved a memorandum, I will give you when we meet.[1]

Mr. Jefferson's appearance is rather prepossessing. He is tall and very thin, a little bent with age, with an intelligent and sprightly countenance. His manners are dignified, but courteous and gentlemanly; and he enters into conversation with great ease and animation.

After two hours tête-à-tête, I rose about six o'clock to take my leave. He invited me to stay all night; but I thought I had already encroached sufficiently on his time, and I was not sure that we should withdraw to the ladies, of whom I had just seen enough to feel persuaded that I should have passed a very agreeable evening with them. While sitting with this philosophical legislator and his polished family, in a handsome saloon, surrounded by instruments of science, valuable specimens of the fine arts, and literary treasures of every nation, and every age, I could not help contrasting my situation with some of those which I had occupied during the preceding month, when sleeping on a bear-skin, on the floor of an Indian hut, listening to the traditions of my Chickasaw or Choctaw host, or dandling on my knee a young Indian warrior, with his miniature belt and mocassins, his necklaces and feathers, and his little bow and arrow, doomed to provoke nothing but a smile. In the course of a few weeks, I had passed from deep forests, whose silence had never been broken by the woodman's axe, to a thickly settled country, where cattle were grazing in extensive meadows, and corn fields waving in the wind; where commerce was planting her towns, science founding her universities, and religion rearing her heaven-directed spires. In the same period, I had traced man through every successive stage of civilization, from the roaming savage, whose ideas scarcely extend beyond the narrow circle of his daily wants, to the statesman who has learnt to grasp the complicated interests of society, and the philosopher, to contemplate the system of the universe.

Note

1. It is with great regret that I feel myself constrained to omit what would, perhaps, have been more generally interesting than any thing these volumes contain. It is not, indeed, probable, that Mr. Jefferson would object to the publication of any thing which he saw fit to communicate in conversation with a stranger; but there is not time to obtain his permission, and without it, delicacy imposes a restraint, which I feel unwilling to break through [Hodgson's note].

From *Letters from North America, Written During a Tour in the United States and Canada,* 2 vols. (London: for Hurst, Robinson, 1824), 1: 313–319.

Memorandum of Mr. Jefferson's Conversations (1824)

DANIEL WEBSTER

Accompanied by George and Anna Ticknor, Daniel Webster (1782–1852) visited Monticello in December 1824. By this time, Webster had already established himself as one of the nation's leading orators and as a leader in the House of Representatives, where he took on such worthy opponents as Henry Clay. They spent five days at Monticello. On the evening after their departure, Webster dictated to Mrs. Ticknor a lengthy account of their conversations, which George Ticknor corroborated. Together, the three attempted to record what Jefferson had said as accurately as possible. The resulting memorandum is one of the most important records of Jefferson's conversation available. Rather than recording their conversation with Jefferson in dialogue form, however, they recorded it as a series of anecdotes, which, in itself, is significant. Jefferson often saved his personal anecdotes to tell family members. That Webster was able to coax several personal anecdotes from Jefferson attests to his rhetorical skill. Having established his own reputation as an orator, Webster was curious about Patrick Henry, the greatest orator of the Revolutionary era. Jefferson related his general impressions of Henry. Jefferson's comments are consistent with and elaborate on what he told William Wirt, Henry's biographer. Webster coaxed many other anecdotes from Jefferson about the American Revolution, his time in France, and his encounter with the comte de Buffon; Webster even managed to solicit Jefferson's opinion on Andrew Jackson. This visit to Monticello did much to change Webster's opinions of Jefferson. Peter Harvey, who compiled a volume of reminiscences of Daniel Webster, observed:

> Mr. Webster was greatly interested in this visit to Jefferson, and he said that very much of the early prejudice which he had imbibed with his political opinions in youth, when he considered Jefferson a great heretic, was dispelled when he came into personal contact with the aged statesman, and saw him in his home. Jefferson's great simplicity impressed him.

> Mr. Webster believed him to be a sincere man, very true to his convictions; and was convinced that much of the abuse heaped upon him by the opposite party, which had accused him of being a demagogue and an anarchist, was unjust. Mr. Webster said to me once, in speaking of Jefferson, that he had more deeply impressed his opinions and theories, as well as his practical ideas of government, upon the legislation and destinies of the country, than any man that had lived. (*Reminiscences and Anecdotes, 212*)

When the following memorandum was first published as part of *The Private Correspondence of Daniel Webster,* it was recognized as one of the best parts of the book. Several reviewers reprinted Webster's character sketch of Jefferson that begins the memorandum.

MR. JEFFERSON IS NOW between eighty-one and eighty-two, above six feet high, of an ample, long frame, rather thin and spare. His head, which is not peculiar in its shape, is set rather forward on his shoulders; and his neck being long, there is, when he is walking or conversing, an habitual protrusion of it. It is still well covered with hair, which having been once red, and now turning gray, is of an indistinct sandy color.

His eyes are small, very light, and now neither brilliant nor striking. His chin is rather long, but not pointed. His nose small, regular in its outline, and the nostrils a little elevated. His mouth is well formed and still filled with teeth; it is strongly compressed, bearing an expression of contentment and benevolence. His complexion, formerly light and freckled, now bears the marks of age and cutaneous affection. His limbs are uncommonly long; his hands and feet very large, and his wrists of an extraordinary size. His walk is not precise and military, but easy and swinging. He stoops a little, not so much from age as from natural formation. When sitting, he appears short, partly from a rather lounging habit of sitting, and partly from the disproportionate length of his limbs.

His dress, when in the house, is a gray surtout coat, kerseymere stuff waistcoat, with an under one faced with some material of a dingy red. His pantaloons are very long and loose, and of the same color as his coat. His stockings are woollen either white or gray; and his shoes of the kind that bear his name. His whole dress is very much neglected, but not slovenly. He wears a common round hat. His dress, when on horseback, is a gray straight-bodied coat and a spencer of the same material, both fastened with large pearl buttons. When we first saw him, he was riding; and, in addition to the above articles of apparel, wore round his throat a knit white woollen tippet, in the place of a cravat, and black velvet gaiters under his pantaloons. His general appearance indicates an extraordinary degree of health, vivacity, and spirit. His sight is still good, for he needs glasses only in the evening. His hearing is generally good, but a number of voices in animated conversation confuses it.

Mr. Jefferson rises in the morning as soon as he can see the hands of his clock, which is directly opposite his bed, and examines his thermometer immediately, as he keeps a regular meteorological diary. He employs himself chiefly in writing till breakfast, which is at nine. From that time, till dinner, he is in his library, excepting that in fair weather he rides on horseback from seven to fourteen miles. Dines at four, returns to the drawing-room at six, when coffee is brought in, and passes the evening till nine in conversation. His habit of retiring at that hour is so strong, that it has become essential to his health and comfort. His diet is simple, but he seems restrained only by his taste. His breakfast is tea and coffee, bread always fresh from the oven, of which he does not seem afraid, with sometimes a slight accompaniment of cold meat. He enjoys his dinner well, taking with his meat a large proportion of vegetables. He has a strong preference for the wines of the continent, of which he has many sorts of excellent quality, having been more than commonly successful in his mode of importing and preserving them. Among others, we found the following, which are very rare in this country, and apparently not at all injured by transportation: L'Ednau, Muscat, Samian, and Blanchette de Limoux. Dinner is served in half Virginian, half French style, in good taste and abundance. No wine is put on the table till the cloth is removed.

In conversation, Mr. Jefferson is easy and natural, and apparently not ambitious; it is not loud, as challenging general attention, but usually addressed to the person next him. The topics, when not selected to suit the character and feelings of his auditor, are those subjects with which his mind seems particularly occupied; and these, at present, may be said to be science and letters, and especially the University of Virginia, which is coming into existence almost entirely from his exertions, and will rise, it is to be hoped, to usefulness and credit under his continued care. When we were with him, his favorite subjects were Greek and Anglo-Saxon, historical recollections of the times and events of the Revolution, and of his residence in France from 1783–4 to 1789.

(In the course of the evening when the preceding was written, from Mr. Webster's dictation, the following anecdotes from Mr. Jefferson's conversation were recalled and written down: —)

Patrick Henry was originally a bar-keeper. He was married very young, and going into some business, on his own account, was a bankrupt before the year was out. When I was about the age of fifteen, I left the school here, to go to the college at Williamsburgh. I stopped a few days at a friend's in the county of Louisa. There I first saw and became acquainted with Patrick Henry. Having spent the Christmas holidays there, I proceeded to Williamsburgh. Some question arose about my admission, as my preparatory studies had not been pursued at the school connected with that institution. This delayed my admission about a fortnight, at which time Henry appeared in Williamsburgh, and applied for a license to practise law, having commenced the study of it at or subsequently to the time of my meeting him in Louisa. There were four examiners, [George] Wythe, [Edmund] Pendleton, Peyton Randolph, and John Randolph; Wythe and Pendleton at once rejected his application. The two Randolphs, by his importunity, were prevailed upon to sign the license; and having obtained their signatures, he applied again to Pendleton, and after much entreaty and many promises of future study, succeeded in obtaining his. He then turned out for a practising lawyer. The first case which brought him into notice, was a contested election, in which he appeared as counsel before a committee of the House of Burgesses. His second was the Parsons cause, already well known. These and similar efforts soon obtained for him so much reputation, that he was elected a member of the legislature. He was as well suited to the times as any man ever was, and it is not now easy to say what we should have done without Patrick Henry. He was far before all in maintaining the spirit of the Revolution. His influence was most extensive with the members from the upper counties, and his boldness and their votes overawed and controlled the more cool or the more timid aristocratic gentlemen of the lower part of the State. His eloquence was peculiar, if indeed it should be called eloquence; for it was impressive and sublime, beyond what can be imagined. Although it was difficult when he had spoken to tell what he had said, yet, while he was speaking, it always seemed directly to the point. When he had spoken in opposition to my opinion, had produced a great effect, and I myself been highly delighted and moved, I have asked myself when he ceased: "What the d—l has he said?" I could never answer the inquiry. His person was of full size, and his manner and voice free and manly. His utterance neither very fast nor very slow. His speeches generally short, from a quarter to a half an hour. His pronunciation was vulgar and vicious, but it was forgotten while he was speaking.

He was a man of very little knowledge of any sort; he read nothing, and had no books. Returning one November from Albemarle court, he borrowed of me Hume's *Essays*, in two volumes, saying he should have leisure in the winter for reading. In the spring he returned them, and declared he had not been able to go further than twenty or thirty pages in the first volume. He wrote almost nothing—he could not write. The resolutions of '75, which have been ascribed to him, have by many been supposed to have been written by Mr. [George] Johnson, who acted as his second on that occasion; but if they were written by Henry himself, they are not such as to prove any power of composition. Neither in politics nor in his profession was he a man of business; he was a man for debate only. His biographer says that he read Plutarch every year. I doubt whether he ever read a volume of it in his life. His temper was excellent, and he generally observed decorum in debate. On one or two occasions I have seen him angry, and his anger was terrible; those who witnessed it, were not disposed to rouse it again. In his opinions he was yielding and practicable and not disposed to differ from his friends. In private conversation, he was agreeable and facetious, and, while in genteel society, appeared to understand all the decencies and proprieties of it; but, in his heart, he preferred low society, and sought it as often as possible. He would hunt in the pine woods of Fluvannah, with overseers, and people of that description, living in a camp for a fortnight at a time without a change of raiment. I have often been astonished at his command of proper language; how he attained the knowledge of it, I never could find out, as he read so little and conversed little with educated men. After all, it must be allowed that he was our leader in the measures of the Revolution, in Virginia. In that respect more was due to him than any other person. If we had not had him we should probably have got on pretty well, as you did, by a number of men of nearly equal talents, but he left us all far behind. His biographer sent the sheets of his work to me as they were printed, and at the end asked for my opinion. I told him it would be a question hereafter, whether his work should be placed on the shelf of history or of panegyric. It is a poor book written in bad taste, and gives so imperfect an idea of Patrick Henry, that it seems intended to show off the writer more than the subject of the work.

Throughout the whole Revolution, Virginia and the four New England States acted together; indeed, they made the Revolution. Their five votes were always to be counted on; but they had to pick up the remaining two for a majority, when and where they could.

About the time of the Boston Port Bill, the patriotic feeling in Virginia had become languid and worn out, from some cause or other. It was thought by some of us to be absolutely necessary to excite the people; but we hardly knew the right means. At length it occurred to us to make grave faces and propose a fast. Some of us, who were the younger members of the assembly, resolved upon the measure. We thought Oliver Cromwell would be a good guide in such a case. So we looked into Rushworth [John Rushworth's *Historical Collections*] and drew up our resolutions after the most pious and praiseworthy examples. It would hardly have been in character for us to present them ourselves. We applied therefore to Mr. [Robert Carter] Nicholas, a grave and religious man; he proposed them in a set and solemn speech; some of us gravely seconded him, and the resolutions were passed unanimously. If any debate had occurred, or if they had been postponed for consideration, there was no chance that they would have been passed. The next morning Lord Botetourt, the governor, summoned the assembly to his presence, and said to them: "I have heard of your proceedings of yesterday, and augur ill of their effects. His Majesty's interest requires that you be dissolved, and you are dissolved." Another election taking place soon afterwards, such was the spirit of the times, that every member of the assembly, without an individual exception, was re-elected.

Our fast produced very considerable effect. We all agreed to go home and see that preachers were provided in our counties, and notice given to our people. I came home to my own county, provided a preacher, and notified the people, who came together in great multitudes, wondering what it meant.

Lord Botetourt was an honorable man. His government had authorized him to make certain assurances to the people here, which he made accordingly. He wrote to the minister that he had made these assurances, and that, unless he should be enabled to fulfil them, he must retire from his situation. This letter he sent unsealed to Peyton Randolph for his inspection. Lord Botetourt's great respectability, his character for integrity, and his general popularity, would have enabled him to embarrass the measures of the patriots exceedingly. His death was, therefore, a fortunate event for the cause of the Revolution. He was the first governor in chief that had ever come over to Virginia. Before his time, we had received only deputies, the governor residing in England, with a salary of five thousand pounds, and paying his deputy one thousand pounds.

When Congress met, Patrick Henry and Richard Henry Lee opened the subject with great ability and eloquence. So much so, that [William] Paca and [Jeremiah Townley] Chase, delegates from Maryland, said to each other as they returned from the House: "We shall not be wanted here; those gentlemen from Virginia will be able to do every thing without us." But neither Henry nor Lee were men of business, and having made strong and eloquent general speeches, they had done all they could.

It was thought advisable that two papers should be drawn up, one, an address to the people of England, and the other, an address, I think, to the king. Committees were raised for these purposes, and Henry was at the head of the first, and Lee of the second.

When the address to the people of England was reported, Congress heard it with utter amazement. It was miserably written and good for nothing. At length Governor [William] Livingston of New Jersey, ventured to break silence. After complimenting the author, he said he thought some other ideas might be usefully added to his draft of the address. Some such paper had been for a considerable time contemplated, and he believed a friend of his had tried his hand in the composition of one. He thought if the subject were again committed, some improvement in the present draft might be made. It was accordingly recommitted, and the address which had been alluded to by Governor Livingston, and which was written by John Jay, was reported by the committee, and adopted as it now appears.

It is, in my opinion, one of the very best state papers which the Revolution produced.

Richard Henry Lee moved the Declaration of Independence, in pursuance of the resolutions of the assembly of Virginia, and only because he was the oldest member of the Virginia delegation.

The Declaration of Independence was written in a house on the north side of Chestnut street, Philadelphia, between third and fourth, not a corner house. Heiskell's tavern, which has been pointed out as the house, is not the true one.

For depth of purpose, zeal, and sagacity, no man in Congress exceeded, if any equalled Sam. Adams; and none did more than he to originate and sustain revolutionary measures in Congress. But he could not speak; he had a hesitating, grunting manner.

John Adams was our Colossus on the floor. He was not graceful, nor elegant, nor remarkably fluent; but he came out, occasionally, with a power of thought and expression that moved us from our seats.

I feel much alarmed at the prospect of seeing General Jackson President. He is one of the most unfit men I know of for such a place. He has had very little respect for laws or constitutions, and is, in fact, an able military chief. His passions are terrible. When I was President of the Senate he was a Senator; and he could never speak on account of the rashness of his feelings. I have seen him attempt it repeatedly, and as often choke with rage. His passions are no doubt cooler now; he has been much tried since I knew him, but he is a dangerous man.

When I was in France, the Marquis de Chastellux carried me over to Buffon's residence in the country, and introduced me to him.

It was Buffon's practice to remain in his study till dinner time, and receive no visitors under any pretence; but his house was open and his grounds, and a servant showed them very civilly, and invited all strangers and friends to remain to dine. We saw Buffon in the garden, but carefully avoided him; but we dined with him, and he proved himself then, as he always did, a man of extraordinary powers in conversation. He did not declaim; he was singularly agreeable.

I was introduced to him as Mr. Jefferson, who, in some notes on Virginia, had combated some of his opinions. Instead of entering into an argument, he took down his last work, presented it to me, and said, "When Mr. Jefferson shall have read this, he will be perfectly satisfied that I am right."

Being about to embark from Philadelphia for France, I observed an uncommonly large panther skin at the door of a hatter's shop. I bought it for half a Jo (sixteen dollars) on the spot, determining to carry it to France to convince Monsieur Buffon of his mistake in relation to this animal; which he had confounded with the cougar. He acknowledged his mistake, and said he would correct it in his next volume.

I attempted also to convince him of his error in relation to the common deer, and the moose of America; he having confounded our deer with the red deer of Europe, and our moose with the reindeer. I told him that our deer had horns two feet long; he replied with warmth, that if I could produce a single specimen, with horns one foot long, he would give up the question. Upon this I wrote to Virginia for the horns of one of our deer, and obtained a very good specimen, four feet long. I told him also that the reindeer could walk under the belly of our moose; but he entirely scouted the idea. Whereupon I wrote to General [John] Sullivan of New Hampshire. I desired him to send me the bones, skin, and antlers of our moose, supposing they could easily be procured by him. Six months afterwards my agent in England advised me that General Sullivan had drawn on him for forty guineas. I had forgotten my request, and wondered why such a draft had been made, but I paid it at once. A little later came a letter from General Sullivan, setting forth the manner in which he had complied with my request. He had been obliged to raise a company of nearly twenty men, had made an excursion towards the White Hills, camping out many nights, and had at last after many difficulties caught my moose, boiled his bones in the desert, stuffed his skin and remitted him to me. This accounted for my debt and convinced Mr. Buffon. He promised in his next volume to set these things right also, but he died directly afterwards.

Madame Houdetot's society was one of the most agreeable in Paris when I was there. She inherited the materials of which it was composed from Madame de Terrier and Madame Geoffrin. St. Lambert was always there, and it was generally believed that every evening on his return home, he wrote down the substance of the conversations he had held there with D'Alembert, Diderot, and the other distinguished persons, who frequented her house. From these conversations he made his books.

I knew the Baron de Grignon very well; he was quite ugly, and one of his legs was shorter than the other; but he was the most agreeable person in French society, and his opinion was always considered decisive in matters relating to the theatre and painting. His persiflage was the keenest and most provoking I ever knew.

Madame Necker was a very sincere and excellent woman, but she was not very pleasant in conversation, for she was subject to what in Virginia we call the "Budge," that is, she was very nervous and fidgety. She could rarely remain long in the same place, or converse long on the same subject. I have known her to get up from table five or six times in the course of the dinner, and walk up and down her saloon to compose herself.

Marmontel was a very amusing man. He dined with me every Thursday for a long time, and I think told some of the most agreeable stories I ever heard in my life. After his death, I found almost all of them in his memoirs, and I dare say he told them so well because he had written them before in his book.

I wish Mr. [John] Pickering would make a radical lexicon. It would do more than anything else in the present state of the matter, to promote the study of Greek among us. [John] Jones's Greek Lexicon is very poor. I have been much disappointed in it. The best I have ever used is the Greek and French one by [Joseph] Planche.

From *The Private Correspondence of Daniel Webster,* ed. Fletcher Webster, 2 vols. (Boston: Little, Brown, 1857), 1: 364–373.

[From the University of Virginia to Monticello] (1828)

Bernhard, Duke of Saxe-Weimar-Eisenach

Born Prince Carl Bernhard of Saxe-Weimar-Eisenach, Duke Bernhard (1792–1862) was the son of Duke Carl August of Saxe-Weimar-Eisenach. An influential figure in German politics, Carl August sought democratic rule, freedom of the press, and the unification of Germany. He also gave his son a liberal education, partly supplied by several prominent men of letters: Goethe, Herder, Schiller. Military studies formed a significant part of his education. Soon travel and the military became Duke Bernhard's twin passions. He joined the army when he was fourteen and subsequently fought for and against Napoleon. After the Battle of Wagram in 1809, Napoleon decorated him. Once Napoleon returned to France after his exile, Bernhard served as a brigade commander in the Allied Army at the battles of Quatre Bras and Waterloo. Bernhard traveled to North America in 1825 and 1826, a journey that brought him to the University of Virginia and Monticello. He critiqued the irregular architecture of the University of Virginia. He did not realize that Jefferson's mixture of styles was deliberate: the architecture was designed as a pedagogical tool to teach different kinds of classical architecture. From the university, Bernhard made his way to Monticello. He arrived just as dinner was being served.

Jefferson rose from the table and came to greet him and his party. The duke was a big, strapping fellow. William Wirt, who had dined with him in Baltimore, described him in a 30 October 1825 letter to his wife, saying Duke Bernhard has "no redundant fat, but [is] brawny, muscular, and of herculean strength. He is about thirty-five years old, and looks like a Russian, or one of those gigantic Cossacks. I dare say he make a magnificent figure in uniform. He speaks English tolerably well; yet he has that apparent dullness of apprehension which always accompanies a defective knowledge of a language" (quoted in Kennedy, *Memoirs of the Life of William Wirt,* 2: 204). Describing the conversation at Monticello, Bernhard shows Jefferson's passion for discussing his time in France but also reveals his ability to shape the conversation to suit his audience. Duke Bernhard wrote up the story of his American travels, which appeared in German in 1828 but was translated into English and published in Philadelphia before the year's end. For the remainder of his life, he indulged his passion for military service and world travel, serving in the military during the Belgian Revolution and touring Europe and Russia extensively. He ultimately took a position as commander-in-chief of the Dutch East Indies Army.

HAVING CROSSED THE BLUE RIDGE, we arrived at a good-looking country house, and a mill called Brown's Farm, situated at the base of the mountains, and took our dinner there. This house is surrounded by fields belonging to it, and from its piazza there is a very fine view of the mountains. From this place we had yet twenty miles to Charlotteville. The road became less hilly, at least we had no more mountains to cross; however, the road continued very rough, and we were rudely jolted. About eight o'clock in the evening we reached Charlotteville, in which the houses appeared to be scattered. In its vicinity is a new establishment for education, called University of Virginia. The next morning we went to see the University, which is one mile distant from the town.

This establishment has been open since March, 1824, and it is said to have already one hundred and thirty students; but a spirit of insubordination has caused many of the pupils to be sent away. The buildings are all new, and yet some of them seem to threaten to fall in, which may be the case with several others also, being chiefly built of wood. The interior of the library was not yet finished, but according to its plan it will be a beautiful one. The dome is made after the model of the Pantheon in Rome, reduced one half. This place is intended for public meetings of the academy: but it is said that an echo is heard in case of loud speaking, which renders the voice of the speaker unintelligible.

Under the rotunda are three elliptical halls, the designation of which is not yet entirely determined. The set of columns on the outside of this building, I was told is to be a very fine one; the capitals were made in Italy.

As for the rest, the ten buildings on the right and left are not at all regularly built, but each of them in a different manner, so that there is no harmony in the whole, which prevents it from having a beautiful and majestic appearance.

The garden walls of the lateral building are also in crooked lines, which gives them a singular but handsome appearance. The buildings have been executed according to Mr. Jefferson's plan, and are his hobby; he is rector of the University, in the construction of which the state of Virginia is said to have laid out considerable sums of money.

We addressed a gentleman whom we met by chance, in order to get some information, and we had every reason to be satisfied with his politeness. It was Dr. Dunglison, professor of medicine. He is an Englishman, and came last year with three other professors from Europe. He showed us the library, which was still inconsiderable, and has been provisionally arranged in a lecture room; it contained some German belles lettres works, among others a series of Kotzebue's calendar of dramatical works. It was said a great quantity of books was coming from Europe.

The university is situated on a hill in a very healthy situation, and there is a very fine view of the Blue Ridge. President Jefferson invited us to a family dinner; but as in Charlotteville there is but a single hackney-coach, and this being absent, we were obliged to go the three miles to Monticello on foot.

We went by a pathway, through well cultivated and enclosed fields, crossed a creek named Rivanna, passing on a trunk of a tree cut in a rough shape, and without rails; then ascended a steep hill overgrown with wood, and came on its top to Mr. Jefferson's house, which is in an open space, walled round with bricks, forming an oblong, whose shorter sides are rounded; on each of the longer sides are portals of four columns.

The unsuccessful waiting for a carriage, and our long walk, caused such a delay, that we found the company at table when we entered; but Mr. Jefferson came very kindly to meet us, forced us to take our seats, and ordered dinner to be served up anew. He was an old man of eighty-six years of age, of tall stature, plain appearance, and long white hair.

In conversation he was very lively, and his spirits, as also his hearing and sight, seemed not to have decreased at all with his advancing age. I found in him a man who retained his faculties remarkably well in his old age, and one would have taken him for a man of sixty. He asked me what I had seen in Virginia. I eulogized all the places, that I was certain would meet with his approbation, and he seemed very much pleased. The company at the table, consisted of the family of his daughter, Mrs. Randolph, and of that of the professor of mathematics at the university, an Englishman, and of his wife [Thomas Hewitt and Sarah Troward Key]. I turned the conversation to the subject of the university, and observed, that this was the favourite topic with Mr. Jefferson; he entertained very sanguine hopes as to the flourishing state of the university in future, and believed that it, and the Harvard University near Boston, would in a very short time be the only institutions, where the youth of the United States would receive a truly classical and solid education. After dinner we intended to take our leave, in order to return to Charlotteville; but Mr. Jefferson would not consent to it. He pressed us to remain for the night at his house. The evening was spent by the fire; a great deal was said about travels, and objects of natural history; the fine arts were also introduced, of which Mr. Jefferson was a great admirer. He spoke also of his travels in France, and the country on the Rhine, where he was very much pleased. His description of Virginia is the best proof what an admirer he is of beauties of nature. He told us that it was only eight months since he could not ride on horseback; otherwise, he rode every day to visit the surrounding country; he entertained, however, hopes of being able to re-commence the next spring his favourite exercise. Between nine and ten o'clock in the evening, the company broke up, and a handsome room was assigned to me.

The next morning I took a walk round the house, and admired the beautiful panorama, which this spot presents. On the left, I saw the Blue Ridge, and between them and Monticello are smaller hills. Charlotteville and the University lay at my feet; before me, the valley of the Rivanna river, which farther on, makes its junction with the James river, and on my right was the flat part of Virginia, the extent of which is lost in distance; behind me was a towering hill, which limited the sight. The interior of the house was plain, and the furniture somewhat of an old fashion. In the entrance was a marble stove with Mr. Jefferson's bust, by Ceracchi. In the rooms hung several copies of the celebrated pictures of the Italian school, views of Monticello, Mount-Vernon, the principal buildings in Washington and Harper's Ferry; there were also an oil painting, and an engraving of the Natural Bridge, views of Niagara by Vanderlin [John Vanderlyn], a sketch of the large picture by Trumbull, representing the surrender at Yorktown, and a pen drawing of Hector's departure, by Benjamin West, presented by him to General [Thaddeus] Kosciuszko, finally, several portraits of Mr. Jefferson, among which the best was that in profile by [Gilbert] Stuart. In the saloon there were two busts, one of Napoleon as first consul, and another of the Emperor Alexander. Mr. Jefferson admired Napoleon's military talents, but did not love him. After breakfast, which we took with the family, we bid the respectable old man farewell, and set out upon our return on foot to Charlotteville.

Mr. Jefferson tendered us the use of his carriage, but I declined, as I preferred walking in a fine and cool morning. In the afternoon we left Charlotteville, in a tolerably good stage, in order to go to Richmond, the chief town of Virginia, distant eighty miles. A student was our travelling companion, and so we had plenty of room. But the stage went only ten miles to a small tavern situated in a wood, and kept by Mrs. Boyd. We passed by not far from Monticello, crossed the Rivanna at a rather deep ford, and remained for some miles on its left bank. The banks were high and rocky in some places. The road was, for the greatest part, through a wood, hilly and rough; in some places it was what they call causeway.

From *Travels through North America, During the Years 1825 and 1826,* 2 vols. (Philadelphia: Carey, Lea and Carey, 1828), 1: 196–199.

Recollections of President Jefferson (1828)

John Bernard

John Bernard (1756–1828) established himself as a leading comedian on the British stage during the last third of the eighteenth century. In 1797, Thomas Wignal, proprietor of the Chestnut Street Theater in Philadelphia, invited him to America. Bernard accepted the lucrative offer, reached Philadelphia later that year, and quickly emerged as one of the finest comedians on the American stage. He remained in the United States for over two decades before returning to England. Though he had an excellent contemporary reputation as a comedic actor, Bernard's most lasting contribution is *Retrospections of America,* a reminiscence presenting a vivid picture of American society and culture of the early nineteenth century. Few commentators are more observant or perceptive; few provide as insightful a view of Jefferson.

Bernard's time in Philadelphia coincided with Jefferson's time as vice president, and the two became friends. Bernard established a Beefsteak Club in Philadelphia, which Jefferson sometimes visited. Bernard occasionally dined at the White House during the Jefferson administration, and *Retrospections of America* testifies to the conviviality of President Jefferson's dinner gatherings. Besides contributing his own witticisms to the dinner conversation, Bernard enjoyed the president's. His memoirs provide a general overview of Jefferson's manner of speaking and record many snippets of conversation that occurred at the president's table: Bernard's memoirs are the source for several quips and anecdotes unrecorded elsewhere. In Bernard's presence, Jefferson retold some of his favorite stories.

THROUGH THE KINDNESS of General Washington I was introduced to Mr. Jefferson, who proved one of my sincerest, though not most fortunate, friends. The coupling of his acquaintance with a speculation involving considerable loss and chagrin cannot, however, prevent my recurring to the period with a degree of pleasure which I trust may prove communicable to the reader. In all the chief requisites of the social character Mr. Jefferson appeared to me to possess few equals. His heart was warmed with a love for the whole human race; a *bonhomie* which fixed your attention the instant he spoke. His information was equally polite and profound, and his conversational powers capable of discussing moral questions of deepest seriousness, or the lightest themes of humor and fancy. Nothing could be more simple than his reasonings, nothing more picturesque and pointed than his descriptions. On all abstract subjects he was plainness itself—a veritable Quaker; but when conveying his views of human nature through their most attractive medium—anecdote—he displayed the grace and brilliance of a courtier. His talents may suggest some idea of his manners. Though, like taste and beauty, manners have no general standard, so that refinement in France is frivolity in Holland, and frankness in Holland is boorishness in France, the citizen of the world perceives that an excess of artificiality is as opposed to human happiness as utter barbarity. But if manners be brought to the one test of general consideration for others, my good friend, the President, would certainly not have been judged deficient by any one. To a just balance of qualities his residence in France had no doubt contributed. He had witnessed an extraordinary contrast—the extremes of society under a polished despotism and in a young republic—and tracing their respective effects on the national welfare, the rooting of his convictions had led to the branching out of his sympathies. During the many pleasant evenings I spent in his society at Washington and Philadelphia, I chiefly attempted to draw out his observations upon the period he had passed in France, where his official situation placed him in juxtaposition with the leading characters of the court, as well as most of the agents of the Revolution. Amid this group he was equally intimate with [Jacques] Neckar and [Honoré Gabriel Riqueti, comte de] Mirabeau, the Duc de Lauzun, and the Abbé Sieyès. Six years a spectator of the gathering of that tornado which began in tears and ended in blood, no man could have written a more animated account of the organization of the Tree of Liberty. Adams, in his boyhood (1755), detected its first shoots in America in the all-engrossing interest of political conversations. Jefferson was destined to witness the effect of its transplantation to Gallic soil. The two great accessories of the French Revolution were the encyclopedists and the patriots, the latter of whom returned from America to make known to their countrymen the enviable condition of a people whose rights were respected. As their verbal accounts must have taken a wider range than literary teachings, it is not too much to assume that these patriots held the match to the explosion, and that Louis, in extending assistance to the Americans, provided for his own dethronement. As Franklin remarked when the outbreak was announced to him, "Ah, they served their apprenticeship in America, and now they mean to set up for themselves." With truer instinct Frederick the Great, when solicited to afford assistance to the Americans, replied, "No, a king I was born, and a king I will remain; it is too much of you to require a man to ruin his own trade."

Mr. Jefferson supported the above supposition by pointing out a chain of sequences among the most striking in modern history. "America," said he, "the child of the Old World, appears destined to become its teacher. Like the heart in the human system, it has received and sent back purified the diseased opinions of England and France. Those countries have fought for its possession in the true spirit of despotism, and have been foiled because the lamb grew up, during the contest, into a lion. We see, in the first instance, English exiles in the cause of freedom settling America and impregnating its moral atmosphere. Then France rearing her standard on the walls of Quebec, and gradually extending her possessions along the margin of the Lakes to the Ohio, and thence onward to the mouth of the Mississippi, with the giant design of spanning the continent from the Arctic Ocean to the Gulf of Mexico; England, rising up at the cry of the colonies, fought through that arduous war which sealed the submission of France with the blood of [James] Wolfe; but after that, inflated with her triumph, we see her next turning round and taxing these very colonists to discharge the burden belonging to other possessions; the colonies resisting; and France, in the hope of recovering Canada, sending them assistance; the independence following, and the Frenchmen returning home to achieve the liberation of their own country. To conclude, England, placed between the fires of two revolutions, and not less admonished by the lurid excesses of the one than invited by the calm and benign glow of the other, to provide for the general happiness of her people, is working out English freedom on the pattern of American independence."

Mr. Jefferson said he had perceived at an early period that Neckar and Mirabeau were two of the most important persons in France. Of both it was impossible to calculate whether they would save the country from a convulsion or throw it into one. They frequently met, and on the most sociable terms, but their manners in company presented a curious contrast. The financier always began the evening with great spirit, and talked animatedly upon all subjects till about nine o'clock, when a shadow stole over his countenance and he sank into silence, absorbed in public considerations only temporarily put aside. The count always sat down under a cloud and brooded, until the wine dissipated his vapors and warmed him into life. For an hour or two he was then a most agreeable companion. He poured out information, poetry, and anecdote, and flashed his sarcasm right and left with the edge and polish of a true Damascene. But he drank furiously, and, as the wine heated him, his ruling interest regained its sway, and his hilarity rose into a species of madness. His eye dilated, his voice choked, he shook his black hair wildly about his face, burst into political prophecies, and struck the table until the glasses rang by way of emphasis, recalling the image of the Sibyl during the throes of inspiration. In a short time he had reached the pinnacle of his social glory—his antagonists had deserted the table, or he was lying under it.

The popularity of this glittering monster to whom property meant license, and power pay, whose life was passed in a state of moral drunkenness, proves that his talents must have been very extraordinary, or that the people were indeed destitute and desperate. In America, where virtue was its own reward, there had been no Mirabeaus in principle, save [Benedict] Arnold. The test of patriotism was there too primitive. And yet the count had the complacency to hint to Mr. Jefferson that if France was destined to become another America, the world should see that there was another Washington, to which the latter replied, with polite ambiguity, "Pardon me, count, but I consider such is the striking originality of your character, you would disdain to imitate any man."

Nor was it with the populace only that Mirabeau had influence; he was also the idol of the women. Why? Although the ugliest man in Europe, his popularity solves the mystery. Conquest with one sex led necessarily to submission from the other. At a convivial party he once remarked to his companions, "They say abroad 'Mirabeau must have a great mind, for the women love him though he is as ugly as the devil.'" As no one answered, he continued, taking a pinch of snuff, "It's very true. I and the devil have always been their favorites."

Mr. Jefferson did not wonder at the shadow on Baron Neckar's countenance, destined as he was to resist singlehanded the erection of the court barricades, and to see the king forwarding by every indirect means the object of his enemies. A reply attributed to the Comte d'Artois well exhibits that spirit which at length unsealed the fountains of the deluge. On the baron observing to him the growing necessity of relieving in some measure the burdens of the people. "My good friend," exclaimed he, "the people are not the only sufferers; we at court have a burden much more difficult to get rid of." "What may that be?" "Our time," was the reply.

My friend quite concurred in the general impression as to the sympathetic weakness of the king and queen, who, in quiet times, would have slid through the world in the fashionable absence of all sense or principle, without exciting praise or blame. The queen, a truly affable creature, was pleased to pay him particular attention, but, as he conceived, more as a curiosity than as a friend. She was always wondering how it was possible the people of America could be happy without a court, and at length said to him, "Surely your great deliverer intends to create nobility?" To which he replied, "Please your majesty, the influence of your own is so powerful that it is the general impression we can do without them."

Mr. Jefferson has put so much evidence upon record, both of his varied talents and his social excellence, that I feel loath to intrude too many recollections; and shall avail myself, therefore, of but a few instances which came within the knowledge of myself and friends.

While he was in Paris a young man waited upon him as a member of a family he knew in Virginia, and by means of a plausible story obtained from him a supply of money. On his return home he mentioned the circumstance to his friends, and discovered it was a gross imposture. But the news did not cost him his composure. "This is the way," said his friend, "in which generosity gets soured; but I wonder, Mr. J., that you gave the money so easily without more inquiry." "Now I think of it, I wonder myself," replied the latter, "but that it is so much pleasanter to *give* than to *refuse.*"

When once at a party where the private delinquencies of a well-known individual formed the subject of conversation, every one present opened in full cry upon the unfortunate buck, except Mr. Jefferson, whose silence was at length interpreted as a disbelief of the charges. A friend asked him the question, "Surely you must be as well aware as ourselves that these are the facts?" "Undoubtedly," he replied, "only I can't see how my calling the man a rascal will help to reclaim him."

He was strikingly happy in illustrations which brought the fullest amount of argument into the smallest compass. When a once-applauding public expatriated Dr. [Joseph] Priestley in his old age, Mr. J. remarked,

"His antagonists think they have quenched his opinions by sending him to America, just as the pope imagined when he shut up Galileo in prison that he had compelled the world to stand still."

His regard for both science and literature was founded on this just view of their respective effects. "I consider," said he to me, "scientific knowledge to be that food which alone can enable the mental functions to acquire vigor and activity; but elegant literature as the wine that should invariably follow, because without it the mind would never rise to the full measure of its enjoyment, the power of sympathizing with itself, after sympathizing with Nature."

In poetry his taste was thoroughly orthodox; Shakespeare and Pope, he said, gave him the perfection of imagination and judgment, both displaying more knowledge of the human heart—the true province of poetry—than he could elsewhere find. His prose favorites were Swift and Bolingbroke. Upon the utility of literature he made another remark that pleased me; "I was bred," said he, "to the law; that gave me a view of the dark side of humanity. Then I read poetry to qualify it with a gaze upon its bright side; and between the two extremes I have contrived through life to draw the due medium. And so," he continued, "substituting history and biography for law, I would have every man form his own estimate of human nature, because it seems to me that precisely the same directing forces should subsist in the social as in the solar system; there should be the same attractive or concentrating power in our hearts to draw us together qualifying the repelling impulse which we gain from our experience and reading."

With specimens of his humor I could fill pages. Hearing from the profound Dr. Rush that he, in company with a well-known wit of Philadelphia, had nearly been lost while proceeding in a packet from New York to Baltimore, Mr. J. replied, "Well, doctor, such a fate would have suited your genius precisely. You, you know, are always for going to the bottom of things; though it would have been inappropriate for our friend H—, who prefers skimming the surface."

Of a piece with this was a remark upon a captain of Virginia militia, who had once been a waiter at a tavern, and who was so heavy a sleeper that, on training days, the company were compelled to discharge a volley under his window before they could wake him. "Ah," said Jefferson, "it would be a much better plan if you were to ring a handbell under his window; then, I'll be bound, he'd at once pop out his head and cry 'Coming! coming.'"

He was deservedly a favorite with the ladies, the elegance of his compliments affording the best proof of his refinement. They had the veritable odor of Versailles. A lady of his acquaintance once congratulated herself upon never feeling cold in the depth of winter. "Go where I will," said she, "I can always fancy it's summer." "And whenever you come under my roof, madam," he replied, "I partake your impression!" On another occasion, a lady at an evening party called his attention to some flowers in her bosom, which were exotics but recently imported. Jefferson, admiring them greatly, inquired their name. She replied by giving their Linnaean designation. "Dear me!" said he, "I thought they were a new species of primrose." "Primrose, Mr. Jefferson?" "Yes, madam, from the snow that's so near them."

Perhaps I cannot conclude these recollections more pleasantly than by relating an anecdote of himself, which he told with great humor as having occurred shortly after his election to the presidency. He was riding one day in the neighborhood of Washington, in his usual plain attire — a black suit verging on brown — when, from a cross-road, a Connecticut farmer trotted up to him, and immediately displayed his provincial spirit of barter by surveying the president's superior steed, and asking him to "swap." Jefferson, however, asked too much money in exchange, so, after a fruitless attempt to draw him into a commercial transaction in respect to the saddle and bridle, the stranger began to favor the president with his history. He had lately quitted "Down East," and was coming South to "explore" a brother, hid away somewhere among the niggers in Virginny. He was anxious, therefore, to obtain all the knowledge he could of the country and the state of politics in parts "contagious" to the seat of government. This wish led directly to the topic of the new president, Thomas Jefferson, who had been elected to that dignity in direct opposition to the said stranger's advice. "I," said he, "support John Adams, a real old New-Englander, after the manner of our forefathers, the Pilgrims of Plymouth Rock. I have smallish faith in these chaps from the nigger states, upon principle. Doesn't it stand to reason, mister, that they must be a largish bit tyrannical?" Jefferson attempted some refutation of the charge, but the farmer scarcely listened to ten words before he rejoined, "Come, come, mister, I guess you don't see the moral sin of niggery; but it ain't only that. This Thomas Jefferson — did you ever see him?" The president nodded. "Well, that's more luck than I've had; but that doesn't matter. Now I hear that this Thomas Jefferson is a very wasteful chap with our hard-earned money" (Jefferson stared), "and you'll allow, mister, that that's unpatriotic upon principle. They tell me he never goes out but he's got clothes on his back that would sell for a plantation, or kiver a wagon-load of immigrants; he's a couple of watches or more, that he never thinks of swapping; rings on all his fingers; and a frill to his shirt big enough to turn a windmill. Now, if you've seen him, mister, you can tell me if that's about right." Jefferson laughed, and replied that, on the contrary, the president was seldom better dressed than himself at that moment. The farmer had his prejudices, and shook his head knowingly as he continued, "Come, come, squire; I see you are a small measure biassed. I guess now this Jefferson's a friend of your'n?" The president confessed it. "I dare say a man you speak to when you please?" Another nod. "Perhaps the smallest end of a relation?" Nod and laugh. "There, now! I guessed it. I knew you could not speak the truth on principle." At this moment they came in view of the president's house, and the farmer inquired who it belonged to. As soon as he received the intelligence he burst into one of those conventional substitutes for oaths which emphasize the language of the Northern lower orders. "Well, now, may I be 'tarnally starved down for mutton broth, if that sight doesn't come over a man like a suspension of the works of natur'. Now, mister, doesn't that prove my words, awfully strong? There's a house as big as Noah's ark? At the smallest count, there's thirty rooms in it. What can any careful chap, 'pon principle, want with more than *six*? I ha'n't got more than *four*. I say this Jefferson's wasting the people's money, and Congress is winking at it, and I guess it's all naked truth about the frill and watches; and I ain't afraid to affirm that it's my guess the inside of that house shows just as much wastefulness as Jefferson a-horseback." To this charge the president could make but one reply—an offer to introduce the farmer to the mansion, and give him ocular conviction. The latter readily consented, and they rode on, Jefferson planning an elaborate lesson of reproof to his calumniator. But, as they approached the gate, some gentlemen, who were engaged to dine with him, stepped forward and exclaimed, "Good-morning, president; you have had a fine day." At the word "president" the farmer, who was trotting on briskly, drew up so short he was near flying over his steed's ears. He turned and stared at Jefferson with a mixture of curiosity and alarm, which drew from the latter a quiet smile of enjoyment. In another instant he had struck his spurs into his horse and was flying away like a whirlwind, fully convinced that he should in some way pay for his temerity. "Hallo, friend!" shouted Jefferson, "won't you go over the house?" "No, thank ye, president," was the reply; "I'll look in when I come back."

Those who consider that the chief magistracy is a dignity which, to obtain its due respect, should be secluded from the common gaze, must admit that here was a proof of the benefit of its exhibition. This farmer echoed the opinions of many upon the president's character, and, in the only way that could have satisfied him, his suspicions were refuted.

Strikingly singular was the series of coincidences which made the destiny of Jefferson and of John Adams a parallel. Both, bred to the law and skilled in their profession, were early advocates, by speech and pen, of the colonial rights. Both went as delegates to the first Congress; together they voted for independence; were members of the committee to frame the "Declaration," and formed the sub-committee to prepare the draught. Both served their country on foreign embassies; both became vice-presidents and presidents; both lived to see the fiftieth anniversary of the freedom they had accomplished, and both died on that great day within an hour of each other! Though placed at the head of contending parties, they were firm friends in private, and spent the evening of their days in the exchange of the best sympathies arising from their common patriotism.

From *Retrospections of America, 1797–1811,* ed. Mrs. Bayle Bernard (New York: Harper, 1887), pp. 232–243.

[A Father's Grief, A Daughter's Memories] (1832)

MARTHA JEFFERSON RANDOLPH

Martha Jefferson Randolph (1772–1836), Thomas Jefferson's oldest daughter, was also one of his closest confidantes. With the death of her mother in 1782, she accompanied her father to Philadelphia the following year when he went there to serve his last term in Congress. He placed her in school in Philadelphia and then went to Annapolis, where Congress was meeting temporarily. Once Congress appointed Jefferson minister to France, she accompanied him from Philadelphia to Boston, where they took passage to France. In Paris, he enrolled her at L'Abbaye Royale de Penthémont, a prestigious convent school. They returned to Virginia in 1789. On 23 February 1790, she married Thomas Mann Randolph. She undertook the task of educating their numerous children. With a reputation as the finest French teacher in the region, she often gave French lessons to other local children. They named their first son after his grandfather: Thomas Jefferson Randolph. The list of names of their other sons — Benjamin Franklin Randolph, George Wythe Randolph, James Madison Randolph, Meriwether Lewis Randolph — read like an honor roll of Jefferson's best friends. Martha also made sure to educate her daughters. She instilled in all of her children a profound respect for their grandfather. The Randolphs made their home at Edgehill, but she spent much of her time at nearby Monticello. Once Jefferson's second presidential term ended and he returned to Monticello, she and her children moved there permanently. After her father's death in 1826, his enormous debts, combined with those of her husband, forced her to sell Monticello, which she wistfully referred to as her "lost home." After her husband's death in 1828, she lived with one or another of her children until her own death in 1836. She wrote the following reminiscence for George Tucker when he was preparing his *Life of Thomas Jefferson* (1837), but B. L. Rayner published it before Tucker as part of *Sketches of the Life, Writings, and Opinions of Thomas Jefferson* (1832).

DURING MY MOTHER'S LIFE he (Jefferson) bestowed much time and attention on our education—our cousins, the Carrs, and myself—and after her death, during the first month of desolation which followed, I was his constant companion while we remained at Monticello . . .

As a nurse no female ever had more tenderness nor anxiety. He nursed my poor mother in turn with aunt Carr and her own sister—sitting up with her and administering her medicines and drink to the last. For four months that she lingered he was never out of calling; when not at her bedside, he was writing in a small room which opened immediately at the head of her bed. A moment before the closing scene, he was led from the room in a state of insensibility by his sister, Mrs. Carr, who, with great difficulty, got him into the library, where he fainted, and remained so long insensible that they feared he never would revive. The scene that followed I did not witness, but the violence of his emotion, when, almost by stealth, I entered his room by night, to this day I dare not describe to myself. He kept his room three weeks, and I was never a moment from his side. He walked almost incessantly night and day, only lying down occasionally, when nature was completely exhausted, on a pallet that had been brought in during his long fainting-fit. My aunts remained constantly with him for some weeks—I do not remember how many. When at last he left his room, he rode out, and from that time he was incessantly on horseback, rambling about the mountain, in the least frequented roads, and just as often through the woods. In those melancholy rambles I was his constant companion—a solitary witness to many a burst of grief, the remembrance of which has consecrated particular scenes of that lost home beyond the power of time to obliterate. [. . .]

In returning, he was detained ten days at Havre de Grace, and, after crossing the Channel, ten more at Cowes, in the Isle of Wight, which were spent in visiting different parts of the island, when the weather permitted: among others, Carisbrook Castle, remarkable for the confinement of Charles the First, and also for a well of uncommon depth. We sailed on the 23d of October, 1789, in company with upwards of thirty vessels who had collected there and been detained, as we were, by contrary winds. Colonel [John] Trumbull, who chartered the ship for my father in London, applied to Mr. [William] Pitt to give orders to prevent his baggage from being searched on his arrival, informing Mr. Pitt at the same time that the application was made without his knowledge. The orders to such an effect were accordingly issued, I presume, as he was spared the usual vexation of such a search. The voyage was quick and not unpleasant. When we arrived on the coast there was so thick a mist as to render it impossible to see a pilot, had any of them been out. After beating about three days, the captain, a bold as well as an experienced seaman, determined to run in at a venture, without having seen the Capes. The ship came near running upon what was conjectured to be the Middle Ground, when anchor was cast at ten o'clock P.M. The wind rose, and the vessel drifted down, dragging her anchor, one or more miles. But she had got within the Capes, while a number which had been less bold were blown off the coast, some of them lost, and all kept out three or four weeks longer. We had to beat up against a strong head-wind, which carried away our topsails; and we were very near being run down by a brig coming out of port, which, having the wind in her favor, was almost upon us before we could get out of the way. We escaped, however, with only the loss of a part of our rigging. My father had been so anxious about his public accounts, that he would not trust them to go until he went with them. We arrived at Norfolk in the forenoon, and in two hours after landing, before an article of our baggage was brought ashore, the vessel took fire, and seemed on the point of being reduced to a mere hull. They were in the act of scuttling her, when some abatement in the flames was discovered, and she was finally saved. So great had been the activity of her crew, and of those belonging to other ships in the harbor who came to their aid, that every thing in her was saved. Our trunks, and perhaps also the papers, had been put in our state-rooms, and the doors incidentally closed by the captain. They were so close that the flames did not penetrate; but the powder in a musket in one of them was silently consumed, and the thickness of the travelling-trunks alone saved their contents from the excessive heat. I understood at the time that the state-rooms alone, of all the internal partitions, escaped burning. Norfolk had not recovered from the effects of the war, and we should have found it difficult to obtain rooms but for the politeness of the gentlemen at the hotel (Lindsay's), who were kind enough to give up their own rooms for our accommodation.

There were no stages in those days. We were indebted to the kindness of our friends for horses; and visiting all on the way homeward, and spending more or less time with them all in turn, we reached Monticello on the 23d of December. The negroes discovered the approach of the carriage as soon as it reached Shadwell, and such a scene I never witnessed in my life.

They collected in crowds around it, and almost drew it up the mountain by hand. The shouting, etc., had been sufficiently obstreperous before, but the moment it arrived at the top it reached the climax. When the door of the carriage was opened, they received him in their arms and bore him to the house, crowding around and kissing his hands and feet—some blubbering and crying—others laughing. It seemed impossible to satisfy their anxiety to touch and kiss the very earth which bore him. These were the first ebullitions of joy for his return, after a long absence, which they would of course feel; but perhaps it is not out of place here to add that they were at all times very devoted in their attachment to him.

From B. L. Rayner, *Sketches of the Life, Writings, and Opinions of Thomas Jefferson with Selections of the Most Valuable Portions of His Voluminous and Unrivaled Private Correspondence* (New York: A. Francis and W. Boardman, 1832), pp. 62–63, 150–152.

[Fond Memories from a Granddaughter] (1839)

Virginia J. Randolph Trist

Born and raised at Monticello, Virginia Jefferson Randolph Trist (1801–1882), the sixth child of Thomas Mann Randolph and Martha Jefferson Randolph, grew up in awe of her grandfather, the president. After she and Nicholas P. Trist were wed at Monticello, they continued to live there. Trist read law with his famous grandfather-in-law and also acted as Jefferson's personal secretary. Trist's responsibilities convinced him of the importance of preparing Jefferson's papers as a record of the man and what he meant to the nation, but he also realized that many stories about Jefferson that circulated orally among family members had never been written down and eventually would be lost if no one recorded them. He had often listened to his wife recall her childhood days at Monticello, and he urged her to write them down. The following letter is the result. She explains how Jefferson encouraged athletic contests among his grandchildren, taught them how to make scrapbooks using poems he clipped from the newspapers, indulged their whims, and inspired them to read, presenting such books as Maria Edgeworth's *Parents' Assistant*. Edgeworth was a special favorite with Virginia and her sisters; their grandfather would give them several other works of hers.

Virginia J. Randolph Trist to Nicholas P. Trist, 26 May 1839

Faithful to my promise, dearest ———, I shall spend an hour every Sunday in writing all my childish recollections of my dear grandfather, which are sufficiently distinct to relate to you. My memory seems crowded with them, and they have the vividness of realities; but all are trifles in themselves, such as I might talk to you by the hour, but when I have taken up my pen, they seem almost too childish to write down. But these remembrances are precious to me, because they are of *him,* and because they restore him to me as he then was, when his cheerfulness and affection were the warm sun in which his family all basked and were invigorated. Cheerfulness, love, benevolence, wisdom, seemed to animate his whole form. His face beamed with them. You remember how active was his step, how lively and even playful were his manners.

I cannot describe the feelings of veneration, admiration and love that existed in my heart towards him. I looked on him as a being too great and good for my comprehension; and yet I felt no fear to approach him, and be taught by him some of the childish sports that I delighted in. When he walked in the garden and would call the children to go with him, we raced after and before him, and we were made perfectly happy by this permission to accompany him. Not one of us in our wildest moods ever placed a foot on one of the garden beds, for that would violate one of his rules, and yet I never heard him utter a harsh word to one of us, or speak in a raised tone of voice, or use a threat. He simply said, "do," or "do not." He would gather fruit for us, seek out the ripest figs, or bring down the cherries from on high above our heads with a long stick, at the end of which there was a hook and a little net bag. . . . One of our earliest amusements was in running races on the terrace, or around the lawn. He placed us according to our ages, giving the youngest and smallest the start of all the others by some yards, and so on, and then he raised his arm high with his white handkerchief in his hand, on which our eager eyes were fixed, and slowly counted three, at which number he dropt the handkerchief and we started off to finish the race by returning to the starting-place and receiving our reward of dried fruit — three figs, prunes or dates to the victor, two to the second, and one to the lagger who came in last. These were our summer sports with him.

I was born the year he was elected President, and except one winter that we spent with him in Washington, I never was with him during that season until after he had retired from office. During his absences, all the children who could write corresponded with him. Their letters were duly answered, and it was a sad mortification to me that I had not learned to write before his return to live at home, and of course had no letter from him. Whenever an opportunity occurred, he sent us books, and he never saw a little story or piece of poetry in a newspaper suited to our ages and tastes, that he did not preserve it and send it to us; and from him we learnt the habit of making these miscellaneous collections by pasting in a little paper book made for the purpose, anything of the sort that we received from him or got otherwise.

On winter evenings, when it grew too dark to read, in the half hour that passed before candles came in, as we all sat round the fire, he taught us several childish games, and would play them with us. I remember that "cross questions," and "I love my love with an A," were two I learned from him;

and we would teach some of ours to him. When the candles were brought, all was quiet immediately, for he took up his book to read, and we would not speak out of a whisper lest we should disturb him, and generally we followed his example and took a book—and I have seen him raise his eyes from his own book and look round on the little circle of readers, and smile and make some remark to mamma about it. When the snow fell we would go out as soon as it stopped to clear it off the terraces with shovels, that he might have his usual walk on them without treading in snow.

He often made us little presents. I remember his giving us *Parents Assistant,* and that we drew lots, and that she who drew the longest straw had the first reading of the book—the next longest straw entitled the drawer to the second reading—the shortest, to the last reading and the ownership of the book. Often he discovered, we knew not how, some cherished object of our desires, and the first intimation we had of his knowing the wish was its unexpected gratification. Sister Anne gave a silk dress to sister Ellen. Cornelia (then eight or ten years old) going up stairs, involuntarily expressed aloud some feelings which possessed her bosom on the occasion, by saying, "I never had a silk dress in my life." The next day a silk dress came from Charlottesville for Cornelia—and (to make the rest of us equally happy) also a pair of pretty dresses for Mary and myself. One day I was passing hastily through the glass door from the hall to the portico; there was a broken pane which caught my muslin dress and tore it sadly. Grandpapa was standing by and saw the disaster. A few days after he came into mamma's sitting room with a bundle in his hand, and said to me, "I have been mending your dress for you." He had himself selected for me another beautiful dress. I had for a long time a great desire to have a guitar. A lady of our neighborhood was going to the West and wished to part with her guitar, but she asked so high a price that I never in my dreams aspired to its possession. One morning on going down to breakfast, I saw the guitar. It had been sent up by Mrs. — for us to look at, and grandpapa told me that if I would promise to learn to play on it I should have it. I never shall forget my ecstasies. I was but fourteen years old and the first wish of my heart was unexpectedly gratified.

From Henry S. Randall, *The Life of Thomas Jefferson,* 3 vols. (New York: Derby and Jackson, 1858), 3: 349–351.

[Of Art and Religion] (1841)

John Trumbull

Like so many other Revolutionary American painters, John Trumbull (1756–1843) went to England to hone his craft. He studied with Benjamin West in London during the early 1780s but came into his own by the middle of the decade. In 1785, Trumbull embarked on a series of paintings depicting important people and events from the Revolutionary War, including *The Death of General Warren at the Battle of Bunker Hill* and *The Death of General Montgomery in the Attack on Quebec.* When Thomas Jefferson came to London in 1786, Trumbull asked him whether he should continue the series. Jefferson encouraged Trumbull to persevere, invited him to Paris, and even offered him a place to stay. Trumbull took Jefferson up on his offer, arriving in Paris later that year and becoming a member of Jefferson's household. In a 14 August 1786 letter, Jefferson announced his arrival to Francis Hopkinson: "Our countryman Trumbull is here, a young painter of the most promising talents. He brought with him his Battle of Bunker's hill and Death of Montgomery to have them engraved here, and we may add, to have them sold; for like Dr. Ramsay's history [David Ramsay's *History of the Revolution in South Carolina*], they are too true to suit the English palate" (*Papers,* 10: 250).

Once Jefferson introduced Trumbull to his contacts in Paris, Trumbull immersed himself in the Parisian art world. The two paintings he brought quickly earned him considerable respect. As Jefferson told Ezra Stiles in a 1 September 1786 letter, Trumbull's paintings "are the admiration of the Connoisseurs. His natural talents of this art seem almost unparalleled" (*Papers,* 10: 317). Trumbull made many friends among the leading artists in Paris and, in turn, introduced Jefferson to them. Jacques-Louis David was one of these friends; Maria Cosway was another. Jefferson and Trumbull became reacquainted in 1793 after both had returned to the United States, but, as Trumbull relates, an unfortunate dinner conversation divided the two.

IN THE SUMMER OF 1785, political duties had called Mr. Jefferson, then minister of the United States in Paris, to London, and there I became acquainted with him. He had a taste for the fine arts, and highly approved my intention of preparing myself for the accomplishment of a national work. He encouraged me to persevere in this pursuit, and kindly invited me to come to Paris, to see and study the fine works there, and to make his house my home, during my stay.

I now availed myself of this invitation, and went to his house, at the Grille de Chaillot, where I was most kindly received by him. My two paintings, the first fruits of my national enterprise, met his warm approbation, and during my visit, I began the composition of the Declaration of Independence, with the assistance of his information and advice. [. . .]

Sunday, August 5th.—Went with Mr. Jefferson and others to see the ceremony of crowning the *rosière* of Sarennes, a village near St. Cloud, four miles from Chaillot. Every year, the most amiable, industrious and virtuous poor girl of the parish is elected, who is received by all the village, and a crowd of strangers, in the church with great solemnity; the service is performed, a sermon preached, and the ceremony of crowning with roses is performed, with the benediction of a bishop. The *rosière* of the year, with the preceding candidates, is arranged on the right of the bishop—their parents and friends with them; the crown of flowers is placed by a little girl, daughter of the seigneur of the parish, with the *benedicite* of the bishop, and accompanied by music; the *rosière* is then conducted home, attended by the clergy, music and company, when she receives three hundred livres—the annual legacy of a clergyman, whose institution this is. Returned to Paris on foot, over the Pont de Neuilly, a very beautiful stone bridge over the Seine; the floor of this bridge is horizontal; it consists of seven arches, which have a beautiful degree of lightness; these arches, which in fact and intrinsically are hemispherical, are sloped from one fourth of the piers on each side to the outer face, so that the arch externally appears to be a very flat ellipse, but within and under the centre of the bridge, they are hemispheres. [. . .]

[Monday, 13 August] Dined, in company with Mr. Jefferson, at the Abbés Chassí and Arnout [Abbés Chalut and Arnoux] in Passy; *a jour maigre*, or fast day, but the luxury of the table in soups, fish and fruits, truly characteristic of the opulent clergy of the times. [. . .]

August 19th.—Here my manuscript fails me; I presume that one if not two sheets, have perished entirely. Of the next fragment, one half of four pages are consumed vertically; that is, half of each line only remains. This begins with the 10th of September, commencing my journey to Frankfort. I very much regret the loss of these twenty days; for, after fifty years, memory unaided, can do little to restore the chasm. I distinctly recollect, however, that this time was occupied with the same industry in examining and reviewing whatever relates to the arts, and that Mr. Jefferson joined our party almost daily; and here commenced his acquaintance with Mrs. Cosway, of whom very respectful mention is made in his published correspondence. In the course of this interval, I became acquainted with the Count de Moustier [François Élie Éléonore], afterwards minister to the United States, and his sister, the Marquise de Brethon [Madame de Bréhan, the count's sister-in-law]. She was a most interesting little woman, who had been married to an abandoned brute, with whom it was impossible for any woman of delicacy, or of any sense of virtue, to live. She was therefore separated from him, and went with the Count, her brother, soon after to the United States, where she became unpopular in consequence of her dispirited, retired, melancholy manners, which, if her domestic history had been known, would, I trust, have endeared her to my fair countrywomen. [. . .]

In the autumn of 1787, I again visited Paris, where I painted the portrait of Mr. Jefferson in the original small Declaration of Independence, Major General [Charles] Ross in the small Sortie from Gibraltar, and the French officers in the Surrender of Lord Cornwallis, at Yorktown in Virginia. I regard these as the best of my small portraits; they were painted from the life, in Mr. Jefferson's house. [. . .]

It has been seen, that in Europe I had been on terms of confidence with Mr. Jefferson; this continued for some time, so that in America, when the first mission to the states of Barbary was determined on, it was, through him, offered to me, and declined; but as the French revolution advanced, my whole soul revolted from the atrocities of France, while he approved or apologized for all. He opposed Washington—I revered him—and a coldness gradually succeeded, until in 1793, he invited me to dine. A few days before, I had offended his friend, Mr. [William Branch] Giles, senator from Virginia, by rendering him ridiculous in the eyes of a lady, to whose favorable opinion he aspired. On entering the drawing-room at Mr. Jefferson's, on the day of the dinner, I found a part of the company already assembled, and among them Mr. Giles. I was scarcely seated, when Giles began to rally me upon the puritanical ancestry and character of New England. I saw there was no other person from New England present, and therefore, although conscious that I was in no degree qualified to manage a religious discussion, yet I felt myself bound to make the attempt, and defend my country on this delicate point, as well as I could.

Whether it had been pre-arranged that a discussion on the Christian religion, in which it should be powerfully ridiculed on the one side, and weakly defended on the other, should be brought forward, as promising amusement to a rather freethinking dinner party, I will not determine; but it had that appearance, and Mr. Giles pushed his raillery, to my no small annoyance, if not to my discomfiture, until dinner was announced. That I hoped would relieve me, by giving a new turn to the conversation, but such was not the case; the company was hardly seated at table, when he renewed his attack with increased asperity, and proceeded so far at last, as to ridicule the character, conduct, and doctrines of the divine founder of our religion—Jefferson in the mean time, smiling and nodding approbation on Mr. Giles, while the rest of the company silently left me and my defense to our fate; until at length my friend, David Franks, (first cashier of the bank of the United States,) took up the argument on my side. Thinking this a fair opportunity for evading further conversation on this subject, I turned to Mr. Jefferson and said, "Sir, this is a strange situation in which I find myself; in a country professing Christianity, and at a table with Christians, as I supposed, I find my religion and myself attacked with severe and almost irresistible wit and raillery, and not a person to aid me in my defense, but my friend Mr. Franks, *who is himself a Jew.*" For a moment, this attempt to parry the discussion appeared to have some effect; but Giles soon returned to the attack, with renewed virulence, and burst out with—"It is all a miserable delusion and priestcraft; I do not believe one word of all they say about a future state of existence, and retribution for actions done here. I do not believe one word of a Supreme Being who takes cognizance of the paltry affairs of this world, and to whom we are responsible for what we do."

I had never before heard, or seen in writing, such a broad and unqualified avowal of atheism. I was at first shocked, and remained a moment silent; but soon rallied and replied, "Mr. Giles, I admire your frankness, and it is but just that I should be equally frank in avowing my sentiments. Sir, in my opinion, the man who can with sincerity make the declaration which you have just made, is perfectly prepared for the commission of every atrocious action, by which he can promise himself the advancement of his own interest, or the gratification of his impure passions, provided he can commit it secretly, and with a reasonable probability of escaping detection by his fellow men. Sir, I would not trust such a man with the honor of a wife, a sister, or a daughter—with my own purse or reputation, or with any thing which I thought valuable. Our acquaintance, sir, is at an end." I rose and left the company, and never after spoke to Mr. Giles.

I have thought it proper to relate this conversation, as helping to elucidate the character of Mr. Jefferson, on the disputed point of want of credulity, as he would call it. In nodding and smiling assent to all the virulence of his friend, Mr. Giles, he appeared to me to avow most distinctly, his entire approbation. From this time my acquaintance with Mr. Jefferson became cold and distant.

From John Trumbull, *Autobiography, Reminiscences and Letters of John Trumbull, from 1756 to 1841* (New York: Wiley and Putnam, 1841), pp. 95–96, 101–102, 116, 117–118, 150–151, 169–172.

[A Visionary Who Loved to Dream Eyes Wide Open] (1841)

AUGUSTUS J. FOSTER

A career diplomat, Augustus J. Foster (1780–1848) was educated at Christ Church, Oxford. After college he traveled through Europe, getting to know such literary figures as Goethe, Schiller, and Madame de Staël, among many other prominent people. Appointed secretary of the legation at Washington, D.C. in 1804, he reached America in December of that year and stayed until 1808. When Congress was not in session, Foster traveled around the United States. In 1807 his travels brought him to Monticello, a visit he recorded in detail. After serving as chargé d'affaires at Stockholm from 1808 through 1810, Foster came back to the United States as minister plenipotentiary in Washington, D.C., but he could do little to prevent the War of 1812. He returned to Great Britain in 1812 and later served as minister plenipotentiary at Copenhagen from 1814 to 1824 and at Turin from 1825 to 1840.

Foster's *Notes on the United States* came into being when, in the words of Richard Beale Davis, "a British diplomat in his mid-fifties decided that he must have his say about the America he had known as a young man" (*Jeffersonian America,* ix). Drawing upon his travel notes, Foster composed a first draft of the work in the mid 1830s. He tinkered with his text for the remainder of the decade, bringing it near enough to completion that he gave John Gibson Lockhart, editor of the *Quarterly Review,* a copy of the manuscript. Lockhart reviewed the manuscript as if it were a published work, but his critical comments are limited to brief remarks interspersed between big chunks of text from Foster's manuscript. Lockhart's review essentially constitutes the first published edition of *Notes on the United States.*

For the *Quarterly Review,* Lockhart quoted much of Foster's impressions of Thomas Jefferson, adding only one interpretive comment of his own. After quoting Foster's description of a newly invented odometer Jefferson used on his carriage, Lockhart observed:

> Jefferson's printed correspondence is full of allusions to polygraphs, and pantographs, and so forth. "I have always observed," says Sir Walter Scott, "that a small taste for mechanics tends to encouraging a sort of trifling self-conceit, founded on knowing what is not worth being known by one who has other matters to employ his mind on, and, in short, forms a trumpery gimcrack kind of a character." —Letter to Miss Joanna Baillie, *Life of Scott,* vol. vi. p. 83.

Lockhart's criticism of Jefferson seems petty, but his words reinforce the influence of Thomas Jefferson Randolph's four-volume edition of his grandfather's writings, which was reprinted in London in 1829 as *Memoirs, Correspondence, and Private Papers of Thomas Jefferson.*

After his retirement from the diplomatic corps, Foster revised his manuscript further, but he was never sufficiently satisfied with it to see it into press and left it unpublished at the time of his death. On 1 August 1848, in a fit of temporary insanity, Foster slit his throat. *Notes on the United States* remained unpublished until 1954, when Richard Beale Davis issued a scholarly edition of the work. Since Davis's edition is readily available, the Monticello section is presented here as John Gibson Lockhart originally presented it for the readers of the *Quarterly Review.*

THE HOUSE HAS TWO PORTICOES of the Doric order, though one of them was not quite completed, and the pediment had, in the meanwhile, to be supported on the stems of four tulip-trees, which are really, when well grown, as beautiful as the fluted shafts of Corinthian pillars. They front north and south: on the ground-floor were four sitting-rooms, two bed-rooms, and the library, which contained several thousand volumes, classed according to subject and language. It was divided into three compartments, in one of which the president had his bed placed in a doorway; and in a recess at the foot of the bed was a horse with forty-eight projecting hands, on which hung his coats and waistcoats, and which he could turn round with a long stick,—a nick-nack that Jefferson was fond of showing, with many other little mechanical inventions; one of which was a sulky upon four wheels, with the spring in the centre, a very rough sort of carriage, but which he preferred to any other, as having been made by an Irish mechanic at Monticello, under his own superintendence, and to praise which was a sure way to prejudice him in your favour. He had also got an odometer, which was fastened upon the axle-tree of the sulky, and would tell the number of miles gone over by the wheels [. . .]

If the library had been thrown open to his guests, the president's country-house would have been as agreeable a place to stay at as any I know; but it was there he sat and wrote, and he did not like, of course, to be disturbed by visitors, who in this part of the world are rather disposed to be indiscreet. The family breakfast-hour was eight o'clock; and after breakfast Mrs. Randolph (the president's daughter) and the other female relations of the house set about cleaning the tea-things and washing the alabaster lamp, which I took to be designed as a catch for popularity. After this operation the president retired to his books; his daughter to give lessons to her children; her husband to his farm; and the guests were left to amuse themselves as they pleased, walking, riding, or shooting. The president took his daily ride at one o'clock, to look at his farm and mill; at four dinner was served up; and in the evening we walked on a wooden terrace, or strolled into the wood, Mr. Jefferson playing with his grandchildren till dusk, when tea was brought in, and afterwards wine and fruit, of which the peaches were excellent. At nine our host withdrew, and everybody else as they pleased [. . .]

Jefferson's opinions in regard to the mental qualities of the negro race were certainly not favourable; he considered them to be as far inferior to the rest of mankind as the mule is to the horse, and as made to carry burthens, while he augured but little good as likely to result from their emancipation.—That the black race is, however, as susceptible of refined civilisation and as capable to the full of profiting by the advantages of education as any other of any shade whatever, must be admitted, in contradiction to Mr. Jefferson's prejudices, by any person who has had the honour to be acquainted with the daughters of Christophe, who was supreme sovereign or emperor of Hayti during eight or nine years, and who spared no kind of expense in getting good European masters for his children. The early and melancholy fate of his sons prevents us from forming a judgment as to what they might have become in consequence of such care, but his daughters are well known at several European courts, and by many individuals of the best European society, especially at the Tuscan and Sardinian capitals, where, in spite of their colour and their rank, which made it difficult for them to mix familiarly in the great world, they were sufficiently seen, nevertheless, to let it be apparent that their wit and understandings, as well as their accomplishments, were of the very highest order. . . .

I thought Mr. Jefferson more of a statesman and man of the world than Mr. Madison, who was rather too much the disputatious pleader; yet the latter was better informed, and, moreover, a social, jovial, and good-humoured companion, full of anecdote, sometimes rather of a loose description, but oftener of a political and historical interest. He was a little man with small features, rather wizened when I saw him, but occasionally lit up with a good-natured smile. He wore a black coat, stockings with shoes buckled, and had his hair powdered, with a tail. Jefferson, on the other hand, was, as before stated, very tall and bony, and affected to despise dress: in conversation, too, he was visionary, and loved to dream eyes open, or, as the Germans say, "zu schwarmen," and it must be admitted that America is the paradise for "Schwarmers," futurity there offering a wide frame for all that the imagination can put into it. If he lived, however, on illusions and mystic philanthropical plans in the country, or in his bed, he was not the less awake or active in taking measures to ensure the triumph of himself and his party at the capital, and I doubt if Washington himself would so certainly have been elected for the third time to the presidential chair, as he would have been had he chosen to be put into nomination for it. But he preferred being consistent, and to follow in this respect the example of his great predecessor, while he had enough of independence of mind and love for even trifling occupations to enable him to bear the change with composure. It must, however, have been a painful necessity that induced him to sell his library. No doubt, it was prudentially done for the interests of his children, and patriotically sold to his country, yet still there was, I fear, also the potent argument of poverty; and it was another great slur upon the character of Congress that they did not vote him the money and refuse to accept the books, at least until after his death. — Such men as Washington and Jefferson, and their contemporaries in the highest stations of their country, having had peculiar claims to its most generous consideration, particularly when we reflect on the nature of the sacrifices which they made in order to establish the Republic, and that such sacrifices never can possibly be equalled by any of their successors — I shall ever look upon it as a proof of degeneracy in the race of men succeeding to that of the founders of American independence that the great Washington was left unburied, otherwise than as we bury a dog — that Jefferson was forced to sell his library in his old age to enable him to live — and that Monroe was almost left to starve, after he, like others, had spent his patrimony in keeping up the respectability of the offices of Secretary of State and President.

From John Gibson Lockhart, "Foster's *Notes on the United States*," *Quarterly Review* 68 (June 1841): 42–44.

[Talking with Jefferson: Two Accounts] (1841 and 1863)

DANIEL PIERCE THOMPSON

Daniel Pierce Thompson (1795–1868), the son of Daniel and Rebekah Thompson, was born in Charlestown, Massachusetts, but moved to Vermont with his parents in 1800. After graduating from Middlebury College in 1820, he left Vermont for Virginia, where he worked as a tutor, read law, and was admitted to the bar. During the summer of 1822, Thompson visited the campus of the University of Virginia, then under construction, where he met Jefferson, who invited him to dinner at Monticello. Thompson readily accepted the invitation. Years later Thompson would write two separate accounts of the experience.

By 1825, Thompson had returned to Vermont and opened a law office in Montpelier, where he went on to fill a series of judicial and legislative positions. As a hobby, Thompson sought out old-timers who had participated in the Revolutionary War. He thus accumulated many anecdotes to use in his literary and historical work. After establishing himself as a career bureaucrat, Thompson could indulge his literary inclinations. In 1835, he published two historical romances, *The Adventures of Timothy Peacock* and *May Martin*. *The Green Mountain Boys* (1839) is generally considered his finest novel. Van Wyck Brooks called it "a homegrown product, if ever literature saw one, as unpretentious as a log-cabin" and "a Yankee tale as brisk and wholesome as any mountain ballad" (*Flowering of New England*, 415). In other words, by the time Thompson published his first account of his interview with Jefferson in 1841, he had already mastered historical romance, something to keep in mind when evaluating the accuracy of his portrayal of the past.

Thompson continued writing novels, but he also tried his hand at local history with *History of the Town of Montpelier* (1860), which gave him an outlet for many of the anecdotes he had accumulated. He continued writing historical novels into the Civil War period but took a break to contribute to *Harper's* a fuller account of his visit with Jefferson. Published in 1863, and taking slavery as a major theme, the article reads like Northern war propaganda as it casts Jefferson in the role of abolitionist. Merrill Peterson recommends treating this article with skepticism (*Jefferson Image,* 480). Despite its obvious political purpose, the article's details jibe with fact. Thompson quotes Jefferson as saying that he had acquired several Anglo-Saxon textbooks for himself; Jefferson's retirement library lists several prominent works treating the Anglo-Saxon language. Furthermore, Jefferson's remarks about Patrick Henry in the article are consistent with what he told Daniel Webster about Patrick Henry. Though flawed by wartime rhetoric and the vagaries of memory, Thompson's second account nevertheless presents a good portrayal of Jefferson in his later years.

The First Meeting of Jefferson and Burr

The following anecdote was related by Mr. Jefferson to the writer, while on a visit to Monticello, in the year 1822. It was told in illustration of an opinion advanced by the former in relation to physiognomy, that although it was but folly to attempt a system of judging character from any particular conformation of features, yet the eye was an unerring index of the soul, and no training on the part of its possessor could prevent it from disclosing his true moral nature to a skilful observer. I will endeavor to repeat the anecdote in the exact words of the illustrious narrator.

During my attendance on some one of the earliest sessions of the Continental Congress at Philadelphia, said Mr. J., I chanced to dine one day at a public house where several distinguished gentlemen from abroad, all entire strangers to me, had just arrived in the city. Among these was a gentleman who became seated directly opposite to me at the table, and who soon attracted my observation by his peculiar and remarkable countenance, and especially by his singularly restless and subtly quivering eye, which to me threw off an expression extremely sinister; for I had ever noted, that an eye of this character indicated moral obliquity of heart, and this kind of eye he possessed in a more eminent degree than any I had ever seen. So strong, indeed, were my impressions in the case, that I felt no hesitation in making up for myself a decided opinion of the true character of the man before me, though, as before mentioned, then unknown to me, even by name.

After retiring to the private room of the friend at whose invitation I had dined there, he asked me, with an air of curiosity, if I noticed the gentleman who sat opposite to me at the table we had just left; and if so, what was my opinion of him?

I replied, that I had not only noticed the man, but formed a decided opinion of him, and that was, that his true character might be expressed in three words—*coldness, cunning,* and *perfidy.*

"Why, sir," said my friend, in surprise, "you cannot know the man of whom you are speaking—it is Mr. Burr, the greatest lawyer in New York."

"I will not alter my opinion for all that," I remarked. "I have never known such an eye as his in an honest man's head; and whatever may be his present eminence, and fair reputation, I will venture the prediction, that he will yet be known as a villain."

In after times, continued Mr. J. to me, I had frequent reason to recall my first impressions of the true character of *Aaron Burr.*

A Talk with Jefferson

During a sojourn in the Old Dominion in the summer of 1822, wishing to visit the buildings of the University of Virginia, then in the process of erection at Charlottesville, and also to visit their illustrious projector, Mr. Jefferson, at his noted residence on the overlooking elevation of Monticello, I procured a letter of introduction to the superintendent of the works, and, repairing to that village, at once delivered my letter to the gentleman to whom it was directed.

"That is Mr. Jefferson," he said, glancing over the letter, and seeing it included the request of an introduction to that personage—"That is Mr. Jefferson whom you see yonder, taking the chisel from the hand of an Italian sculptor and showing him how to turn a volute of the capital on which he is engaged."

"Why, does Mr. Jefferson go into sculpture in so practical a manner as that?" I asked, in some surprise.

"Yes," was the reply, "yes, often, when he detects faulty work. Indeed we consider him the best workman on the ground. But here he comes. I will introduce you; and when he leaves the place, as he probably is about to do, I will go the rounds of the works with you."

Mr. Jefferson—a tall, straight, sandy-complexioned man, wearing a coat of Virginia cloth, surmounting a buff vest and broadcloth pants—advanced with an elastic step and serene countenance, when I was introduced, and greeted with the sweet, winning smile which so peculiarly distinguished him, and which, doubtless, was one of the secrets of his great personal popularity and magnetic power over all whom he would conciliate.

"You will dine with me at Monticello today, I trust," he said. "I must ride down the river a couple of miles, to see to the repairing of the foundation of my mills there, which the rascally workmen slighted when laid in my absence while in office. But I shall return to meet you at the dinner-table."

So saying, he, though then about eighty years of age, mounted the young blooded horse that was now led up for him with the agility of a boy, and galloped away to his destination.

We will pass over our delightful ride along up the spiral road to the top of the broad, dome-shaped Monticello, the unique mansion that surmounted it, the museum picture-gallery, and library; and, lastly, the plain Virginia dinner, presided over by the distinguished head of the household, and graced by the presence of his interesting grandchildren, Master and Misses Randolph. We will pass over all these as foreign to the object of this article, which is to report some of the most remarkable of the utterances with which we were about to be favored.

As we rose from the dinner-table, Mr. Jefferson led me at once to the eastern portico of the house, which was then just beginning to be thrown into the shade, and bade me be seated, with the remark that he had "finished his labors and studies for the day, and had now nothing to do but talk."

"In examining the plan of our University, with its buildings finished and in progress, you noticed, doubtless, that of the different structures designed for professors' houses, no two are of the same order of architecture; and that these houses are to be at least numerous enough to represent the whole of the five orders. The object of this is to furnish correct models for public buildings and private residences, so that students educated here, or their friends visiting here, may carry away with them, and this be the means of spreading, a true architectural taste among the people of Virginia."

"You contemplate, I am told, Sir, the establishment of some professorships which are rarely, if ever, to be found in our American colleges."

"Yes, especially one of the Saxon language, a knowledge of which, as the foundation of the English, I deem no less indispensable than that of Greek and Latin. I have put myself in correspondence with several gentlemen in England on the subject, and they have recommended two or three different individuals for this professorship. But so difficult is it, even in England, to find anyone a proper judge of the competency of another in this language, and so anxious am I that this post should be well filled, that I resolved I would know something of the language myself before finally engaging any one, that, by a personal examination, I may be enabled to form a pretty safe general judgment of the competency of applicants. And for this purpose I, last spring, procured from England a full set of Saxon elementary books, and have ever since devoted two hours each day to the study of the language; and in a few months more I hope to feel myself prepared to meet such applicants in conference. I design, also, that *all* the professorships should be filled by the most eminent men; and with this object I have invited Mr. [Nathaniel] Bowditch, of Salem, Massachusetts, to come and occupy the chair of Mathematics, since I consider Mr. Bowditch to be the second mathematician in the world, Laplace being doubtless the first."

"Do you design a Medical Department in the university?"

"I think not. Anatomy, to be sure, is a science, but I have no confidence in *Materia Medica,* which I have long since banished from my family, choosing rather to rely on nursing and nature for a cure. My attention was first called to this subject when I was Minister to France. During my residence in Paris my daughter was seized with a typhus fever, and I sent for a physician, who was called the most eminent and successful one in the city. He came, examined the patient, gave some directions about nursing, and departed, giving no medicine and leaving none to be given. The same course was taken the next day, and the next, when, growing uneasy, I said to him,

"'Doctor, you don't appear to be doing any thing for my daughter. What is the reason?'

"'The reason is, I wish her to get well. I had supposed you knew what my system of practice was, or you would not have sent for me.'

"'No; what is it?'

"'To have the most careful nursing, leave the disease to wear itself out, and let nature do the rest, but give no medicine.'

"Well, Sir, though still uneasy, I acquiesced in the course, and the result was, my daughter recovered with a constitution uninjured by mineral medicine. Since then—a period of nearly thirty years—I have been my own doctor, and scrupulously following the system of the French physician, have practiced not only in my own family, but among the colored people on my plantation, taking them all through the worst of fevers, and never losing a single patient.

"You see," said Mr. Jefferson, after a pause, indicating that he had no more to say on the subject that had been under consideration—"you see that ancient looking building down yonder in front of us, a little removed from the foot of this eminence? That should be an object of interest to strangers. That was the old home of the noted Patrick Henry."

"It is indeed an object of interest to me, Sir. It would be so at *any* time; and it is especially so at this, as I have just been reading William Wirt's Life of Henry; and I shall have the opportunity of ascertaining from one, who is so competent to judge, how far my impression that the biography was overcolored is well grounded."

"In some respects it doubtless *is* overcolored, but in others scarcely colored up to what was the reality. Mr. Wirt makes Henry a statesman and a lawyer: neither of these was true. Henry was a bold and sincere patriot, but no statesman. And his opinion on a law point was absolutely not worth one single brass farthing. But as to the effect of his oratory, Mr. Wirt has hardly done him justice. His power over an audience was wonderful, and to myself, I confess almost incomprehensible. Men were frenzied under his appeals, and seemed to become the mere machines of his will. I have never witnessed anything like it either in Europe or America. And I doubt whether there ever was in America any such exhibition of the power of a speaker over an audience, with the exception, perhaps, of Whitfield, the greatest pulpit orator, doubtless, of all modern times. And Henry, like Whitfield, should have been a preacher. Had he been one, he would have been a prodigy. But what, you will ask, was the secret of this singular power? That is a question which, among thinking men, has before been often asked, but never to my mind satisfactorily answered. It certainly was not from any peculiar richness of thought or force of his ideas; for his speeches when analyzed by the thinking hearer, as soon as he could divest himself of the peculiar effect of their delivery, were seen to amount to but very little. I have myself sat and listened to one of his speeches with a strange thrill of pleasure, yielded myself involuntarily to the influence, shut up my eyes, and sat it out to the end like one in a trance, and then, as I aroused myself from the thrall, I have asked myself, *Now what has the man said to produce such an effect, even on myself, guarded as I was?* But I never could tell. No, that effect was not produced by the force of intellect, but the faculty of completely seizing the sympathies of the hearers, or rather perhaps some magnetic power over them, which was the peculiar gift of the man, and which has been rarely or never possessed by any individual, to the same extent, in this country before. Henry was no scholar, and read scarcely anything. I recollect he, one fall, came up here, and saying he had been thinking he would read some during the approaching winter, asked me to lend him a book. I lent him a volume of Hume's *Essays*. He brought it back the next spring, when I asked him if he had read it? 'No,' he replied. 'I tried to read it two or three times, but I never could get through more than a page or so before I fell asleep.' And yet for all his indolence, and his aversion to acquiring what he called book knowledge, Henry had a great soul and a comprehensive intellect, which, on all occasions sufficently important to arouse his highest faculties, he brought into action with the strength of a giant. Indeed I hardly know what Virginia would have done without the powerful impetus he imparted to the great political revolution of 1776."

"Yes," I here remarked, "Patrick Henry's services in our great political revolution are everywhere acknowledged; and in reading Wirt's glowing account of those services and of his intense love of freedom, I could not forbear asking an opponent in argument the question I would also like to ask you, and that is, where would Henry, if now alive, with his old keen appreciation of human rights, where would Henry be found in the *social* revolution, or rather the revolution in the domestic institutions of his native State, which, with somewhat divided opinions, you are now inaugurating? — I allude to the institution of slavery, in connection with the States Convention call in part to provide for its gradual abolishment."

"Where would Henry be found, if alive, at this crisis, would you ask? It would require no gift of prophecy in me to answer that question. He would be found with those with whom, side by side, he once labored in the matter so strenuously — Mr. Madison, myself, and many others of Virginia's most enlightened statesmen. Henry was, at that time, even more determined in his opposition to slavery than the rest of us. The Legislature of Virginia, the first of all the States to take any definite anti-slavery action, as early as 1778, through the influence of Patrick Henry and the few leading men who felt like him, and like him had the moral courage to take a bold and decided stand on the subject, abolished the slave traffic in this State by law. And besides the all-important aid Henry contributed to this measure, he caused his opinions and influence to be heeded and felt by the framers of the Constitution of the United States, an influential portion of whom, under the lead of Mr. Madison, thought that they had so guarded that instrument that it should afford the remotest sanction to slavery, but rather invite the after prohibitory action of Congress. And when Congress, in response to our known sentiments, subsequently prohibited the further introduction of slaves after a certain time, Mr. Madison thought, and we all thought, we had effectually accomplished the great desideratum of giving slavery its death-blow, or the blow at least under which the institution could only linger a few years to perish from the land, which it had already begun to blight with its malicious influence. But we soon found ourselves sadly mistaken. When the time arrived on which all had counted for its rapid decline, we saw it taking deeper root than ever. The cupidity of an influential class, taking advantage of the thoughtlessness of other classes, had prevailed. And so it has gone on, till this terrible incubus on the prosperity and true welfare of the South is swelling up to mountain proportions. This, of late years, has constituted the burden of my anxieties and last spring I had several conversations with Mr. Madison on the subject, when, finding ourselves perfectly agreed in views and sentiments, we both resolved we would make one more effort before we died to rid our State of this unspeakable evil before too late. And the result of our movement was the proposition for the gradual emancipation of all the slaves of Virginia, which is soon to be presented for the action of the approaching State Convention for making all expedient alterations in our Constitution, and which, with the strong backing promised us, we have fondly hoped might be adopted. And yet we should not be too sanguine of such an auspicious result. The same causes that have hitherto led to the defeat of every such movement may again conspire to bring this to the same fate, and we shall be compelled to leave the stage of life with our vistas of the earthly future darkened by the presages of the doom, which, if not averted by emancipation, must sooner or later fall, not only on our own beloved State, but the whole South, in the ruin of their people or in the overthrow of their republican liberties, in consequence of the inevitable workings of that most unfortunate institution."

The measure was not destined to prevail, and we are now in a position to estimate the deep foresight embodied in the prophecy of the author of the Declaration of Independence.

"The First Meeting of Jefferson and Burr," *United States Magazine and Democratic Review* 9 (October 1841): 358–359.

"A Talk with Jefferson," *Harper's New Monthly Magazine* 26 (May 1863): 833–835.

[A Man of Easy and Ingratiating Manners] (1849)

Francis T. Brooke

Born at Smithfield in Spotsylvania County, Virginia, Francis T. Brooke (1763–1851) joined the Continental Army as a lieutenant at sixteen and served in Virginia and the southern theater for the remainder of the Revolutionary War. While in command of the magazine at Westham, Virginia, Brooke first met Thomas Jefferson, then serving as governor, who came to Westham with Archibald Blair, clerk of the council. In *A Narrative of My Life* (1849), written seventy years after the fact, Brooke is imprecise about dates, but Jefferson recorded visiting the iron foundry at Westham on 30 March 1780, where the public arsenal and weapons factory were located, so this may have been when they met (*Jefferson's Memorandum Books*, 1: 494).

Restless after the war, Brooke studied history and medicine before settling on a career in law. He obtained his law license in 1788 and started a practice but turned to politics the following decade, being elected to the House of Delegates in 1794 and the senate of Virginia in 1800. When the Virginia Senate unanimously elected him its speaker two years later, Jefferson sent Brooke a copy of *A Manual of Parliamentary Practice* (1801), the handbook of parliamentary procedure he had compiled for the use of the U.S. Senate. The Virginia Senate was one of many legislative bodies across the United States and, indeed, around the world that adopted Jefferson's *Manual*.

Brooke appreciated President Jefferson's opinion about Mary Champe Carter, the woman Brooke would marry on 14 February 1804. That same year Brooke became a judge of the General Court of Virginia and, in 1811, the Virginia Court of Appeals. Twenty years later, when the court was renamed the Supreme Court of Appeals, Judge Brooke was still serving on its bench, which he continued to do until his death twenty years after that.

As a veteran officer of the Revolutionary War, Brooke was active in the Society of the Cincinnati, serving as the vice president of the Cincinnati Society of Virginia. In 1807, the Virginia Society resolved that it would eventually present its funds to Washington Academy (later, Washington and Lee University) provided it maintain a military school at its campus in Lexington, Virginia. Unsure whether Washington Academy could meet this condition, Thomas

Jefferson and Joseph C. Cabell, his aide-de-camp in the financial planning for the University of Virginia or, as it was called in the planning stages, Central College, thought they might secure the funds. They approached Brooke, who promised to do what he could. In an 8 December 1817 letter to Jefferson, Cabell remarked, "Judge Brooke is very friendly to our cause" (*Early History of the University of Virginia*, 87).

HAVING BEEN SET ON SHORE on the north side of the river, when we arrived in Richmond, I was ordered to take the command of the Magazine and Laboratory at Westham, seven miles above that place. [. . .]

In a few days after I took the command of the Magazine, I saw Mr. Jefferson, then Governor of the State, for the first time. He came to Westham with one of his council, Mr. Blair, whom I had known before, and who informed me they wanted to go into the Magazine. I replied they could not, on which they introduced me to Mr. Jefferson as the Governor. I turned out the guard, he was saluted, and permitted to go in. They were looking for flints for the Army of the South, and of the North, and found an abundant supply. [. . .]

The shock I received on the death of my wife, I cannot well describe; but my father had left me a legacy better than property, his fine alacrity of spirits (God bless him), which have never forsaken me; and in the summer afterwards, I was advised to go to the Virginia Springs, and began to look out for another wife, to supply the place to my children of their mother. While at the Warm Springs, with Mr. Giles and some others, a carriage arrived with ladies; there is something in destiny, for as soon as I took hold of the hand of Mary Champe Carter (though I had seen her before and admired her very much), I felt that she would amply supply the place of my lost wife. I began my attentions to her from that moment. In person and in face she was very beautiful. Mr. Jefferson said of her, "She is the most beautiful woman I have ever seen, either in France or in this country." [. . .]

I knew Mr. Jefferson very well. The first time I saw him was at the Magazine, at Westham, above Richmond, as I have mentioned before. I was afterwards often at Monticello, and saw much of him there; and while he was President of the United States. He was a man of easy and ingratiating manners: he was very partial to me, and I corresponded with him while I was Vice-President, of the Society of Cincinnati: he wished the funds of that Society to be appropriated to his Central College, near Charlottesville; and on one occasion I obtained an order for a meeting of the Society, to that effect; but in my absence the order was rescinded, and the funds appropriated to the Washington College, at Lexington, to which Gen. Washington had given his shares in the James River Company, which the State had presented him with. Mr. Jefferson never would discuss any proposition if you differed with him, for he said he thought discussion rather rivetted opinions than changed them. When I was elected Speaker of the Senate of Virginia, he sent me his parliamentary manual, with a very flattering note wafered in it, which is now in the possession of my son Robert. Of Mr. Madison, I personally did not know as much; his manners were not so fine or insinuating as Mr. Jefferson's; he was devoted to Mr. Jefferson but differed with him in some respects; he never shunned discussion, but courted it — told many excellent anecdotes of times past — and was among the purest and ablest statesmen we ever had.

From Francis T. Brooke, "A Narrative of My Life for My Family," in *Some Prominent Virginia Families,* ed. Louise Pecquet du Bellet, 4 vols. (Lynchburg: J. P. Bell, 1907), 2: 346, 360–361, 366. The narrative was first published privately for family members only.

[The Last Days of Thomas Jefferson] (1852)

ROBLEY DUNGLISON

By the time Francis Gilmer recruited him to be a professor at the newly established University of Virginia, Dr. Robley Dunglison (1798–1869) had already established himself as one of the leading physicians in England. In 1824, he published *Commentaries on Diseases of the Stomach and Bowels of Children.* After an arduous journey, Robley and Harriet Dunglison reached Virginia in early 1825 in time for the university's first term. Dunglison taught a variety of medical subjects—anatomy, history of medicine, materia medica, pharmacy, physiology, and surgery—but the University of Virginia did not initially grant a medical degree. Dunglison also became Jefferson's personal physician during the last year of his life. Dunglison's knowledge and professionalism helped Jefferson overcome a lifelong belligerence to medical men. He was the attending physician during Jefferson's final illness, and his story of Jefferson's death constitutes one of the fullest firsthand accounts. Dunglison remained at the University of Virginia after Jefferson's death, but in 1833 he left for the University of Maryland and eventually came to the Jefferson Medical College of Philadelphia, where he served as Professor of the Institutes of Medicine and Medical Jurisprudence from 1836 to 1868 and dean of the medical faculty from 1854 to 1868. Throughout his career, he wrote numerous medical treatises and textbooks. Late in life, he wrote his autobiography, the source of the following text, which he left unpublished at the time of his death. In short, the man Jefferson hired to teach medicine went on to become one of the most distinguished professors of medicine in the United States during the nineteenth century.

OUR ARRIVAL WAS MADE KNOWN to Mr. Jefferson by his grandson; and on the following morning we were visited by Mr. Nicholas P. Trist, who had a short time before married one of Mr. Jefferson's granddaughters—Miss Virginia Randolph—and who was residing with Mr. Jefferson at Monticello. Soon afterwards, the venerable ex President presented himself and welcomed us with dignity and kindness for which he was celebrated. He was then eighty-two years old, with his intellectual powers unshaken by age; and the physical man so active, that he rode to and from Monticello and took exercise on foot with all the activity of one twenty or thirty years younger. He sympathized with us on the discomforts of our long voyage; and on the disagreeable journey we must have passed over the Virginia roads; and depicted to us the great distress he had felt lest we had been lost at sea; for he had almost given us up when my letter arrived with the joyful intelligence that we were safe. Mr. [George] Long, the Professor of Ancient Languages, and Dr. [George] Blaetterman, the Professor of Modern Languages, both of whom had been chosen in London by Mr. Gilmer had judiciously taken passage in regular packets to New York and had arrived a considerable time before us.

As it was not convenient for us to remain in Charlottesville, a distance of a mile and a half from the University by a road almost impassable for the pedestrian, and of the most wretched character for beasts of burden, we took board and lodging at one of the "hotels" of the University, as they were called, which were destined to furnish meals to the students; and remained there until our goods arrived from Richmond, which, along with the necessaries we were able to procure in Charlottesville, enabled us to occupy our own pavilion. It was not long before we were able to sleep in it; but somewhat longer before our bedsteads arrived, until which time we slept on the floor. This was the most trying period of our residence at the University of Virginia. We had not yet succeeded in procuring valuable domestics, and had to put up with those of the most inferior kind; for the better class were in employment. The market people had scarcely begun to present themselves, and it was therefore no easy matter to procure the material for subsistence; but still, everything promised well. The houses were much better finished than we had expected to find them, and would have been far more commodious, had Mr. Jefferson consulted his excellent and competent daughter — Mrs. Randolph — in regard to the interior arrangements, instead of planning the architectural exterior first, and leaving the interior to shift for itself. Closets would have interfered with the symmetry of the rooms or passages, and hence there were none in most of the houses; and in the one which was furnished with a closet, it was told as an anecdote of Mr. Jefferson, that not suspecting it according to his general arrangements, he opened the door and walked into it on his way out of the pavilion.

He was fond of architecture and anxious that the Rotunda and the different pavilions should present specimens of the various orders; and although, from the necessity of building them of brick and wood, the effect was greatly diminished, it was, on the whole, agreeable. The heavy cornices in the interior of the rooms—of the Palladian style—were, however, anything but pleasing. Undoubtedly, too, the desire for having everything architecturally correct according to his taste, induced him in more cases than the one I have mentioned to sacrifice convenience. He could not but admit the anomaly of having windows arranged as in modern habitations, but farther than this it was difficult to induce him to go, and when I consulted him in regard to a distinct building for anatomical purposes, which he agreed to, he at the same time told me, that he must choose the position and the architectural arrangement externally, whilst all the interior arrangements should be left to me. [. . .]

Not long after my arrival at the University, Mr. Jefferson found it necessary to consult me in regard to a condition of great irritability of the bladder under which he had suffered for some time, and which inconvenienced him greatly by the frequent calls to discharge his urine. Few, perhaps, attain that advanced age without suffering more or less from disease of the urinary organs. On examining the urethra I found that the prostatic portion was affected with stricture, accompanied and apparently produced by enlargement of the prostate gland. This required the use of the bougie [a thin flexible surgical instrument made of waxed linen, india rubber, or metal to insert into the orifices of the body for the purpose of dilation], which he soon learned to pass himself; one of the smallest size being inserted at first with difficulty; but as the urethra became gradually enlarged his intervals became prolonged; and his inconvenience greatly diminished. This condition interfered, however, materially with his horseback exercise to which he had been accustomed on his excellent and gentle horse Eagle—long a favourite with his illustrious master. Mr. Jefferson was considered to have little faith in physic; and has often told me he would rather trust to the unaided, or rather uninterfered with, efforts of nature than to physicians in general. "It is not," he was wont to observe, "to physic that I object so much as physicians." Occasionally, too, he would speak jocularly especially to the unprofessional of medical practice; and on one occasion gave offense where most assuredly if the same thing had been said to me no offense would have been taken. In the presence of Dr. [Charles] Everett, afterwards private secretary to Mr. [James] Monroe, who was sensitive and somewhat cynical, and moreover not particularly partial to Mr. Jefferson, he remarked, that whenever he saw three physicans together he looked up to discover whether there was not a turkey buzzard in the neighborhood. The annoyance of the Doctor I am told was manifest. To me when it was recounted it seemed a harmless jest.

But whatever may have been Mr. Jefferson's notions of physic and physicians, it is but justice to say, that he was one of the most attentive and respectful of patients. He bore suffering inflicted upon him for remedial purposes with fortitude; and in my visits shewed me by memoranda the regularity with which he had taken the prescribed remedies at the appointed times. From the very first, indeed, he kindly gave me his entire confidence and at no time wished to have anyone associated with me. It was about this time that Mr. Short wrote to him urging that he should consult Dr. [Philip Syng] Physick in Philadelphia. His reply to Mr. [William] Short—who communicated it to my venerable friend Mr. [Peter Stephen] Du Ponceau—who mentioned it to me with great satisfaction upwards of fifteen years afterwards—was, that he had his Dr. Physick near him in whom he reposed his trust.

I generally visited him at Monticello two or three times a week and always had my seat at table on his left hand. His daughter Mrs. Randolph or one of the grandaughters took the head of the table; he himself sat near the other end, and almost always some visitor was present. The pilgrimage to Monticello was a favourite one with him who aspired to the rank of patriot and philanthropist; but it was too often undertaken for idle curiosity; and could not under such circumstances have afforded pleasure to, whilst it entailed unrequited expense on, its distinguished proprietor. More than once, indeed, the annoyance has been a subject of regretful animadversion. Monticello, like Montpelier, the seat of Mr. Madison, was some miles distant from any tavern and hence without sufficient consideration the traveler not only availed himself of the hospitality of the Ex Presidents but inflicted upon them the expense of his quadrupeds; on one occasion at Montpelier, when my wife and myself were paying a visit to Mr. and Mrs. Madison, no fewer than nine horses were entertained during the night; and in reply to some observations, which the circumstances engendered, Mr. Madison remarked, that whilst he was delighted with the society of the owners he confessed he had not as much feeling for their horses.

Sitting one evening with Mr. Jefferson on the porch at Monticello, two gigs drove up each containing a gentleman and a lady. It appeared to me to be evidently the desire of the party to be invited to stay the night. One of the gentlemen came up to the porch and saluted Mr. Jefferson, stating, that they claimed the privilege of American citizens in paying their respects to the Ex-President and inspecting Monticello. Mr. Jefferson received them with marked politeness, and told them they were at liberty to look at everything around, but as they did not receive an invitation to spend the night, they left in the dusk and returned to Charlottesville. Mr. Jefferson, on that occasion, could scarcely avoid an expression of impatience at the repeated, though complimentary, intrusions to which he was exposed.

At all times dignified and by no means easy of approach to all, he was generally communicative to those on whom he could rely; and in his own house was occasionally free in his speech even to imprudence to those of whom he did not know enough to be satisfied that an improper use might not be made of his candour. As an early example of this, I recollect a person from Rhode Island visiting the University, and being introduced to Mr. Jefferson by one of my colleagues. This person did not impress me favorably; and when I rode up to Monticello I found no better impression had been made by him on Mr. Jefferson and Mrs. Randolph. His adhesiveness was such, that he occupied the valuable time of Mr. Jefferson the whole morning, and stayed to dinner; and during their conversations Mr. Jefferson was apprehensive, that he had said something which might have been misunderstood and be incorrectly repeated. He therefore asked of me to find the gentleman, if he had not left Charlottesville, and request him to pay another visit to Monticello. He had left, however, when I returned, but I never discovered that he had abused the frankness of Mr. Jefferson. Mr. Jefferson took the opportunity of saying to me how cautious his friends ought to be in regard to the persons they introduce to him. [. . .]

In the spring of 1826, the health of Mr. Jefferson became more impaired; his nutrition fell off; and, at the approach of summer, he was troubled with diarrhea, to which he had been liable for some years; ever since—as he believed—he had resorted to the Virginia Springs—especially the White Sulphur and had freely used the waters internally and externally for a psoric eruption, which he had acquired in his journeying between Monticello and Washington, and which did not readily yield to the ordinary remedies. I had prescribed for this affection early in June, and he had improved somewhat; but on the 24th of that month, he wrote me the last note I received from him begging of me to visit him as he was not so well. This note was perhaps the last he penned. On the same day, however, he wrote an excellent letter to General [Roger] Weightman, in reply to an invitation to celebrate, in Washington, the 50th anniversary of the Declaration of Independence which he declined on the ground of indisposition. This, Professor [George] Tucker says, was probably his last letter. It has all the striking characteristics of his vigorous and unfaded intellect.

The tone of the note I received from him satisfied me of the propriety of visiting him immediately, and having mentioned the circumstance to Mr. Tucker, he proposed to accompany me. I immediately saw, that the affection was making a decided impression on his bodily powers, and, as Mr. Tucker has properly remarked in his life of the distinguished individual, was apprehensive that the attack would prove fatal. Nor did Mr. Jefferson himself indulge any other opinion. From this time his strength gradually diminished and he had to remain in bed. The evacuation became less numerous but it was manifest that his powers were failing.

At this time he was visited by Major [Henry] Lee, a well known political writer, whose feelings towards Mr. Jefferson had never been—I believe—very favorable; and whose moral character was certainly far from being without reproach. He had an interview with Mr. Jefferson, and found him so clear in intellect; and vigorous in discourse, that he expressed to me his feelings, that he would recover. I told him my anticipations were of the most gloomy kind, as I had already stated to the family; how much then ought I to have been surprised, when I saw in the *Richmond Enquirer* the particulars of Major Lee's visit, with the assertion, that I told him I thought he would recover. He did not, however, add what was nevertheless a fact—his having suggested to the family that they ought not to trust the life of such a distinguished individual wholly to the hands of a foreigner!—a sentiment which I have no doubt was more offensive to Mr. Jefferson's excellent daughter than it was to me.

Until the 2nd and 3rd of July he spoke freely of his approaching death; made all his arrangements with his grandson, Mr. Randolph, in regard to his private affairs, and expressed his anxiety for the prosperity of the University; and his confidence in the exertions in its behalf of Mr. Madison and the other visitors. He repeatedly, too, mentioned his obligations to me for my attention to him. During the last week of his existence, I remained at Monticello; and one of the last remarks he made was to me. In the course of the day and night of the 2nd of July, he was affected with stupor; with intervals of wakefulness and consciousness; but on the 3rd, the stupor became almost permanent. About seven o'clock in the evening of that day, he awoke, and seeing me standing at his bedside, exclaimed "Ah! Doctor are you still there?" in a voice, however, that was husky and indistinct. He then asked "Is it the 4th?" to which I replied "It soon will be." These were the last words I heard him utter. In Mr. [William] Wirt's eulogy of him, it is said that he clasped his hands and said "*Nunc dimittis*" ["Now lettest thou depart"]. No such expression was heard by me; and if any other person had heard it, it would certainly have been communicated to me. Until toward the middle of the day—the 4th—he remained in the same state, or nearly so; wholly unconscious to everything that was passing around him. His circulation was gradually, however, becoming more languid; and for some hours prior to dissolution, the pulse at the wrist was imperceptible. About one o'clock he ceased to exist.

From "The Autobiographical Ana of Robley Dunglison, M.D.," ed. Samuel X. Radbill, *Transactions of the American Philosophical Society,* new ser. 53 (1963): 22–23, 26–27, 32–33.

[What Jefferson Was Like as a Grandfather, *ca.* 1856]

Ellen W. Randolph Coolidge

The fourth child of Thomas and Martha Randolph, Ellen Wayles Randolph Coolidge (1796–1876) was Thomas Jefferson's favorite granddaughter. An avid reader and a good letter writer, she captured her grandfather's heart. He contributed to Ellen's intellectual interests by giving her many books, including her first copy of Shakespeare. She often accompanied him on trips to Poplar Forest, his vacation retreat in Bedford County. Her letter to biographer Henry S. Randall recounting their Poplar Forest experiences constitutes the fullest account available—but by no means the only one. Ellen's feisty sister Cornelia sometimes went along, and her letters present a much different picture. Whereas Ellen's reminiscence makes the trip to Poplar Forest a beautiful experience, Cornelia's letters, written at the time, complain of the tedium of the journey and the seediness of the roadside taverns. Cornelia's letters reveal how idealized Ellen's reminiscence is.

When Joseph Coolidge, a young Boston merchant, visited Monticello in 1824, Ellen caught his eye. They spent much time together during that visit and corresponded after he left. Joseph Coolidge returned the following year, and, on 27 May 1825, he married Ellen in the parlor of Monticello. Together they left Monticello for Boston. They decided to travel by land so Joseph could show his bride the American countryside, but they sent Ellen's things by sea. Sadly, everything she sent was lost at sea, including her library. Heartbroken by the loss, she expressed her sadness in a letter to Jefferson. As partial compensation, he sent her a portable desk—the very desk on which he had written the Declaration of Independence: not a bad replacement gift! After Ellen left Monticello, her grandfather often gazed wistfully toward her empty chair. Whenever her sisters saw him doing this, one of them would hurry and take her seat. None of them could take Ellen's place in her grandfather's heart.

Ellen W. Randolph Coolidge to Henry S. Randall, *ca.* 1856

When he returned from Washington, in 1809, I was a child, and of that period I have childish recollections. He seemed to return to private life with great satisfaction. At last he was his own master and could, he hoped, dispose of his time as he pleased, and indulge his love of country life. You know how greatly he preferred it to town life. You recollect as far back as his *Notes on Virginia,* he says: "Those who labor in the earth are the chosen people of God." With regard to the tastes and wishes which he carried with him into the country, his love of reading alone would have made leisure and retirement delightful to him. Books were at all times his chosen companions, and his acquaintance with many languages gave him great power of selection. He read Homer, Virgil, Dante, Corneille, Cervantes, as he read Shakspeare and Milton. In his youth he had loved poetry, but by the time I was old enough to observe, he had lost his taste for it, except for Homer and the great Athenian tragics, which he continued to the last to enjoy. He went over the works of Eschylus, Sophocles and Euripides, not very long before I left him. Of history he was very fond, and this he studied in all languages, though always, I think, preferring the ancients. In fact, he derived more pleasure from his acquaintance with Greek and Latin than from any other resource of literature, and I have often heard him express his gratitude to his father for causing him to receive a classical education. I saw him more frequently with a volume of the classics in his hand than with any other book. Still he read new publications as they came out, never missed the new number of a review, especially of the Edinburgh, and kept himself acquainted with what was being done, said, or thought in the world from which he had retired.

He loved farming and gardening, the fields, the orchards, and his asparagus beds. Every day he rode through his plantation and walked in his garden. In the cultivation of the last he took great pleasure. Of flowers, too, he was very fond. One of my early recollections is of the attention which he paid to his flower-beds. He kept up a correspondence with persons in the large cities, particularly, I think, in Philadelphia, for the purpose of receiving supplies of roots and seeds both for his kitchen and flower garden. I remember well when he first returned to Monticello, how immediately he began to prepare new beds for his flowers. He had these beds laid off on the lawn, under the windows, and many a time I have run after him when he went out to direct the work, accompanied by one of his gardeners, generally Wormley, armed with spade and hoe, whilst he himself carried the measuring-line. I was too young to aid him, except in a small way, but my sister, Mrs. [Anne C. Randolph] Bankhead, then a young and beautiful woman, . . . was his active and useful assistant. I remember the planting of the first hyacinths and tulips, and their subsequent growth. The roots arrived, labelled each one with a fancy name. There was Marcus Aurelius, and the King of the Gold Mine, the Roman Empress, and the Queen of the Amazons, Psyche, the God of Love, etc., etc., etc. Eagerly, and with childish delight, I studied this brilliant nomenclature, and wondered what strange and surprisingly beautiful creations I should see rising from the ground when spring returned, and these precious roots were committed to the earth under my grandfather's own eye, with his beautiful granddaughter Anne standing by his side, and a crowd of happy young faces, of younger grandchildren, clustering round to see the progress, and inquire anxiously the name of each separate deposit. Then, when spring returned, how eagerly we watched the first appearance of the shoots above ground. Each root was marked with its own name written on a bit of stick by its side, and what joy it was for one of us to discover the tender green breaking through the mould, and run to grandpapa to announce, that we really believed Marcus Aurelius was coming up, or the Queen of the Amazons was above ground! With how much pleasure compounded of our pleasure and his own, on the new birth, he would immediately go out to verify the fact, and praise us for our diligent watchfulness. Then, when the flowers were in bloom, and we were in ecstasies over the rich purple and crimson, or pure white, or delicate lilac, or pale yellow of the blossoms, how he would sympathize in our admiration, or discuss with my mother and elder sister new groupings and combinations and contrasts. Oh, these were happy moments for us and for him!

It was in the morning, immediately after our early breakfast, that he used to visit his flower-beds and his garden. As the day, in summer, grew warmer, he retired to his own apartments, which consisted of a bed-chamber and library opening into each other. Here he remained until about one o'clock, occupied in reading, writing, looking over papers, etc. My mother would sometimes send me with a message to him. A gentle knock, a call of "come in," and I would enter, with a mixed feeling of love and reverence, and some pride in being the bearer of a communication to one whom I approached with all the affection of a child, and something of the loyalty of a subject. Our mother educated all her children to look up to her father, as she looked up to him herself—literally looked up, as to one standing on an eminence of greatness and goodness. And it is no small proof of his real elevation, that as we grew older and better able to judge for ourselves, we were more and more confirmed in the opinions we had formed of it.

About one o'clock my grandfather rode out, and was absent perhaps two hours; when he returned to prepare for his dinner, which was about half-past three o'clock. He sat some time at table, and after dinner, returned for a while to his room, from which he emerged before sunset to walk on the terrace or the lawn, to see his grandchildren run races, or to converse with his family and friends. The evenings, after candle-light, he passed with us, till about ten o'clock. He had his own chair and his own candle a little apart from the rest, where he sat reading, if there were no guests to require his attention, but often laying his book on his little round table or his knee, whilst he talked with my mother, the elder members of the family, or any child old enough to make one of the family-party.

Ellen W. Randolph Coolidge to Henry S. Randall, 18 February 1856

The house at Poplar Forest was very pretty and pleasant. It was of brick, one story in front, and, owing to the falling of the ground, two in the rear. It was an exact octagon, with a centre-hall twenty feet square, lighted from above. This was a beautiful room, and served as a dining-room. Round it were grouped a bright drawing-room looking south, my grandfather's own chamber, three other bedrooms, and a pantry. A terrace extended from one side of the house; there was a portico in front connected by a vestibule with the centre room, and in the rear a verandah, on which the drawing-room opened, with its windows to the floor. . . .

Mr. Jefferson, from the time of his return home in 1809, was in the habit of visiting this Bedford plantation, but it was some years before the house was ready for the reception of his family. It was furnished in the simplest manner, but had a very tasty air; there was nothing common or second-rate about any part of the establishment, although there was no appearance of expense. As soon as the house was habitable, my grandfather began to take the ladies of his family, generally two at a time, with him, whenever he went. His first visit of a fortnight or three weeks was in the spring—the second, of about six weeks, in early or late autumn. We have staid as much as two months at a time. My mother went occasionally—not very often—for she had too much to do at home. I . . . generally accompanied him with one of my younger sisters. Mr. Jefferson greatly enjoyed these visits. The crowd at Monticello of friends and strangers, of stationary or ever-varying guests, the coming and going, the incessant calls upon his own time and attention, the want of leisure that such a state of things entailed as a necessary consequence, the bustle and hurry of an almost perpetual round of company, wearied and harassed him in the end, whatever pleasure he may have taken, and it was sometimes great, in the society and conversation of his guests. At Poplar Forest he found in a pleasant home, rest, leisure, power to carry on his favorite pursuits—to think, to study, to read—whilst the presence of part of his family took away all character of solitude from his retreat. His young granddaughters were there to enliven it for him, to make his tea, preside over his dinner table, accompany him in his walks, in his occasional drives, and be with him at the time he most enjoyed society, from tea till bed time. The weather was generally fine (the autumn climate of this part of Virginia is delightful, and even the spring is pleasant), the neighbors, who were to a man exceedingly attached to him, were very friendly, without being oppressive in their attentions. There were some excellent people among those Bedford neighbors of ours, and something touching in their affection for their old friend, whose arrival they watched for with pleasant anticipation, and hailed with a sort of loyal satisfaction. It was no sooner known in the neighborhood that Mr. Jefferson had arrived, than our neighbors hastened to help our housekeeping with all kinds of fruit, vegetables, poultry, game (I remember once a quarter of a bear's cub) the product of rich farms and an abundant country.

By and by the gentlemen came dropping in—the ladies soon followed—we were invited out to dine, and the neighbors came to dine with us—but not often enough to consume much time, or interrupt our home occupations. I remember among these neighbors a certain "Parson" Clay, as he was called, who must have been an Episcopal clergyman before the Revolution, to whose four sons my grandfather used to lend books, and who astonished me with their names of Cyrus, Odin, Julius and Paul.

My grandfather was very happy during these sojourns in a comparatively simple and secluded district—far from noise and news—of both of which he got too much at Monticello; and we, his grand-daughters, were very happy too. It was a pleasant change for us, a variety in life and manners.

We saw, too, more of our dear grandfather at those times than at any other. He was most desirous that we should find congenial occupations, and we had books, drawing materials, embroidery, and never felt time heavy on our hands. He interested himself in all we did, thought, or read. He would talk to us about his own youth and early friends, and tell us stories of former days. He seemed really to take as much pleasure in these conversations with us, as if we had been older and wiser people. Such was the influence of his affectionate, cheerful temper, that his grandchildren were as much at their ease with him, as if they had not loved and honored and revered him more than any other earthly being. I . . . not only listened with intense interest to all he said, but answered with perfect freedom, told my own opinions and impressions, gave him my own views of things, asked questions, made remarks, and, in short, felt as free and as happy as if I had been with companions of my own age. My grandfather missed my mother of course. Her company had become very necessary to him, but her absence seemed the only drawback on his unalloyed satisfaction during these short and highly prized intervals of rest and leisure.

Our days at Poplar Forest were cheerful and uneventful. We met in the morning for an early breakfast, which, like all his other meals, he took leisurely. Whilst sipping his coffee or tea he talked with us, and if there was anything unusual to be done, arranged our plans for the day. The forenoon, whilst we followed our own desires, he passed in the drawing room with his books. With the exception of an occasional visitor, he was seldom interrupted until the hour of his ride. We dined about three, and as he liked to sit over his wine (he never took more than three glasses, and these after, and not during dinner), I always remained at table till he rose. His conversation was at this time particularly pleasant—easy, flowing, and full of anecdote. After dinner he again retired for some hours, and later in the afternoon walked with us on the terrace, conversing in the same delightful manner, being sometimes animated, and sometimes earnest. We did not leave him again till bed-time, but gave him his tea, and brought out our books or work. He would take his book from which he would occasionally look up to make a remark, to question us about what we were reading, or perhaps to read aloud to us from his own book, some passage which had struck him, and of which he wished to give us the benefit. About ten o'clock he rose to go, when we kissed him with warm, loving, grateful hearts, and went to our rest blessing God for such a friend.

Mr. Jefferson had decidedly one of the evenest and most cheerful tempers I ever knew. He enjoyed a jest, provided it were to give pain to no one, and we were always glad to have any pleasant little anecdote for him—when he would laugh as cheerily as we could do ourselves, and enter into the spirit of the thing with as much gaiety.

It was pleasant to see him in company with the country gentlemen of the neighborhood, they treated him with so much affectionate and respectful frankness—were so much at their ease with him, whilst they held him in such high honor. Their wives too were as happy as queens to receive him, and when he called or dined with them, were brimful of satisfaction and hospitable devotion. This frank and free homage, paid by independent people, who had nothing to gain, to one whose public character had merited their approbation, and whose private virtues they loved and revered, was equally honorable to those who rendered and him who received it.

Our journeys to and from Bedford, were almost always pleasant. The weather at the season of our visit was good of course, though we were once or twice caught by an early winter. The roads were not bad for country roads. My grandfather travelled in his own carriage, with his own horses, his faithful Burwell on horseback by his side. It took us nearly three days to make the hundred miles. We always stopped at the same simple country inns, where the country-people were as much pleased to see the "Squire," as they always called Mr. Jefferson, as they could have been to meet their own best friends. They set out for him the best they had, gave him the nicest room, and seemed to hail his passage as an event most interesting to themselves. These were pleasant times, but I have dwelt on them long enough.

From Henry S. Randall, *The Life of Thomas Jefferson*, 3 vols. (New York: Derby and Jackson, 1858), 3: 346–347, 342–344.

[The Life and Death of Thomas Jefferson, *ca.* 1857]

THOMAS JEFFERSON RANDOLPH

Born at Monticello and named for his illustrious grandfather, Thomas Jefferson Randolph (1792–1875) traveled to Philadelphia in his teens, where he received a good education in anatomy, botany, and natural history. Randolph also demonstrated an aptitude for financial matters and, in his early twenties, took over the management of his grandfather's affairs. After their marriage on 6 March 1815, he and his wife, Jane Hollins Nicholas, lived at Monticello, but they moved to nearby Tufton in 1817, where they raised a large family. In addition to assuming reponsibility for his grandfather's financial affairs, he also oversaw the finances of his father, Thomas Mann Randolph, and his father-in-law, Wilson Cary Nicholas. In short, Thomas Jefferson Randolph faced a considerable challenge. As executor of his grandfather's estate, he had to cope with enormous debts, which he eventually paid, though he had to sell Monticello to do so. A happier aspect of his role as executor was overseeing his grandfather's papers. Randolph sifted through them and published the first collected edition of Jefferson's writings, *Memoir, Correspondence, and Miscellanies, from the Papers of Thomas Jefferson* (1829), which was reprinted in London that same year under a slightly different title and in Boston the following year. Randolph's edition of his grandfather's papers strongly shaped nineteenth-century attitudes toward Jefferson.

Thomas Jefferson Randolph to Henry S. Randall, *ca.* 1857

Dear Sir:
In compliance with your request, I have committed to paper my reminiscences of Mr. Jefferson, as they, still green and fresh in my memory, have occurred to me. I was thirty-four years old when he died. My mother was his eldest and, for the last twenty-two years of his life, his only child; she lived with him from her birth to his death, except in his absence on public service, at Philadelphia and Washington; having lost her mother at ten years old, she was his inseparable companion until her marriage; he had sought to supply her loss with all the watchful solicitude of a mother's ten-

derness; her children were to him as the younger members of his family, having lived with him from their infancy. I being fifteen years older than my brothers, the duty devolved on me to place myself in the breach of his pecuniary embarrassments, and shield him, living and dead, from their practical effects. He never failed to comply with a pecuniary engagement; his creditors were all paid. It was unimportant to them whether they were paid from the proceeds of the sales of his property, or the sacrifices and toil of his descendants. I was more intimate with him than with any man I have ever known; his character invited such intimacy — soft and feminine in his affections to his family, he entered into and sympathized with all their feelings, winning them to paths of virtue by the soothing gentleness of his manner. His private apartments were open to me at all times, I saw him under all circumstances. While he lived, and since, I have reviewed with severe scrutiny those interviews, and I must say, that I never heard from him the expression of one thought, feeling or sentiment inconsistent with the highest moral standard, or the purest Christian charity in its most enlarged sense. His moral character was of the highest order, founded upon the purest and sternest models of antiquity, softened, chastened and developed by the influences of the all-pervading benevolence of the doctrines of Christ — which he had intensely and admiringly studied. As a proof of this, he left two codifications of the morals of Jesus — one for himself, and another for the Indians; the first of which I now possess, viz., a blank volume, red morocco, gilt, lettered on the back "The Morals of Jesus" — into which he pasted extracts in Greek, Latin, French and English, taken textually from the four Gospels, and so arranged that he could run his eye over the readings of the same verse in four languages. The boldness and self-confidence of his mind was the best guaranty of his truthfulness — he never uttered an untruth himself, or used duplicity, and he contemned it in others — no end, with him, could sanctify falsehood.

In his contemplative moments, his mind turned to religion, which he studied thoroughly. He had seen and read much of the abuses and perversions of Christianity; he abhorred those abuses and their authors, and denounced them without reserve. He was regular in his attendance on church, taking his prayerbook with him. He drew the plan of the Episcopal Church in Charlottesville — was one of the largest contributors to its erection, and contributed regularly to the support of its minister. I paid, after his death, his subscription of $200 to the erection of the Presbyterian church in the same village. A gentleman of some distinction calling on him, and expressing his disbelief in the truths of the Bible, his reply was, "Then, sir, you have studied it to little purpose." He was guilty of no profanity himself, and did not tolerate it in others—he detested impiety, and his favorite quotation for his young friends as a basis for their morals, was the xv. psalm of David. He did not permit cards in his house—he knew no game with them. Of his peculiar religious opinions, his family know no more than the world. If asked by one of them, his opinion on any religious subject, his uniform reply was, that it was a subject each was bound to study assiduously for himself, unbiased by the opinions of others—it was a matter solely of conscience; after thorough investigation, they were responsible for the righteousness, but not the rightfulness of their opinions; that the expression of his opinion might influence theirs, and he would not give it! He held it to be an invasion of the freedom of religious opinion, to attempt to subject the opinions of any man to the ordeal of public judgment; he would not submit to it in his own case, nor sanction it in another—he considered that religious opinions should be judged by the fruits they produced—if they produced good men, they must be good. My mother was educated in a convent—the best school of the day—in Paris; she took up a girlish desire to join the Catholic church, and wrote to her father to ask his permission. He called for her, took her home, and placed her in the gay society of the court of Louis XVI., where all such thoughts quickly vanished. His calling for her was the only intimation she ever had of the receipt of her letter, the subject was never alluded to by him.

His codification of the Morals of Jesus was not known to his family before his death, and they learnt from a letter addressed to a friend, that he was in the habit of reading nightly from it, before going to bed. His report as Rector of the Board of Visitors of the University of Virginia, to the Legislature, places in its proper view, his sense of the importance of religious instruction. [. . .]

His family, by whom he was surrounded, and who saw him in all the unguarded privacy of private life, believed him to be the purest of men. His precepts were those of truth and virtue. "Be just, be true, love your neighbor as yourself, and your country more than yourself," were among his favorite maxims, and they recognized in him a truthful exemplar of the precepts he taught. He said he had left the government of his country "with hands as clean as they were empty." His family circle knew that with calm serenity he had left the theatre of life, with a conscience as unsullied as his life had been just and upright. The beauty of his character was exhibited in the bosom of his family, where he delighted to indulge in all the fervor and delicacy of feminine feeling. Upon his death, there were found carefully preserved in a little sanctum sanctorum, locks of hair and other memorials of his wife and the children he had lost, with words of fond endearment written in his own hand upon the envelopes of the little mementoes. Before he lost his taste for the violin, in winter evenings, he would play on it, having his grandchildren dancing around him. In summer he would station them for their little races on the lawn — give the signal for the start — be the arbiter of the contest, and award the prizes.

His manner was dignified, reserved with strangers, but frank and cordial with his friends; his conversation cheerful, often sportive, and illustrated by anecdotes. He spoke only of the good qualities of men, which induced the belief that he knew little of them, but no one knew them better. I had formed this opinion, and on hearing him speak very favorably of men with defects known to myself, stated them to him, when he asked if I supposed he had not observed them, adding others not noted by me, and evincing much more accurate knowledge of the individual character than I possessed, observing, "My habit is to speak only of men's good qualities." When he believed that either men or measures were adverse to Republican institutions, he spoke of them with open and unqualified condemnation.

Standing himself on an elevated position, from his talents, education, fortune and political station, he was emphatically the friend of the working-man. On passing the home of a neighbor (Mr. Jesse Lewis), a blacksmith, remarkable for his probity, his integrity and his industry, and too wise, when past the meridian of life, to be ashamed to work at the trade that had made his fortune, he often remarked of him, "it is such men as that who constitute the wealth of a nation, not millionaires."

He never indulged in controversial conversation, because it often excited unpleasant feeling, and illustrated its inutility by the anecdote of two men who sat down candidly to discuss a subject, and each converted the other. His maxim was, that every man had a right to his own opinion on all subjects, and others were bound to respect that right; hence, in conversation, if any one expressed a decided opinion differing from his own, he made no reply, but changed the subject; he believed men could always find subjects enough to converse on, in which they agreed in opinion, omitting those upon which they differed; unreserved and candid himself, he was a listener, encouraging others to converse. His tact in the management of men was great; he inquiringly followed out adverse opinions to their results, leaving it to their friends to note the error into which it led them, taking up their doubts as important suggestions, never permitting a person to place himself upon the defensive, or if he did, changing the subject, so as not to fix him in a wrong opinion by controverting it. With men of fertile and ingenious minds, fond of suggesting objections to propositions stated, he would sometimes suggest the opposite of the conclusion to which he desired them to come, then assent to the force of their objections, and thus lead them to convert themselves. If information was sought, he gave it freely; if doubts were suggested, he explained them without reserve, never objecting to the scrutiny or canvass of his own opinions. As a public man, his friends complained that he spoke too freely, communicating more than they thought prudent. His powers of conversation were great, yet he always turned it to subjects most familiar to those with whom he conversed, whether laborer, mechanic or other; and if they displayed sound judgment and a knowledge of the subject, entered the information they gave, under appropriate heads, for reference, embodying thus a mass of facts upon the practical details of every-day life. His capacity to acquire knowledge was of the highest order; his application intense and untiring—his system and arrangement for the preservation of, and reference to the sources of his acquirements, most methodical and exact. The Hon. Littleton Waller Tazewell told me, that when a young man, his father being in the Senate, and Mr. Jefferson Vice-President, some case of impeachment coming on, he was sent with a note to Mr. Jefferson, asking some references to authorities on the subject. On the delivery of the note, he took a note-book from a drawer and instantly copied the references. On delivering them to his father, the latter observed he believed he had sent him chapter and verse for everything written on the subject. Of his voluminous correspondence, embracing upwards of forty thousand letters, written and received, and the private and public accounts of his whole life, he could in a moment lay his hand on any letter or receipt. Shortly after his death, Mr. Madison expressed to me the opinion, that Mr. Jefferson would be found to be the most learned man that had ever devoted so much time to public life. He was economical, exact, and methodical in his expenses and accounts. The account books, now in my possession, of his Maitre d'Hotel, at Paris and Washington, show the minutest details of household expenditure, and notes and figures in his own hand-writing, exhibit the closest personal inspection by himself, and a monthly analysis in a tabularized form of the expenditures in each item. His own numerous account books show the entry at the time, in his own hand, of each expenditure, however minute.

His manners were of that polished school of the Colonial Government, so remarkable in its day — under no circumstances violating any of those minor conventional observances which constitute the well-bred gentleman, courteous and considerate to all persons. On riding out with him, when a lad, we met a negro who bowed to us; he returned his bow, I did not; turning to me he asked, "Do you permit a negro to be more of a gentleman than yourself?"

There was a little emulation endeavored to be excited among the older gentlemen of the neighborhood, in their gardening; and he who had peas first, announced his success by an invitation to the others to dine with him. A wealthy neighbor, without children, and fond of horticulture, generally triumphed. Mr. Jefferson, on one occasion had them first, and when his family reminded him that it was his right to invite the company, he replied "No, say nothing about it, it will be more agreeable to our friend to think that he never fails." In his person he was neat in the extreme. In early life, his dress, equipage, and appointments were fastidiously appropriate to his rank. As he grew old, although preserving his extreme neatness, his dress was plainer, and he was more indifferent to the appearance of his equipage. When at Paris, Philadelphia, and Washington, his furniture, table, servants, equipage and the *tout ensemble* of his establishment, were deemed highly appropriate to the position he held. He was a gentleman everywhere. On entering the Presidency, he determined not to have weekly levees, like his predecessors, and so announced. His political opponents determined that he should continue the custom. On the first levee day, he rode out at his usual hour of one o'clock, returning at three, and on entering the President's house, booted, whip in hand, soiled with his ride, found himself in a crowd of ladies and gentlemen, fashionably dressed for the occasion. He greeted them with all the ease and courtesy of expected guests that he had been prepared to receive, exhibiting not the slightest indication of annoyance. They never again tried the experiment. At home, he desired to live like his neighbors, in the plain hospitality of a Virginia gentleman. It was a source of continued and deep regret to him, that the number of strangers who visited him, kept his neighbors from him; he said, "he had to exchange the society of his friends and neighbors for those whom he had never seen before, and never expected to see again."

Mr. Jefferson's hair, when young, was of a reddish cast, sandy as he advanced in years—his eye, hazel—dying in his 84th year, he had not lost a tooth, or had one defective; his skin, thin, peeling from his face on exposure to the sun, and giving it a tettered appearance; the superficial veins so weak, as upon the slightest blow, to cause extensive suffusions of blood, in early life, upon standing to write for any length of time, bursting beneath the skin: it, however, gave him no inconvenience. His countenance was mild and benignant, and attractive to strangers. While President, returning on horseback from court, with company whom he had invited to dinner, and who were, all but one or two, riding ahead of him, on reaching a stream over which there was no bridge, a man asked him to take him up behind and carry him over. The gentlemen in the rear coming up just as Mr. Jefferson had put him down and rode on, asked the man how it happened that he had permitted the others to pass without asking them? He replied, "From their looks I did not like to ask them—the old gentleman looked as if he would do it, and I asked him." He was very much surprised to hear that he had ridden behind the President of the United States. Mr. Jefferson's stature was commanding, six feet two and a half inches in height, well formed, indicating strength, activity, and robust health; his carriage, erect; step firm and elastic, which he preserved to his death; his temper, naturally strong, under perfect control—his courage, cool and impassive—no one ever knew him exhibit trepidation—his moral courage of the highest order—his will, firm and inflexible—it was remarked of him that he never abandoned a plan, a principle, or a friend. A bold and fearless rider, you saw at a glance, from his easy and confident seat, that he was master of his horse, which was usually the fine blood horse of Virginia. The only impatience of temper he ever exhibited, was with his horse, which he subdued to his will by a fearless application of the whip, on the slightest manifestation of restiveness. He retained to the last his fondness for riding on horseback; he rode within three weeks of his death, when from disease, debility and age, he mounted with difficulty. He rode with confidence, and never permitted a servant to accompany him; he was fond of solitary rides and musing, and said that the presence of a servant annoyed him. He held in little esteem the education that made men ignorant and helpless as to the common necessities of life; and he exemplified it by an incident which occurred to a young gentleman returned from Europe, where be had been educated. On riding out with his companions, the strap of his girth broke, at the hole of the buckle; and they, perceiving it an accident easily remedied, rode on and left him. A plain man coming up and seeing that his horse had made a circular path in the road in his impatience to get on, asked if he could aid him? "Oh, sir," replied the young man, "if you could only assist me to get it up to the next hole." "Suppose you let it out a hole or two on the other side," said the man.

His habits were regular and systematic. He was a miser of his time, rose always at dawn, wrote and read until breakfast, breakfasted early, and dined from three to four — after breakfast read for half an hour in his public rooms or portico, in summer — visited his garden and workshops — returned to his writing and reading till one, when he rode on horseback to three or half past — dined, and gave the evening to his family and company — retired at nine, and to bed from ten to eleven. He said in his last illness, that the sun had not caught him in bed for fifty years. He always made his own fire. He drank water but once a day, a single glass, when he returned from his ride. He ate heartily, and much vegetable food, preferring French cookery, because it made the meats more tender. He never drank ardent spirits or strong wines — such was his aversion to ardent spirits that when, in his last illness, his physician desired him to use brandy as an astringent, he could not induce him to take it strong enough.

He inherited from his father 1,900 acres of land, and some negroes. He commenced the practice of the law soon after he came of age. When he married, in his 29th year, he had increased his estate to 5,000 acres, all paid for. His accounts show a receipt of $3,000 a year from his practice at the bar, and $2,000 from his farms, a large income at that day. The death of his father-in-law ensuing soon after his marriage, he acquired a large addition to his estate, but the share of debt which fell to him was £8,749 12*s*. He sold property immediately to pay it. The payments for this property were made in paper money, which he deposited in the loan office, and received it back again at a depreciation out to him, of one for forty. He sold again in 1785 and 1792, to discharge the debt, with its accumulated interest. This swept nearly half of his estate. He was absent from his estate, as Minister to France, Secretary of State, Vice-President and President from 1782 to 1809 — 27 years, with the exception of four years, from 1793 to 1797, which he devoted to his farms. He returned in his old age to be hunted down by the reputation he had won in the service of his country. Twelve years before his death, he remarked to me, in conversation, that if he lived long enough he would beggar his family—that the number of persons he was compelled to entertain would devour his estate; many bringing letters from his ancient friends, and all coming with respectful feelings, he could not shut his door in their faces. A heavy loss by indorsing for a friend in 1819, and the extreme depression in the value of property, when it became necessary to bring his into market, completed the catastrophe, and verified his anticipations.

Mr. Jefferson had suffered for several years before his death, from a diarrhoea, which he concealed from his family, lest it might give them uneasiness. Not aware of it, I was surprised, in conversation with him, in March, 1826, to hear him in speaking of an event likely to occur about midsummer, say doubtingly, that he *might* live to that time. About the middle of June, hearing that he had sent for his physician, Dr. Dunglison, of the University of Virginia, I went immediately to see him, and found him out in his public rooms. Before leaving the house, he sent a servant to me, to come to his room, whereupon he handed me a paper, which he desired me to examine, remarking, "don't delay, there is no time to be lost." He gradually declined, but would only have his servants sleeping near him: being disturbed only at nine, twelve, and four o'clock in the night, he needed little nursing. Becoming uneasy about him, I entered his room, unobserved, to pass the night. Coming round inadvertently to assist him, he chided me, saying that being actively employed all day, I needed repose. On my replying that it was more agreeable to me to be with him, he acquiesced, and I did not leave him again. A day or two after, my brother-in-law (Mr. Trist) was admitted. His servants, ourselves, and the Doctor became his sole nurses. My mother sat with him during the day, but he would not permit her to sit up at night. His family had to decline for him numerous tenders of service, from kind and affectionate friends and neighbors, fearing and seeing that it would excite him to conversation injurious to him in his weak condition. He suffered no pain, but gradually sunk from debility. His mind was always clear—it never wandered. He conversed freely, and gave directions as to his private affairs. His manner was that of a person going on a necessary journey—evincing neither satisfaction nor regret. He remarked upon the tendency of his mind to recur back to the scenes of the Revolution. Many incidents he would relate, in his usual cheerful manner, insensibly diverting my mind from his dying condition, he remarked that the curtains of his bed had been purchased from the first cargo that arrived after the peace of 1782. Upon my expressing the opinion, on one occasion, that he was somewhat better, he turned to me, and said, "do not imagine for a moment that I feel the smallest solicitude about the result; I am like an old watch, with a pinion worn out here, and a wheel there, until it can go no longer." On another occasion, when he was unusually ill, he observed to the Doctor, "A few hours more, Doctor, and it will be all over." Upon being suddenly aroused from sleep, by a noise in the room, he asked if he had heard the name of Mr. [Frederick] Hatch mentioned — the minister whose church he attended. On my replying in the negative, he observed, as he turned over, "I have no objection to see him, as a kind and good neighbor." The impression made upon my mind at the moment was, that his religious opinions having been formed upon mature study and reflection, he had no doubts upon his mind, and therefore did not desire the attendance of a clergyman; I have never since doubted the correctness of the impression then taken. His parting interview with the different members of his family, was calm and composed; impressing admonitions upon them, the cardinal points of which were to pursue virtue, be true and truthful. My youngest brother, in his eighth year, seeming not to comprehend the scene, he turned to me with a smile and said, "George does not understand what all this means." He would speculate upon the person who would succeed him as Rector of the University of Virginia, and concluded that Mr. Madison would be appointed. With all the deep pathos of exalted friendship he spoke of his purity, his virtues, his wisdom, his learning, and his great abilities. The friendship of these great men was of an extraordinary character — they had been born, lived, and died within twenty-five miles of each other — they visited frequently through their whole lives. At twenty-three years old, Mr. Jefferson had been consulted on Mr. Madison's course of study — he then fifteen. Thus commenced a friendship as remarkable for its duration as it was for the fidelity and warmth of its feelings. The admiration of each for the wisdom, abilities, and purity of the other was unlimited. Their habit of reliance upon mutual counsel, equalled the sincerity of their affection, and the devotion of their esteem.

In speaking of the calumnies which his enemies had uttered against his public and private character, with such unmitigated and untiring bitterness, he said, that he had not considered them as abusing him; they had never known *him*. They had created an imaginary being clothed with odious attributes, to whom they had given his name; and it was against that creature of their imaginations they had levelled their anathemas.

On Monday, the third of July, his slumbers were evidently those of approaching dissolution; he slept until evening, when upon awaking he seemed to imagine it was morning, and remarked, that he had slept all night without being disturbed—"This is the fourth of July." He soon sunk again into sleep, and on being aroused at nine, to take his medicine, he remarked in a clear distinct voice, "No, Doctor, nothing more." The omission of the dose of laudanum administered every night during his illness, caused his slumbers to be disturbed and dreamy; he sat up in his sleep and went through all the forms of writing; spoke of the Committee of Safety, saying it ought to be warned. As twelve o'clock at night approached, we anxiously desired that his death should be hallowed by the Anniversary of Independence. At fifteen minutes before twelve we stood noting the minute hand of the watch, hoping a few minutes of prolonged life. At four A. M. he called the servants in attendance, with a strong and clear voice, perfectly conscious of his wants. He did not speak again. About ten he fixed his eyes intently upon me, indicating some want, which most painfully, I could not understand, until his attached servant, Burwell, observed that his head was not so much elevated as he usually desired it, for his habit was to lie with it very much elevated. Upon restoring it to its usual position, he seemed satisfied. About eleven, again fixing his eyes upon me, and moving his lips, I applied a wet sponge to his mouth, which he sucked and appeared to relish—this was the last evidence he gave of consciousness. He ceased to breathe, without a struggle, fifty minutes past meridian—July 4th, 1826. I closed his eyes with my own hands. He was at all times, during his illness, perfectly assured of his approaching end, his mind ever clear, and at no moment did he evince the least solicitude about the result; he was as calm and composed as when in health. He died a pure and good man. It is for others to speak of his greatness. He desired that his interment should be private, without parade, and our wish was to comply with his request, and no notice of the hour of interment, or invitations were issued. His body was borne privately from his dwelling, by his family and servants, but his neighbors and friends anxious to pay the last tribute of respect and affection to one whom they had loved and honored, waited for it in crowds at the grave.

From Henry S. Randall, *The Life of Thomas Jefferson,* 3 vols. (New York: Derby and Jackson, 1858), 3: 671–676, 543–544.

[Daily Life at Monticello] (1862)

EDMUND BACON

Edmund Bacon (1785–1866), a native of Albemarle County, was the overseer at Monticello from 1806 until 1822. The following year Bacon and his family moved to Kentucky, where he farmed successfully until his death four decades later. In the early 1860s, the Reverend Hamilton W. Pierson, president of Cumberland College, looked up Bacon and solicited his memories of Jefferson, which he published as *Jefferson at Monticello* (1862). Contemporary readers quickly recognized the value of the information it contained. Henry Flagg French concluded, "On the whole, we find our favorable impression of Jefferson, as a large-hearted, progressive, considerate, unselfish, kindly natured man, confirmed by this volume. It has nothing to do with his opinions, political or religious, but gives us an agreeable sketch of the philosopher and statesman at home, most beloved and revered by those who knew him best. There is no position where a great man appears more truly noble, than at the head of his family, on his own homestead" (*New England Farmer* 14 [1862]: 230).

MR. JEFFERSON WAS six feet two and a half inches high, well proportioned, and straight as a gunbarrel. He was like a fine horse—he had no surplus flesh. He had an iron constitution, and was very strong. He had a machine for measuring strength. There were very few men that I have seen try it, that were as strong in the arms as his son-in-law, Col. Thomas Mann Randolph; but Mr. Jefferson was stronger than he. He always enjoyed the best of health. I don't think he was ever really sick, until his last sickness. His skin was very clear and pure—just like he was in principle. He had blue eyes. His countenance was always mild and pleasant. You never saw it ruffled. No odds what happened, it always maintained the same expression. When I was sometimes very much fretted and disturbed, his countenance was perfectly unmoved. I remember one case in particular. We had about eleven thousand bushels of wheat in the mill, and coopers and every thing else employed. There was a big freshet—the first after the dam was finished. It was raining powerfully. I got up early in the morning, and went up to the dam. While I stood there, it began to break, and I stood and saw the freshet sweep it all away. I never felt worse. I did not know what we should do. I went up to see Mr. Jefferson. He had just come from breakfast. "Well, sir," said he, "have you heard from the river?" I said, "Yes, sir; I have just come from there with very bad news. The milldam is all swept away." "Well, sir," said he, just as calm and quiet as though nothing had happened, "we can't make a new dam this summer, but we will get Lewis' ferry-boat, with our own, and get the hands from all the quarters, and boat in rock enough in place of the dam, to answer for the present and next summer. I will send to Baltimore and get ship-bolts, and we will make a dam that the freshet can't wash away." He then went on and explained to me in detail just how he would have the dam built. We repaired the dam as he suggested, and the next summer we made a new dam, that I reckon must be there yet.

Mr. Jefferson was always an early riser—arose at daybreak, or before. The sun never found him in bed. I used sometimes to think, when I went up there *very* early in the morning, that I would find him in bed; but there he would be before me, walking on the terrace.

He never had a servant make a fire in his room in the morning, or at any other time, when he was at home. He always had a box filled with nice dry wood in his room, and when he wanted fire he would open it and put on the wood. He would always have a good many ashes in his fireplace, and when he went out he would cover up his fire very carefully, and when he came back he would uncover the coals and make on a fire for himself.

He did not use tobacco in any form. He never used a profane word or any thing like it. He never played cards. I never saw a card in the house at Monticello, and I had particular orders from him to suppress card-playing among the negroes, who, you know, are generally very fond of it. I never saw any dancing in his house, and if there had been any there during the twenty years I was with him I should certainly have known it. He was never a great eater, but what he did eat he wanted to be very choice. He never eat much hog-meat. He often told me, as I was giving out meat for the servants, that what I gave one of them for a week would be more than he would use in six months. When he was coming home from Washington I generally knew it, and got ready for him, and waited at the house to give him the keys. After saying, "How are all?" and talking awhile, he would say, "What have you got that is good?" I knew mighty well what suited him. He was especially fond of Guinea fowls; and for meat he preferred good beef, mutton, and lambs. Those broadtailed sheep I told you about made the finest mutton I ever saw. Meriwether Lewis' mother made very nice hams, and every year I used to get a few from her for his special use. He was very fond of vegetables and fruit, and raised every variety of them. He was very ingenious. He invented a plough that was considered a great improvement on any that had ever been used. He got a great many premiums and medals for it. He planned his own carriage, buildings, garden, fences, and a good many other things. He was nearly always busy upon some plan or model.

Every day, just as regularly as the day came, unless the weather was very bad, he would have his horse brought out and take his ride. The boy who took care of his horse knew what time he started, and would bring him out for him, and hitch him in his place. He generally started about nine o'clock. He was an uncommonly fine rider—sat easily upon his horse, and always had him in the most perfect control. After he returned from Washington he generally rode Brimmer or Tecumseh until I bought Eagle for him of Capt. John Graves, of Louisa Co., just before I left him.

He was always very neat in his dress, wore short breeches and bright shoe buckles. When he rode on horseback he had a pair of overalls that he always put on.

Mr. Jefferson never debarred himself from hearing any preacher that came along. There was a Mr. Hiter, a Baptist preacher, that used to preach occasionally at the Charlottesville Court House. He had no regular church, but was a kind of missionary—rode all over the country and preached. He wasn't much of a preacher, was uneducated, but he was a good man. Everybody had confidence in him, and they went to hear him on that account. Mr. Jefferson's nephews Peter Carr, Sam. Carr, and Dabney Carr thought a great deal of him. I have often heard them talk about him. Mr. Jefferson nearly always went to hear him when he came around. I remember his being there one day in particular. His servant came with him and brought a seat—a kind of camp stool, upon which he sat. After Mr. Jefferson got old and feeble, a servant used to go with him over the plantation, and carry that stool, so that he could sit down while he was waiting and attending to any kind of work that was going on. After the sermon there was a proposition to pass round the hat and raise money to buy the preacher a horse. Mr. Jefferson did not wait for the hat. I saw him unbutton his overalls, and get his hand into his pocket, and take out a handful of silver, I don't know how much. He then walked across the Court House to Mr. Hiter, and gave it into his hand. He bowed very politely to Mr. Jefferson, and seemed to be very much pleased.

Mr. Jefferson was very liberal and kind to the poor. When he would come from Washington, the poor people all about the country would find it out immediately, and would come in crowds to Monticello to beg him. He would give them notes to me, directing me what to give them. I knew them all a great deal better than he did. Many of them I knew were not worthy—were just lazy, good-for-nothing people, and I would not give them any thing. When I saw Mr. Jefferson I told him who they were, and that he ought not to encourage them in their laziness. He told me that when they came to him and told him their pitiful tales, he could not refuse them, and he did not know what to do. I told him to send them to me. He did so, but they never would come. They knew what to expect.

In, I think, the year 1816, there was a very severe frost, and the corn was almost destroyed. It was so badly injured that it would hardly make bread, and it was thought that the stock was injured by eating it. There was a neighborhood at the base of the Blue Ridge where the frost did not injure the corn. They had a good crop, and the people were obliged to give them just what they were disposed to ask for it. I went up there and bought thirty barrels for Mr. Jefferson of a Mr. Massey—gave him ten dollars a barrel for it. That spring the poor trifling people came in crowds for corn. I sent the wagon after what I had bought, and by the time it would get back, Mr. Jefferson had given out so many of his little orders that it would pretty much take the load. I could hardly get it hauled as fast as he would give it away. I went to Mr. Jefferson and told him it never would do; we could not give ten dollars a barrel for corn, and haul it thirty miles, and give it away after that fashion. He said, What can I do? These people tell me they have no corn, and it will not do to let them suffer. I told him again, I could tell him what to do. Just send them all to me. I knew them all a great deal better than he did, and would give to all that were really deserving. [. . .]

Mr. Jefferson had four children. Two of them died very young. The other two, Martha and Maria, were in France with him while he was Minister. They were in school there. Martha married Col. Thomas Mann Randolph, afterwards Governor of Virginia. Maria married John W. Eppes. He afterwards went to Congress. He was a very fine-looking man, and a great favorite with everybody. Mrs. Eppes died very young, and was buried at Monticello. She had one boy, Frank Eppes, a fine little fellow. He used to stay at Monticello a good deal.

I knew Mrs. Randolph as well as I ever knew any person out of my own family. Few such women ever lived. I never saw her equal. I was with Mr. Jefferson twenty years and saw her frequently every week. I never saw her at all out of temper. I can truly say that I never saw two such persons in this respect as she and her father. Sometimes he would refer me to her, or she would refer me to him, a half dozen times in a day. Mrs. Randolph was more like her father than any lady I ever saw. She was nearly as tall as he, and had the same clear, bright complexion, and blue eyes. I have rode over the plantation, I reckon, a thousand times with Mr. Jefferson, and when he was not talking he was nearly always humming some tune, or singing in a low tone to himself. And it was just so with Mrs. Randolph. As she was attending to her duties about the house, she seemed to be always in a happy mood. She had always her father's pleasant smile, and was nearly always humming some tune. I have never seen her at all disturbed by any amount of care and trouble.

Mr. Jefferson was the most industrious person I ever saw in my life. All the time I was with him I had full permission to visit his room whenever I thought it necessary to see him on any business. I knew how to get into his room at any time of day or night. I have sometimes gone into his room when he was in bed, but aside from that I never went into it but twice in the whole twenty years I was with him, that I did not find him employed. I never saw him sitting idle in his room but twice. Once he was suffering with the toothache; and once, in returning from his Bedford farm, he had slept in a room where some of the glass had been broken out of the window, and the wind had blown upon him and given him a kind of neuralgia. At all other times he was either reading, writing, talking, working upon some model, or doing something else.

Mrs. Randolph was just like her father in this respect. She was always busy. If she wasn't reading or writing, she was always doing something. She used to sit in Mr. Jefferson's room a great deal, and sew, or read, or talk, as he would be busy about something else. As her daughters grew up, she taught them to be industrious like herself. They used to take turns each day in giving out to the servants, and superintending the housekeeping. I knew all her children just as well as I did my own. There were six daughters and five sons. Let me see if I can remember their names. The boys were Thomas Jefferson, James Madison, Benjamin Franklin, Meriwether Lewis, and George Wythe. The daughters were Anne, Ellen, Virginia, Cornelia, and a little thing that could just run about when I came away. Her name was Septimis, or something like that [Septimia]. Only two of them were married when I came away. Jeff, married Jane Nicholas, daughter of Gov. Wilson C. Nicholas, and Anne married Charles S. Bankhead. Anne, Ellen, and Meriwether Lewis had the fresh rosy countenance of the Jefferson family. The rest of the family, as far as I can remember—I don't remember about the little ones—had the Randolph complexion, which was dark and Indian-like. You know they claim to be descended from Pocahontas. Virginia and Cornelia were tall, active, and fine looking, with very dark complexions.

Mr. Jefferson was perfectly devoted to his grandchildren, and they to him. They delighted to follow him about over the grounds and garden, and he took great pleasure in talking with them, and giving them advice, and directing their sports. I have heard him tell them enough of times that nobody should live without some useful employment. I always raised my boys to work. Mr. Jefferson knew this, and it pleased him. On Saturdays, when they were not in school, they often cut coal wood for the nailery. They could cut a cord a day and earn fifty cents. Governor Randolph once told them that if they would cut off the bushes from a certain field, he would give them twenty dollars. His boys would often go and work with them like little Turks on Saturdays, so that my boys could go with them a-fishing. After a while they finished their job and got their pay. Mr. Jefferson heard of it. One evening I heard him talking with his grandchildren about it. He told them my boys had got twenty dollars—more money than any of them had got; that they had earned it themselves, and said a great deal in their praise, and in regard to the importance of industrious habits. Meriwether Lewis was a very bright little fellow. I always thought him the most sprightly of all the Randolph children. He spoke up and said, "Why, grandpa, if we should work like Fielding and Thomas, our hands would get so rough and sore that we could not hold our books. And we need not work so. We shall be rich, and all we want is a good education, so that we shall be prepared to associate with wealthy and intelligent people." "Ah!" said Mr. Jefferson, and I have thought of the remark a thousand times since, "those that expect to get through the world without industry, because they are rich, will be greatly mistaken. The people that *do* work will soon get possession of all their property." I have heard him give those children a great deal of good advice. I remember, once, hearing him tell them that they should never laugh in a loud, boisterous manner in company, or in the presence of strangers. That was his own habit.

He took great pleasure in the sports and plays of his grandchildren. I have often seen him direct them and enjoy them greatly. The large lawn back of the house was a fine place for their plays. They very often ran races, and he would give the word for them to start, and decide who was the winner. Another play was stealing goods. They would divide into two parties, and lay down their coats, hats, knives, and other things, and each party would try to get all that the other had. If they were caught in the attempt to steal they were made prisoners. I have seen Mr. Jefferson laugh heartily to see this play go on. The children about the country used to enjoy coming there. It was a fine place for them to play, and in the fruit season there was always the greatest quantities of good fruit. Jeff. Randolph used very often to bring his schoolmates there. [. . .]

I visited Mr. Jefferson at Washington three times while he was President. My first visit was soon after his inauguration. I went to take his carriage horses. The second time I went he had got very much displeased with two of his servants, Davy and Fanny, and he wished me to take them to Alexandria and sell them. They were married, and had got into a terrible quarrel. Davy was jealous of his wife, and, I reckon, with good reason. When I got there, they learned what I had come for, and they were in great trouble. They wept, and begged, and made good promises, and made such an ado, that they begged the old gentleman out of it. But it was a good lesson for them. I never heard any more complaint of them; and when I left Mr. Jefferson, I left them both at Monticello.

The last time I visited Mr. Jefferson in Washington, I stayed there sixteen days. This was when I went to help him settle up his business, and move home his goods and servants. He had eleven servants with him from Monticello. He had a French cook in Washington named Julien, and he took Eda and Fanny there, to learn French cookery. He always preferred French cookery. Eda and Fanny were afterwards his cooks at Monticello.

Some days I was very busy attending to packing up his goods, getting in his bills, and settling up his business. Other days I had very little to do, and I would go up to the Capitol. I haven't been in Washington since the British played the wild there in the war of 1812. When I was there, the President's house was surrounded with a high rock wall, and there was an iron gate immediately in front of it, and from that gate to the Capitol the street was just as straight as a gun-barrel. Nearly all the houses were on that street. I took a great deal of pleasure in going to the Capitol and hearing the debates.

Mr. Jefferson often told me that the office of Vice-President was far preferable to that of President. He was perfectly tired out with company. He had a very long dining-room, and his table was chock-full every one of the sixteen days I was there. There were Congressmen, foreigners, and all sorts of people to dine with him. He dined at four o'clock, and they generally sat and talked until night. It used to worry me to sit so long, and I finally quit when I got through eating, and went off and left them.

The first thing in the morning there, was to go to market. There was no market then in Washington. Mr. Jefferson's steward was a Frenchman named Lamar. He was a very smart man, was well educated, and as much of a gentleman in his appearance as any man. His carriage driver was an Irishman named [Joseph] Dougherty. He would get out the wagon early in the morning, and Lamar would go with him to Georgetown to market. I have all my life been in the habit of getting up about four o'clock in the morning, and I went with them very often. Lamar told me that it often took fifty dollars to pay for what marketing they would use in a day. Mr. Jefferson's salary did not support him while he was President.

We got loaded up ready to start home, and I left Washington on the third of March. Mr. Jefferson stayed to attend the inauguration, but overtook us before we got home. I had three wagons from Monticello—two six-mule teams loaded with boxes, and the other four sorrel Chickasaw horses, and the wagon pretty much loaded with shrubbery from Maine's nursery. The servants rode on these wagons. I had the carriage horses and carriage, and rode behind them.

On our way home we had a tremendous snowstorm. It snowed very fast, and when we reached Culpepper Court House it was half-leg deep. A large crowd of people had collected there, expecting that the President would be along. When I rode up, they thought I was the President, and shouted and hurrahed tremendously. When I got out of the carriage, they laughed very heartily at their mistake. There was a platform along the whole front of the tavern, and it was full of people. Some of them had been waiting a good while, and drinking a good deal, and they made so much noise that they scared the horses, and Diomede backed, and tread upon my foot, and lamed me so that I could hardly get into the carriage the next morning. There was one very tall old fellow that was noisier than any of the rest, who said he was bound to see the President — "Old Tom," he called him. They asked me when he would be along, and I told them I thought he would certainly be along that night, and I looked for him every moment. The tavern was kept by an old man named [Benjamin] Shackleford. I told him to have a large fire built in a private room, as Mr. Jefferson would be very cold when he got there, and he did so. I soon heard shouting, went out, and Mr. Jefferson was in sight. He was in a one-horse vehicle — a phaeton — with a driver, and a servant on horseback. When he came up, there was great cheering again. I motioned to him to follow me; took him straight to his room, and locked the door. The tall old fellow came and knocked very often, but I would not let him in. I told Mr. Jefferson not to mind him, he was drunk. Finally the door was opened, and they rushed in and filled the room. It was as full as I ever saw a bar-room. He stood up, and made a short address to them. Afterwards some of them told him how they had mistaken me for him. He went on next day, and reached Monticello before we did, so that I did not see the large reception that the people of Albemarle gave him when he got home.

Mr. Jefferson had a very large library. When the British burnt Washington, the library that belonged to Congress was destroyed, and Mr. Jefferson sold them his. He directed me to have it packed in boxes and sent to Washington. John Hemings, one of his servants, made the boxes, and Burwell and I packed them up mostly. [James] Dinsmore helped us some, and the girls, Ellen, Virginia, and Cornelia would come in sometimes and sort them out, and help us a good deal. There was an immense quantity of them. There were sixteen wagon loads. I engaged the teams. Each wagon was to carry three thousand pounds for a load, and to have four dollars a day for delivering them in Washington. If they carried more than three thousand pounds, they were to have extra pay. There were all kinds of books — books in a great many languages that I knew nothing about. There were a great many religious books among them — more than I have ever seen anywhere else. All the time Mr. Jefferson was President I had the keys to his library, and I could go in and look over the books, and take out any one that I wished, and read and return it. I have written a good many letters from that library to Mr. Jefferson in Washington. Mr. Jefferson had a sofa or lounge upon which he could sit or recline, and a small table on rollers, upon which he could write, or lay his books. Sometimes he would draw this table up before the sofa, and sit and read or write; and other times he would recline on his sofa, with his table rolled up the sofa, astride it. He had a large Bible, which nearly always lay at the head of his sofa. Many and many a time I have gone into his room and found him reading that Bible. You remember I told you about riding all night from Richmond, after selling that flour, and going into his room very early in the morning, and paying over to him the new United States Bank money. *That* was one of the times that I found him with the big Bible open before him on his little table, and he busy reading it. And I have seen him reading it in that way many a time. Some people, you know, say he was an atheist. Now if he was an atheist, what did he want with all those religious books, and why did he spend so much of his time reading his Bible?

When Chancellor Wythe died, he willed to Mr. Jefferson his library. It was very large, and nearly filled up the room of the one he sold to Congress. Mr. Jefferson studied law with Chancellor Wythe. They thought a great deal of each other. [. . .]

After Mr. Jefferson returned from Washington, he was for years crowded with visitors, and they almost ate him out of house and home. They were there all times of the year; but about the middle of June the travel would commence from the lower part of the State to the Springs, and then there was a perfect throng of visitors. They travelled in their own carriages, and came in gangs — the whole family, with carriage and riding-horses and servants; sometimes three or four such gangs at a time. We had thirty-six stalls for horses, and only used about ten of them for the stock we kept there. Very often all of the rest were full, and I had to send horses off to another place. I have often sent a wagon-load of hay up to the stable, and the next morning there would not be enough left to make a hen's-nest. I have killed a fine beef, and it would all be eaten in a day or two. There was no tavern in all that country that had so much company. Mrs. Randolph, who always lived with Mr. Jefferson after his return from Washington, and kept house for him, was very often greatly perplexed to entertain them. I have known her many and many a time to have every bed in the house full, and she would send to my wife and borrow all her beds — she had six spare beds — to accommodate her visitors. I finally told the servant who had charge of the stable, to only give the visitors' horses half allowance. Somehow or other

Mr. Jefferson heard of this; I never could tell how, unless it was through some of the visitors' servants. He countermanded my orders.

One great reason why Mr. Jefferson built his house at Poplar Forest, in Bedford County, was that he might go there in the summer to get rid of entertaining so much company. He knew that it more than used up all his income from the plantation and every thing else, but he was so kind and polite that he received all his visitors with a smile, and made them welcome. They pretended to come out of respect and regard to him, but *I think* that the fact that they saved a tavern bill had a good deal to do with it, with a good many of them. I can assure you I got tired of seeing them come, and waiting on them.

From Hamilton W. Pierson, *Jefferson at Monticello: The Private Life of Thomas Jefferson* (New York: Charles Scribner, 1862), pp. 70–76, 85–90, 112–120, 124–125.

Thomas Jefferson (1868)

Henry Tutwiler

A member of the first class to enter the University of Virginia, Henry Tutwiler (1807–1884) took what he learned there and applied it during his own outstanding career as an educator. Born in Harrisburg, Tutwiler studied at the University of Virginia from 1825 to 1829, when he became the first student to earn a master's degree from the institution. He took a broad range of classes, studying ancient languages with George Long and also taking science courses. When the University of Alabama opened its doors in 1831, Tutwiler was hired as its professor of ancient languages. He taught at other Alabama colleges until 1847, when he established a private school at Green Springs, which he would continue to run until two years before his death. Characterizing Tutwiler's educational approach, Thomas McAdory Owen observed, "When languages were taught by the most formal and antiquated methods, he used natural and living methods. He taught science by experiment when textbook teaching was the rule. He made the foundation of character the chief end of education, each pupil being treated as an individual, protesting against the Procrustean bed to which each student must be fitted whatever his natural endowments" (*History of Alabama*, 4: 1695). This description sounds quite similar to Thomas Jefferson's approach to education. According to Thomas Chalmers McCorvey, Tutwiler's experience at the University of Virginia profoundly influenced the history of education in Alabama.

When McCorvey published his study in the early twentieth century, he was unaware of the personal reminiscence of Thomas Jefferson that Tutwiler had published in 1868 as part of a series of articles in the *Mobile Sunday Times*, but this reminiscence reinforces McCorvey's thesis regarding the impact Jefferson had on Tutwiler. Few issues of the *Mobile Sunday Times* survive, but *Southern Opinion*, a weekly Richmond paper, reprinted the article, which Jay Hubbell discovered in the mid twentieth century (*The South in American Literature*, 128). Tutwiler's reminiscence indicates that Jefferson frequently came to campus and enjoyed speaking with students after the University of Virginia opened its doors. He often invited them to his home for dinner. Tutwiler's account of the conversation around the dinner table at Monticello provides important evidence about Jefferson's intellectual life: he disliked modern fiction, he enjoyed talking about his time in France, and he often recommended books for the students to read.

EVERY AUTHENTICK ANECDOTE relating to those who have acted a conspicuous part in their country's history is worthy of preservation. A few personal reminiscences of Mr. Jefferson may be interesting to your readers. I was a student at the University of Virginia during the latter years of Mr. Jefferson's life, and at the time of his death. His deep devotion to this child of his old age, is known to all. Indeed one of his claims to the lasting gratitude of his countrymen is based upon this institution. This is shown by the inscription prepared by himself and, by his direction, placed upon his monument: "Here was buried Thomas Jefferson, Authour of the Declaration of American Independence, of the Statute of Virginia for Religious Freedom, and Father of the University of Virginia." In the summer and autumn of 1825 Mr. Jefferson was in the habit of making frequent visits to the University, about four miles from Monticello, and he generally came on horseback, unattended. He was then eighty-two years of age. I well remember the first time I ever saw him. I was in the Proctor's office, when a tall, venerable gentleman, plainly dressed, entered the room, in a quiet, unobtrusive manner, and took a seat in my corner. Mr. [Arthur] Brockenbrough, the Proctor, was busy at the time and did not observe his entrance. I thought that it was a plain country farmer, who had called to see the Proctor on business; but a fellow-student who was with me, and who had seen Mr. Jefferson before, took occasion, in a private way, to let me know who it was, and I then observed him more closely. I thought that I had never seen a countenance that exhibited more of the kindliest feelings of the heart. Afterwards, I saw him frequently riding along the Eastern Range, as it is called, on which I had a room, sometimes on horseback, and once or twice in a *landau,* accompanied by his grand-daughters. It was the first time I had ever seen a vehicle of the kind where the driver rode one of the horses, and it excited my boyish curiosity. It was I believe, brought by him from France.

Mr. Jefferson was in the habit of inviting some of the students, generally four or five, to dine with him at Monticello on Sundays. This day was selected because it would not interfere with their attendance on the lectures in the school of the University. The names were taken in regular order from the Proctor's book, and the invitations were given through one of his grandsons, Ben or Lewis, who were then students in the University. Geo. W. [Randolph], our Confederate Secretary of War, was at the time only thirteen years of age, and was at school in Massachusetts. I had a dear friend and roommate, now no more, a brother of the late Dr. Gessner Harrison. He was one of the most pious young men I ever knew. When he was invited to the Sunday dinner he did not go, nor did he send any excuse, hoping that his absence would not be noted. But it was a rule with Mr. Jefferson, whenever a student did not attend to renew the invitation for the following Sunday, and it was done in this case. Finding that his invitation was still declined, he learned, through his grandson, the cause and sent a special invitation to this young man and some others on a week day. The invitation was accepted.

Some time after Mr. J's death, young H. and myself, with several other students, made a visit to Monticello. After going through the house, and just as we were leaving it, Burwell, Mr. J's favorite servant who acted as cicerone on these occasions, detained me a moment, and asked me if that was not young H. who had declined Mr. J.'s invitation to dine with him on Sunday. On my answering him in the affirmative, he said, "Mr. Jefferson thought a great deal of that young man."

I mention this little incident to show the tender regard which Mr. Jefferson had for the conscientious scruples of others, and the high estimate which he placed upon one who acted upon those scruples. Burwell had, no doubt, heard Mr. Jefferson commend the consistency of that youth.

Mr. Jefferson had a wonderful tact in making everyone, even the youngest, feel at ease in his company. One soon forgot that he was in the presence of a man who had acted so distinguished part in the foundation and formation of a new and mighty Republick. It would seem as if he knew something personal in regard to each student, and by asking him questions concerning his immediate neighbourhood, or in regard to his studies at the University, he made each one feel that he was imparting information to his distinguished host. I well remember the day on which it was my good fortune to dine with him. Many of the accidents are still fresh in my memory, although more than forty years have elapsed. There were only four of us from the University. He received us in his drawing-room, and, while we were examining the portraits and busts which adorn its walls, he had some interesting anecdote to tell in regard to most of them. When we came to the portrait of General Washington, he remarked that the General could not be called a handsome man, but on horseback he was one of the most graceful figures he had ever seen. He amused us very much with an account of interviews which took place between Madam de Stael and himself when he was in Paris and of the laughable mistakes which she would make in her attempt to speak English.

His daughter, Mrs. Randolph, presided at the dinner table, and her daughters were also present, all of them being members of his family. The conversation happening to turn on novel-reading, Mrs. Randolph remarked that she could never get her father to read through a novel. She said that when *Ivanhoe* came out, she was so much fascinated by it that she thought her father would certainly be interested in it, and begged him to read it for her sake. He promised to do so, and began it, but was not able to get more than half through. Mr. Jefferson smiled, and said that he had found it the dullest and driest reading he had ever tried.

We were surpirsed to hear Mrs. Randolph say that she found Blackstone almost as interesting as a novel. Mr. Jefferson admired Blackstone as a writer, but could not bear his "Tory principles," as he called them. Indeed, so much was he opposed to these, that it was not until after his death that Blackstone was admitted as a textbook into the Law School of the University.—Coke was his favourite, and he thought that no one could be a sound lawyer who was not well versed in the *Institutes.* He felt the same antipathy to Hume's *History of England,* and hesitated about admitting this work into the University Library.—He used to say that the reading of Hume would make an English Tory, and that the transition to an American Tory was an easy one. He never failed to recommend to the youthful student, as an antidote to Hume, Brodie's *British Empire*; the latter, he said, had "pulverized" Hume.

"Thomas Jefferson," *Southern Opinion,* 17 October 1868.

[Jefferson and the Boy Professor] (1875)

George Long

Professor George Long (1800–1879) wrote this reminiscence at the request of one of his first students at the University of Virginia, Henry Tutwiler. Educated at Cambridge University, Long was hired as professor of ancient languages at the University of Virginia. He enjoyed his time in Virginia. His method of teaching Latin and Greek pleased students, including his most renowned student, Edgar Allan Poe. Long had a passion for geography, and he used to incorporate lessons in ancient geography as he taught Latin and Greek. He also enjoyed talking about classical literature with Jefferson. In 1828, Lord Brougham invited Long to serve as professor of Greek at the newly founded University of London (later University College, London). Long accepted the position and returned to England. A prolific writer, Long produced numerous scholarly works over the course of his lengthy career. In his *Essays in Criticism* (1865), Matthew Arnold said that Long "treats Marcus Aurelius's writings, as he treats all the other remains of Greek and Roman antiquity which he touches, not as a dead and dry matter of learning, but as documents with a side of modern applicability and living interest, and valuable mainly so far as this side in them can be made clear" (257). Arnold's words apply to Thomas Jefferson, as well.

From George Long to Henry Tutwiler, 30 May 1875

Early in December 1824 I travelled from Washington to Fredericksburg, where I stayed all night. I do not know how I was known, but a gentleman called on me, and asked me to his house, and I spent a pleasant evening. I saw some young Virginian ladies there and I thought they were very charming. I was amused with the curiosity which my new friends showed to hear some news about England. A gentleman came up to me, and asked how I left Mr. [Thomas] Campbell, the poet. Luckily I had lately called on him in London on some business about a relative of his who thought of emigrating to America, and I could therefore give a satisfactory answer. At Fredericksburg I first tasted corn bread, and I used it all the time that I lived in Virginia. I wish that I could have it now.

From Fredericksburg I had a two days' rather unpleasant journey to Charlottesville in the stage coach. The roads were bad, the accommodation not good, and the company very indifferent. The young men of the present day can hardly conceive what this road was then, for I suppose that there is now a railroad the whole distance.

At Charlottesville, I mean of course the University near it, I lived at least two months in the house which was assigned to me, in great solitude and during bad weather. It would have been still worse, if I had not experienced the kindness of the Proctor, Mr. Brockenbrough, whose wife's sister I afterwards married. The other professors had embarked in an English vessel for Norfolk, and they had a very long passage. The ship was described to me as something like an old hay stack: it could just float and go before the wind. I had more wisely embarked in one of the New York American packets from Liverpool. Since that time the English have learned to build good ships for the American trade. When my brother professors arrived at the University, they found me eating corn bread and already a Virginian in tastes and habits. Things were rather rough, but I have always had and still have the faculty of making myself happy under any circumstances.

A few days after my arrival at Charlottesville I walked up to Monticello to see Mr. Jefferson. I made myself known to his servant, and was introduced into his great room. In a few minutes a tall dignified old man entered, and after looking at me a moment said, Are you the new professor of antient languages? I replied that I was. He observed, You are very young: to which I answered, I shall grow older. He smiled, and said, That was true. He was evidently somewhat startled at my youthful and boyish appearance; and I could plainly see that he was disappointed. We fell to talking and I stayed to dine with him. He was grave and rather cold in his manner, but he was very polite; and I was pleased with his simple Virginian dress, and his conversation free from all affectation. I remember this interview as well as if it took place yesterday.

During my solitary residence before the University opened I visited Monticello several times and occasionally passed the night there. I thought that he became better satisfied with the boy professor; and we talked on all subjects. He saw that I took great interest in the geography of America and in the story of the revolution; and he told me much about it, but in a very modest way as to himself. He showed me the original draft of the Declaration of Independence; and he could clearly see that I was in habits, as I have always been and still am, a man who preferred plain republican institutions to the outward show and splendour of European kingdoms—when I say "republican institutions," I mean genuine republican, for a republican may have the name, and very little besides that I value.

I often saw Mr. Jefferson between this time and his death. When he came on his horse to the University, he generally called on me. His thoughts were always about this new place of education of which he was really the founder; and though the first few years of the University were not quite satisfactory, he confidently looked forward to the future and to the advantages which the state would derive from the young men who were educated in the University of Virginia.

I remember well a long conversation which I once had with Mr. Jefferson on George Washington. He spoke of him freely and generously, as of a man of great and noble character. Mr. [George] Tucker in his life of Jefferson has given the character of George Washington as Jefferson wrote it; and it is perhaps certain that the character was written at the time when Mr. Jefferson spoke of Washington to me, though he told me something more than the written character contains, but nothing that is contradictory to it. The character is exceedingly well written, and it proves that as a mere writer Jefferson might have excelled most men of his day.

I discovered that Mr. Jefferson was well acquainted with Polybius, who is not a good writer, but a man of excellent sense and the soundest judgment. The last time that I saw Mr. Jefferson when he was suffering from a complaint which caused his death, he was reading Pliny's letters, and we had some talk about a passage. A few weeks after when I was at the Sweet Springs during the summer vacation, I heard of his death. There was much foolish display on the occasion in Virginia, and some extravagant bombastic orations, one of them by a man whom I knew. Those who had more sense showed their feeling in another way. The man who had done so much for Virginia and the United States was honoured for his services, for his talents, and his grand and simple character. He ought to be revered by all who enjoy the advantage of being educated in his University, and ever remembered as one of the great men whom Virginia has produced. His great deeds are recorded in the epitaph which he wrote for his own tomb.

From *Letters of George Long,* ed. Thomas Fitzhugh (Charlottesville: University of Virginia Library, 1917), pp. 21–24.

"Once the Slave of Thomas Jefferson" (1898)

PETER F. FOSSETT

Throughout his long life, Peter F. Fossett (1815–1901) retained fond memories of his adolescent encounters with Thomas Jefferson. The son of Joseph Fossett and Edith Hern, Peter Fossett, a house slave at Monticello, came to know his master during adolescence. Jefferson died when Fossett was eleven, an age when experience takes hold of the memory with great tenacity. After Jefferson's death, Fossett was sold in the January 1827 auction. Whereas Jefferson encouraged the youth's intellectual interests and even permitted him to assemble a small library of his own, Colonel John Jones, Fossett's new owner, threatened to whip the boy when he caught him with a book. Regardless, Fossett continued reading on the sly and shared his knowledge with fellow slaves on the Jones plantation. Joseph Fossett, who had secured his own freedom and that of other family members, eventually helped Peter obtain his freedom and brought him to Cincinnati, where Peter worked as a caterer before becoming pastor of the First Baptist Church in Cumminsville. The following interview, which originally appeared in the New York *Sunday World* (30 January 1898) and is reprinted here for the first time, is the most detailed interview Peter Fossett granted, but not the only one. Two years later, a pseudonymous correspondent of *The Colored American* (23 June 1900) known only as "Monticello" related his interview with Fossett, who had returned to Charlottesville for a visit. The *Colored American* interview confirms many of the details from this earlier interview. Peter Fossett is generally considered the most reliable witness among Jefferson's former slaves. The author of his obituary in the Washington *Evening Times* (7 January 1901), commented: "Of the many who have in recent years claimed to have lived at Monticello as a servant in the lifetime of Jefferson, old Peter was probably the only one who did not romance."

THE REV. PETER F. FOSSETT, of this city [Cincinnati], is probably the last surviving slave of Thomas Jefferson. Mr. Fossett is a very intelligent colored man. He is eighty-three years old and lives at No. 313 Stone Street in a comfortable, well furnished and well provided home. It was there that a *Sunday*

World reporter found the kindly old gentleman to-day, well preserved in mind and body, spending the winter of his days in comfort and happiness. He is held in great regard by colored people and is loved by all the white ministers of Cincinnati, who know him well and esteem him highly.

Recently Mr. Fossett was invited to deliver an address before the Cincinnati Baptist Ministers' Association and in his speech he told the story of his early days, giving many reminiscences of the great founder of the Democratic party. In conversation with the *Sunday World* reporter he went into greater detail and chatted entertainingly about his life in "Ole Virginny."

"I was born," he said, "at Monticello, Jefferson's beautiful Virginia home, on June 6, 1815, just before Waterloo. Jefferson was an ideal master. He was a democrat in practice as well as theory, was opposed to the slave trade, tried to keep it out of the Territories beyond the Ohio River and was in favor of freeing the slaves in Virginia. In 1787 he introduced that famous 'Jefferson proviso' in Congress, prohibiting slavery in all the Northwestern Territory, comprising the States of Ohio, Indiana, Illinois and Missouri. He had made all arrangements to free his slaves at his death by making three prizes of his property, etc.

"I well remember the visit of Gen. Lafayette to Monticello. The whole place was in gala array in his honor. He was met at Red Gate and escorted to Monticello by the Jefferson Guards and the Virginia Militia. The latter consisted of all the schoolboys in the county, who had been drilled for the occasion, armed with sharp pointed sticks tipped with pikes. The meeting between Jefferson and Lafayette was most affectionate. They fell into each other's arms with these words: 'My dear Lafayette,' 'My dear Jefferson,' and wept.

"Mrs. Patsy Randolph, who had been Martha Ann Jefferson, received Lafayette with grace and dignity befitting a queen, welcoming him to the hospitality of the home of her father. They all listened to the addresses that followed. Even the slaves wept. A youth of eighteen made the address on behalf of the juvenile soldiers, and, I think, Gen. Chestin Cox, in behalf of the citizens.

"The next day occurred the visit to the University, which had just been finished except the dome. There was a grand procession that day and the slaves had a holiday. First came the Jefferson Guards, then the carriage bearing Mr. Jefferson, with Gen. Lafayette on his right, with ex-President Monroe and Mr. Madison sitting opposite them. In the second carriage was Gen. Chestin Cox, President of the University Faculty. On his right sat George Washington Lafayette, son of the General, and opposite them were Thomas Jefferson Randolph, the grandson of Mr. Jefferson, and Gen. Lavassor. Surrounding these two carriages were the Virginia Militia.

"Thomas Jefferson Randolph was orator of the day, and there were addresses by all the great men present.

"There was never such a time in Virginia as during the visit of Gen. Lafayette. Two years after this Mr. Jefferson died. Then began our troubles. We were scattered all over the country, never to meet each other again until we meet in another world. A peculiar fact about his house servants was that we were all related to one another, and as a matter of fact we did not need to know that we were slaves. As a boy I was not only brought up differently, but dressed unlike the plantation boys. My grandmother was free, and I remember the first suit she gave me. It was of blue nankeen cloth, red morocco hat and red morocco shoes. To complete this unique costume, my father added a silver watch.

"At Monticello we always had the house full of company. Not only did Jefferson's own countrymen visit him, but people from all parts of Europe came to see his wonderful home. On the first floor was Mr. Jefferson's study, called the 'green room.' Here such men as Madison, Monroe and others were wont to discuss the problems of the day. I was too young to know much about these great men, but I remember seeing them and being in the same house with them.

"Mr. Madison used to come and stay for days with Mr. Jefferson. He was a very learned man, as was Mr. Jefferson also. He was a kindly looking old gentleman, and his coming was looked for with pleasure by the older servants for he never left without leaving each of them a substantial reminder of his visit.

"Mr. Monroe did not live as far from our home as Mr. Madison, and his visits were more frequent. While he was a wise and great man, and a friend of Mr. Jefferson, their companionship was not as close as that existing between Mr. Jefferson and Madison. He was more of a statesman than a scientist, while Madison and Jefferson were both. On the north terrace of Monticello was the telescope, and it was here that Madison and Jefferson spent a great deal of their time. One day while Mr. Jefferson was looking through his telescope to see how the work was progressing over at Pan Top, one of his plantations, he saw 500 soldiers, headed by Col. Tarleton, and led by a traitor whose name I have forgotten, coming up the north side of the mountain to capture him along with the Congress which was being held at Charlottesville.

"He hastily called up his servants, told them to collect and hide the silver, and gathered his valuable papers. My mother's uncle saddled his horse and took him up to Carter's Mountain, where Mr. Jefferson hid in the hollow of an old tree. He had told his butler to hoist the flag over the dome of his home while the soldiers were there and to take it down when they had gone. This he did. My father's aunt hid the silver in the potato cellar. When the soldiers came up she was standing over the keyhole. The house was searched and nothing could be found. They came to her and with arms drawn demanded that she should tell them where the silver was. She denied knowing anything about it. Then they turned their attention to the wine cellar, broke all the casks and with their swords cut all the tops off the bottles of wine that stood on the shelves. The rare old wine that he had sent to France for covered the floor to the depth of three steps.

"They caroused around the place for about three hours, and one of the soldiers rode up into the house on his horse, and the beautiful floor of the music room, inlaid with gothic fret-work, still bore the prints of the horse's shoes when I left Monticello.

"His summer residence, Poplar Forest, where he spent three months in each year, was a Mecca for all the great men of the world, and the Indians also. In those days they ran the wisest and best men for office, and not the most unscrupulous, as now. At 10 o'clock every day he went to the University and returned at 2 for dinner. Many times have I ordered his horse, a large chestnut bay, which bore the name of Eagle. As for the social enjoyment of the men of those days the people of this time do not begin to come up to it. Weddings, parties, barbecues and the like, even the slaves participated in.

"As a master Jefferson was kind and indulgent. Under his management his slaves were seldom punished, except for stealing and fighting. They were tried for any offense as at court and allowed to make their own defense. The slave children were nursed until they were three years old, and left with their parents until thirteen. They were then sent to the overseers' wives to learn trades. Every male child's father received $5 at its birth.

"Jefferson was a man of sober habits, although his cellars were stocked with wines. No one ever saw him under the influence of liquor. His servants about the house were tasked. If you did your task well you were rewarded; if not, punished. Mrs. Randolph would not let any of the young ladies go anywhere with gentlemen with the exception of their brothers, unless a colored servant accompanied them. On July 4, 1826, exactly fifty years after the signing of the Declaration of Independence, Jefferson and Adams died. I was eleven years old.

"Sorrow came not only to the homes of two great men who had been such fast friends in life as Jefferson and Adams, but to the slaves of Thomas Jefferson. The story of my own life is like a fairy tale, and you would not believe me if I told to you the scenes enacted during my life of slavery. It passes through my mind like a dream. Born and reared as free, not knowing that I was a slave, then suddenly, at the death of Jefferson, put upon an auction block and sold to strangers. I then commenced an eventful life.

"I was sold to Col. John R. Jones. My father was freed by the Legislature of Virginia. At the request of Mr. Jefferson, my father made an agreement with Mr. Jones that when he was able to raise the amount that Col. Jones paid for me he would give me back to my father, and he also promised to let me learn the blacksmith trade with my father as soon as I was old enough. My father then made a bargain with two sons of Col. Jones — William Jones and James Lawrence Jones — to teach me. They attended the University of Virginia.

"Mr. Jefferson allowed his grandson to teach any of his slaves who desired to learn, and Lewis Randolph first taught me how to read. When I was sold to Col. Jones I took my books along with me. One day I was kneeling before the fireplace spelling the word 'baker,' when Col. Jones opened the door, and I shall never forget the scene as long as I live.

"'What have you got there, sir?' were his words.

"I told him.

"'If I ever catch you with a book in your hands, thirty-and-nine lashes on your bare back.' He took the book and threw it into the fire, then called up his sons and told them that if they ever taught me they would receive the same punishment. But they helped me all they could, as did his daughter Ariadne.

"Among my things was a copy-book that my father gave me, and which I kept hid in the bottom of my trunk. I used to get permission to take a bath, and by the dying embers I learned to write. The first copy was this sentence, 'Art improves nature.'

"Col. Jones, when he bought me, promised my father to let him have me when he could raise the money, but in 1833 he refused to let him have me on any conditions. Mrs. Jones declared that she would sooner part with one of her own children. They had become very attached to me, and then I was a very valuable servant, notwithstanding that all the time I was teaching all the people around me to read and write, and even venturing to write free passes and sending slaves away from their masters. Of course they did not know this, or they would not have thought me so valuable.

"Amid these scenes it was during my stay with Col. Jones that I first saw my state as a sinner. The white Baptists where I lived had no church. They held services in the Court-House and sometimes in the Episcopal Church. The Baptist churches were all in the country near some creek convenient for baptizing. It was in these churches during the summer that they held three-day and ten-day meetings, at which many were converted, and here their greatest revivals took place.

"It was during one of these meetings that I was convicted of my sins from a sermon preached by Cumberland George. I was converted at a two weeks' meeting at Piney Grove. Mrs. Jones, my mistress, was called the mother of the Baptist church, and our house was the stopping place for all the preachers. It was here when they were holding these meetings that my eyes were opened.

"I well remember the struggle they had in the great controversy with Alexander Campbell. Two eloquent young preachers — Lindsay Coleman and James Goss — the pride and hope of the Baptist denomination, took Campbell's side, and tried to take the church from them. The people belonging to the church had a church meeting which lasted for a week, day and night. Every time a vote was taken it was a tie. If it had not been for that young hero, Robert Ryland, who was chaplain at the University of Virginia, they would have succeeded. At last Col. Nimrod Branham, the moderator, who was on the fence, gave the casting vote, and the regular Baptists retained possession of the church.

"Col. Jones had by this time become very fond of me, and would not arrange any terms by which I could gain my freedom. He respected me, and would not let me see him take his 'bitters.' He was surprised and pleased to find that I did not touch liquor. Being with and coming from such a family as Mr. Jefferson's, I knew more than they did about many things. This also raised me in their esteem. My sister Isabel was also left a slave in Virginia.

I wrote her a free pass, sent her to Boston, and made an attempt to gain my own freedom. The first time I failed and had to return. My parents were here in Ohio and I wanted to be with them and be free, so I resolved to get free or die in the attempt. I started the second time, was caught, handcuffed, and taken back and carried to Richmond and put in jail. For the second time I was put up on the auction block and sold like a horse. But friends from among my master's best friends bought me in and sent me to my father in Cincinnati, and I am here to-day."

Concerning the taking of a life mask of Jefferson at Monticello, in 1825, Mr. Fossett said: "I never saw the bust made from this life mask, but I remember when the mask was taken. I was then ten years old. The man who took the mask covered Mr. Jefferson's head, shoulders, arms and body down to the waist with clay or plaster of some kind. He left holes for the nose and eyes. Somehow or other he left the plaster on too long and it got too hard. He had to take a chisel to knock it off and when he got it off Mr. Jefferson was greatly exhausted.

"The report got around that Mr. Jefferson had been killed, and there was the greatest excitement until we all saw Mr. Jefferson again alive and well. I see a magazine writer says there was no trouble about taking the life mask, but I know better, for I was there and remember well the excitement it caused everywhere."

"Once the Slave of Thomas Jefferson," New York *Sunday World,* 30 January 1898.

Permissions

[An Italian Friend Remembers Virginia and France] by Philip Mazzei comes from "Memoirs of the Life and Voyages of Doctor Philip Mazzei," trans. E. C. Branchi, *William and Mary College Quarterly Historical Magazine,* 2d ser. 9 (July 1929): 163–164, 168; 10 (January 1930): 14–15. Reprinted by permission of Special Collections, Earl Greg Swem Library, William and Mary College.

[The Last Days of Thomas Jefferson] by Robley Dunglison comes from "The Autobiographical Ana of Robley Dunglison, M.D.," ed. Samuel X. Radbill, *Transactions of the American Philosophical Society,* new ser. vol. 53, part 8 (1963): 22–23, 26–27, 32–33. Reprinted by permission of the American Philosophical Society.

Selected Bibliography

The following bibliography presents a list of works cited in the headnotes to all of the documents included in this collection. Much biographical information for the headnotes comes from the *American National Biography,* the *Dictionary of Virginia Biography,* and the *Oxford Dictionary of National Biography,* which are not cited otherwise.

Adams, John. "Revolutionary Speeches, Orations, &c." *Niles' Weekly Register* 11 (18 January 1817): 337.

Arnold, Matthew. *Essays in Criticism.* London: Macmillan, 1865.

Brooks, Van Wyck. *The Flowering of New England, 1815–1865.* New York: E. P. Dutton, 1936.

Cabell, Nathaniel Francis, ed. *Early History of the University of Virginia as Contained in the Letters of Thomas Jefferson and Joseph C. Cabell.* Richmond: J. W. Randolph, 1856.

Cappon, Lester J., ed. *The Adams-Jefferson Letters: The Complete Correspondence between Thomas Jefferson and Abigail and John Adams.* 1959. Reprinted. Chapel Hill: University of North Carolina Press, 1987.

"Death of Jefferson's Servant," *Evening Times* [Washington, D.C.] (7 January 1901): 5.

Foster, Augustus J. *Jeffersonian America: Notes on the United States of America, Collected in the Years 1805–6–7 and 11–12.* Ed. Richard Beale Davis. San Marino, CA: Huntington Library, 1954.

French, Henry Flagg. "Jefferson at Monticello." *New England Farmer* 14 (May 1862): 230.

Garraty, John A., and Mark C. Carnes, eds. *American National Biography.* 26 vols. New York: Oxford University Press, 1999.

Gray, Francis Calley. *Thomas Jefferson in 1814: Being an Account of a Visit to Monticello, Virginia.* Boston: The Club of Odd Volumes, 1924.

Hall, Francis. *Travels in Canada, and the United States, in 1816 and 1817.* London: Longman, Hurst, Rees, Ormse, & Brown, 1818.

"Hall's Travels in Canada and the United States." *Monthly Magazine; or British Register* 45 (July 1818): 626.

Harvey, Peter. *Reminiscences and Anecdotes of Daniel Webster.* Boston: Little, Brown, 1877.

Hayes, Kevin J. *The Road to Monticello: The Life and Mind of Thomas Jefferson.* New York: Oxford University Press, 2008.

Hubbell, Jay B. *The South in American Literature, 1607–1900.* Durham: Duke University Press, 1954.

Jefferson, Issac. "Memoirs of a Monticello Slave." *Jefferson at Monticello.* Ed. James Adam Bear. Charlottesville: University Press of Virginia, 1967. 1–24.

Jefferson, Thomas. *Jefferson's Memorandum Books: Accounts, with Legal Records and Miscellany, 1767–1826.* Ed. James A. Bear, Jr. and Lucia C. Stanton. 2 vols. Princeton: Princeton University Press, 1997.

———. *Memoir, Correspondence, and Miscellanies, from the Papers of Thomas Jefferson.* Ed. Thomas Jefferson Randolph. 4 vols. Charlottesville: F. Carr, and Co., 1829.

———. *Memoirs, Correspondence, and Private Papers of Thomas Jefferson.* Ed. Thomas Jefferson Randolph. 4 vols. London: H. Colburn and R. Bentley, 1829.

———. *The Papers of Thomas Jefferson.* Ed. Julian P. Boyd, et al. 37 vols. to date. Princeton: Princeton University Press, 1950–.

———. *The Papers of Thomas Jefferson: Retirement Series.* Ed. J. Jefferson Looney, et al. 7 vols. to date. Princeton: Princeton University Press, 2004–.

———. *The Works of Thomas Jefferson.* Ed. Paul Leicester Ford. 12 vols. New York: G. P. Putnam's Sons, 1904–1905.

Kennedy, John P. *Memoirs of the Life of William Wirt, Attorney General of the United States.* 2 vols. Philadelphia: Lea and Blanchard, 1849.

Kneebone, John T., J. Jefferson Looney, Brent Tarter, and Sandra Gioia Treadway, eds. *Dictionary of Virginia Biography.* 3 vols. to date. Richmond: Library of Virginia, 1998–.

Matthew, H. C. G., and Brian Harrison, eds. *Oxford Dictionary of National Biography.* 60 vols. New York: Oxford University Press, 2004.

McCorvey, Thomas Chalmers. *Henry Tutwiler, and the Influence of the University of Virginia on Education in Alabama.* Montgomery: Alabama Historical Society, 1905.

Mitchill, Samuel L. *A Discourse on the Character and Services of Thomas Jefferson, More Especially as Promoter of the Natural and Physical Sciences: Pronounced by Request before the New-York Lyceum of Natural History on the 11th October 1826.* New York: G. and C. Carvill, 1826.

Monticello, pseud. "Charlottesville, Va., Letter." *The Colored American* (23 June 1900): 9.

Montlezun, baron de. *Souvenirs des Antilles: Voyage en 1815 et 1816, aux États-Unis, et dans l'Archipel Caraibe aperçu de Philadelphie et New-Yorck; descriptions de la Trinidad, la Grenade, Saint-Vincent, Sainte-Lucie, Martinique, Guadeloupe, Marie-Galante, Saint-Christophe, Sainte-Croix et Saint Thomas.* 2 vols. Paris: Gide fils, 1818.

Owen, Thomas McAdory. *History of Alabama and Dictionary of Alabama Biography.* 4 vols. Chicago: S. J. Clarke, 1921.

Pearse, Hugh. *The Hearseys: Five Generations of an Anglo-Indian Family.* Edinburgh: William Blackwood, 1905.

Pecquet du Bellet, Louise. *Some Prominent Virginia Families.* 4 vols. Lynchburg: J. P. Bell, 1907.

Peterson, Merrill D. *The Jefferson Image in the American Mind.* New York: Oxford University Press, 1960.

———, ed. *Visitors to Monticello.* Charlottesville: University Press of Virginia, 1989.

Randall, Henry S. *The Life of Thomas Jefferson.* 3 vols. New York: Derby and Jackson, 1858.

Smith, Margaret Bayard. *A Winter in Washington; or, Memoirs of the Seymour Family.* 2 vols. New York: E. Bliss and E. White, 1824.

Smith, Paul Hubert, and Ronald M. Gephart, eds. *Letters of Delegates to Congress, 1774–1789.* 26 vols. Washington: Library of Congress, 1976–2000.

Smith, Sydney. *The Works of the Rev. Sydney Smith.* 3 vols. London: Longman, Orme, Brown, Green, and Longmans, 1839.

Sowerby, E. Millicent. *Catalogue of the Library of Thomas Jefferson.* 5 vols. Washington: Library of Congress, 1952–1959.

Sparks, Jared. "Hodgson's Remarks on America." *North American Review* 43 (April 1824): 221–234.

Tucker, George. *The Life of Thomas Jefferson, Third President of the United States. With Parts of his Correspondence Never before Published, and Notices of His Opinions on Questions of Civil Government, National Policy, and Constitutional Law.* 2 vols. Philadelphia: Carey, Lea & Blanchard, 1837.

Varriere, J. M., and L. C. Moffett. "A Frenchman Visits Albemarle, 1816." *Papers of the Albemarle County Historical Society* 5 (1944–1945): 39–55.

Warden, David B. *A Statistical, Political, and Historical Account of the United States of North America; from the Period of Their First Colonization to the Present Day.* 3 vols. Edinburgh: for A. Constable, 1819.

Index

WRITERS IN THEIR OWN TIME BOOKS

Alcott in Her Own Time
Edited by Daniel Shealy

Emerson in His Own Time
Edited by Ronald A. Bosco and Joel Myerson

Franklin in His Own Time
Edited by Kevin J. Hayes and Isabelle Bour

Fuller in Her Own Time
Edited by Joel Myerson

Hawthorne in His Own Time
Edited by Ronald A. Bosco and Jillmarie Murphy

Jefferson in His Own Time
Edited by Kevin J. Hayes

Lincoln in His Own Time
Edited by Harold K. Bush, Jr.

Poe in His Own Time
Edited by Benjamin F. Fisher

Stowe in Her Own Time
Edited by Susan Belasco

Thoreau in His Own Time
Edited by Sandra Harbert Petrulionis

Twain in His Own Time
Edited by Gary Scharnhorst

Whitman in His Own Time
Edited by Joel Myerson